EQUAL EDUCATION UNDER LAW

Legal Rights and Federal Policy in the Post-*Brown* Era

ROSEMARY C. SALOMONE

ST. MARTIN'S PRESS
New York

© 1986 Rosemary C. Salomone

All rights reserved.
For information, write:
Scholarly & Reference Division,
St. Martin's Press, Inc., 175 Fifth Avenue, New York, NY 10010

Printed in the U. S. A.

ISBN 0-312-25763-5
ISBN 0-312-25764-3 (pbk.)

Library of Congress Cataloging-in-Publication Data

Salomone, Rosemary C.
  Equal education under law.

  "July 1985."
  Bibliography: p. 253
  Includes index.
  1. Discrimination in education—Law and legislation—
United States. I. Title.
KF4155.S25 1986   344.73'0798   85-22221
ISBN 0-312-25763-5   347.304798
ISBN 0-312-25764-3 (pbk.)

To Joe

Contents

VI
THE RECENT FEDERAL RETREAT:
A New Ideology for a New Federalism   *168*

VII
MORAL VISION, FEDERAL POLICY, AND
EDUCATIONAL RIGHTS   *193*

Preface

A preface permits the author to state not only what a book is, but what it is not. With that license in hand, I will begin by dispelling any misconceptions about what this book is or should be.

First of all, the book does not cover the whole range of questions raised in the equality debate. In fact, limited as it is to the issue of student rights at the elementary and secondary level, the discussion never touches on such significant concerns as affirmative action and reverse discrimination. These are best left to works on employment discrimination or admissions policies in higher education or to more theoretical analyses of equality and public policy.

While the book is framed in the context of compensatory education, it is not an apologia for the specific strategies that have evolved under that rubric. Rather, it examines these strategies with a critical eye and attempts to sort out those features that have proven more successful than others. Nevertheless, the book is not a blueprint for educational reform. Unlike most contemporary scholarship on the federal role, it tends to be more descriptive than prescriptive. It moves us backward with a historical perspective in order to ultimately move us forward in formulating workable and reasonable policy.

This leads us from what the book is not to what it attempts to be. Essentially, it represents an effort to examine the equality question thirty years down the road from *Brown v. Board of Education*. It aims to cut through the demagoguery of the recent federal retreat and to revitalize the national interest in promoting both excellence and equality as compatible ends. It holds fast to the underlying commitment of *Brown,* our vision of a just society, while bringing us down from the clouds of well-intentioned but overly ambitious social goals.

With that basic premise made clear, the analysis is at best critical but certainly no more objective than could be expected. We all see history through the lens of our personal ideology. I hope to have brought to this analysis the objectivity of a scholar, the passion of an advocate, and the pragmatism of a practitioner. My own perspective on equality and the federal role has been forged from three decades of impressions and experiences—from childhood memories of the evening news and the National Guard quelling the school desegregation riots in Little Rock, to more than a decade of teaching and developing federally funded programs in disadvantaged neighborhoods in New York City, and finally to the past five years of reflecting and reassessing far above the fray. These latter years have offered me the distance to develop some objectivity and the time to examine the issues from an interdisciplinary perspective. But most important of all, they have permitted me to test my ideas before class after class of students eager to question, challenge, and search for the truth in the context of a rapidly changing economic and political climate.

What initially motivated me to analyze and synthesize the voluminous materials contained in this work was an invitation to prepare a report in 1982 entitled *Public Policy and the Law* for the Desegregation Assistance Centers of Region II of the U.S. Department of Education. Those centers are funded under Title IV of the Civil Rights Act of 1964 and include Rutgers University (sex desegregation), New York University (race desegregation), and Teachers College, Columbia University (national origin desegregation). Various Harvard-administered grants from the Spencer Foundation (Graduate School of Education), the Milton Fund (School of Medicine), and the Mark DeWolfe Howe Fund (School of Law) quickened the pace of the research. Finally, a sabbatical from Harvard and a graduate fellowship at Columbia University School of Law during the 1983–84 academic year added depth to the manuscript in progress and permitted me to expand, refine, and complete the research into its present form. I especially thank Vince Blasi, Peter Strauss, and Walter Gellhorn for making that year possible and productive.

Aside from institutional support, a number of scholars, litigators, and practitioners have contributed to the conception and development of this work. Included among these are Courtney Cazden, Patricia Albjerg Graham, Kent Greenawalt, Harold (Doc) Howe II, Francis Keppel, Margaret Kohn, Edwin Martin, Michael Rebell, Roger Rice, William Taylor, and my husband, Joseph Viteritti. Their comments and suggestions have added depth and accuracy to the final product. Any errors or omissions I reserve to myself. A note of recognition must go to the students of the Harvard Graduate School of Education who served as able research assistants at various stages of this project, and especially to Karin Froom who assisted me in the final year of revisions and updates. Her willingness to search the depths of the Harvard libraries helped immeasurably to move this project along in a spirited way. A word of thanks also goes to Martha Metzler and Michele Rosen whose word-processing skills and even temperament saw the manuscript through from beginning to end. Finally, my appreciation goes to Kermit Hummel of St. Martin's Press whose commitment to this project and to Debra Hudak whose cooperation made the final stages relatively painless.

I never intended this book to spur an educational revolution. But I do hope it affords its audience a broad understanding of how public policy, legal rights, and social responsibility are all intertwined. From there they can form their own judgments about a responsible federal role in education. If the books does no more than return equality to the discourse of reform, it will have been worth the effort.

R.C.S.
July 1985

Introduction

Education first molds, and afterwards sustains the various modes of government (and) ought to be regulated by the general consent, and not abandoned to the blind decision of chance and idle caprice."

—Aristotle, *Politics*

Individual Interests and the Collective Good

For the ancient Greeks, education was a collective interest of the highest order. It was the process by which a community might preserve and transmit its physical and intellectual character. Education represented for them a general consciousness of shared values. But they realized that community values do not remain static over time. As values change, so does education.[1]

American public schooling has drawn from this notion of the common ethos and its history has been driven by changing public values. But superimposed on the classical idea of the *polis* is a characteristically American passion for individualism. As the centripetal force of community has pushed educational policy toward the center of collective good, so the centrifugal force of individual liberty has pulled outward in diverse directions. Similar to classical thought, American society has come to deem an educated citizenry as a prerequisite to democratic government. But it also values education as an effective vehicle for social mobility. Whether viewed in the narrow sense of basic literacy or in the broader sense of information processing, critical thinking, and socialization, we believe that education increases informed participation in

1

governmental decision making and that it enhances life's opportunities for personal fulfillment and economic rewards.

The governance structure of education reflects this two-fold mission. Our decentralized system of public schooling is quite distinct from the highly centralized systems of western Europe. From its inception, American education has been a diffuse enterprise driven by a strong political culture of local control. The framers of the United States Constitution, in their efforts to prevent the tyranny of the majority and to preserve the pluralistic spirit of the fledgling nation, reserved certain matters to the states. Implicit among these was education. The states subsequently incorporated educational provisions in their own constitutions and enacted compulsory education laws.[2] And so education was raised above a public benefit to the level of a guaranteed state right. The states further created local school districts and delegated to them the responsibility to manage the daily operation of the schools. Along with that function came the power to raise educational revenue through local taxation.

Local operation and state/local funding would make education more responsive to local community preferences within broadly defined curricular and administrative standards established by the state. For state government, the primary concern was to provide a basic level of education to the largest numbers possible. As for the federal role, American resistance to a national education policy rendered federal involvement far more remote. In fact, the United States Office of Education, established during the Reconstruction Era, did little more than compile obscure statistical reports for the first century of its existence. The federal government was clearly not in the business of education.

Early Federal Involvement

Until the mid-twentieth century, the federal government treaded gingerly on educational ground, never regulating but merely stimulating local activity primarily through categorical grants, especially in times of national crisis. The Morill Act, passed in 1862 during the Civil War, provided aid to college-level scientific, engineering, and agricultural programs. The

Smith-Hughes Act for vocational education, the first federal aid program to elementary and secondary schools, was enacted in 1917 during World War I as part of President Wilson's preparedness program.

During World War II, Congress passed the Lanham Act to provide assistance to localities whose property tax base was affected by federal ownership of land such as military bases. That legislation was expanded a decade later during the Korean War. This program, which has come to be known as "impact aid," stands unique as a source of general and not categorical federal funding for education. More recently, in response to Cold War concerns, Congress passed the National Defense Education Act in 1958 with its focus on mathematics, science, and foreign languages—a program clearly targeted at the most talented students.[3] And thus education in this country evolved as a matter of local function, state responsibility, and federal concern.

From "Brown" to the "Great Society"

In mid-twentieth century America witnessed a cataclysmic event that would change the power configuration and focus of public education for the next quarter-century. It is here that the modern era of education policy began with the Supreme Court's decision in *Brown v. Board of Education*.[4] Speaking in a unanimous voice, the early Warren Court stated in 1954 that because of "the importance of education to our democratic society . . . the opportunity of an education . . . where the state has undertaken to provide it, is a right which must be made available to all on equal terms."[5] That pronouncement, in fact, gave legal weight and moral force to an era of social reform and unprecedented federal involvement with the equality principle as its guide.

The Court in *Brown* tried to make the ideals of liberalism a reality for all. By announcing that racially segregated schools are inherently unequal, the Court acknowledged the worth of the black population and aimed to liberate the individual from the domination of government interference. In the context of that decision and the year 1954, equal educational opportunity clearly meant, at a minimum, equal treatment to an education in a nonsegregated setting. Whatever else the concept might mean has never been resolved by Congress, by the federal courts, or by society at large. Yet the Court in *Brown* laid the groundwork for equality to guide numerous public policy decisions in the years to come.

The *Brown* decision and its controversial mandate lay largely quiescent for a decade. In the mid-1960s, in the wake of Sputnik, poverty and race riots, and exploding demographics, Lyndon Johnson and his War on Poverty successfully and dramatically expanded the federal role in educational policy.[6] With equality of educational opportunity as their policy objective, liberal partisans of the Great Society programs justified their proposals on a theory of education as "investment in human capital."[7]

This large-scale federal involvement grew out of Johnson's domestic policy. That policy advanced a two-pronged attack on combating the effects of poverty and promoting equal educational opportunity—what has since been called a *carrot and stick* approach. The first step was to enact a series of prohibitions to assure the equal treatment of minority members of society. The second was to use the power of the federal purse to induce compliance.

In 1964 Congress enacted the Civil Rights Act. Title VI[8] of this Act prohibits discrimination on the basis of race, color, and national origin in federally assisted programs. Applied to education, this provision allayed fears in Congress that federal funds might be spent in support of racially segregated educational programs. Title VI thereby lifted the long-standing desegregation barrier to federal aid. The Johnson Administration then artfully pieced together a fragile coalition of education interest groups including states, local school districts, education reformers, private schools, and advocates for the disadvantaged. Each group received a piece of the funding action.[9]

In order to achieve broad political consensus in Congress, proponents of compensatory education couched its overriding purpose in a societal benefit theory. As stated by Congressman Carl Perkins, "If we can reduce the costs of crime, delinquency, unemployment and welfare in the future by well-directed spending on education, now certainly on this count alone, we will have made a sound investment."[10] The rationale was as follows: educational failure is mainly the result of poverty; the poor tend to reside in certain geographic areas; extra government assistance will afford them equal access to educational opportunity which, in turn, will develop them into productive members of society. For the Great Society reformers, "education was a paying investment" not only in our economic well-being but in our national survival. They also spoke of equality in the context of educational excellence. Federal aid would obliterate "deviations in the quality of schools among communities."[11] As stated by Francis Keppel, then Commissioner of Education, at the heart of the federal initiative was a desire "to strengthen the quality and equality of educational opportunity at its points of critical weakness."[12] But underlying compensatory education was an unstated assumption that society was to blame for the economically and impoverished condition of minority groups and had to pay the price for a long history of neglect, discrimination, and disenfranchisement.

The Johnson Administration was keenly aware that such a dramatic expansion in the federal role would be received at the state and local levels as a mixed blessing and with a suspect eye. And so from the onset, the Administration underscored the primacy of the state role and clarified the limited purpose of federal involvement. In his message before Congress in January 1965, Lyndon Johnson expressly stated, "Federal assistance does not mean Federal control." Quoting the late Senator Robert Taft, he went on to note, "Education is primarily a State function—but . . . the Federal Government has a secondary obligation to see that there is a basic floor under those essential services for all adults and children in the United States."[13] Both Keppel and Perkins echoed that perspective whereby "the Federal Government must participate—not toward domination, but as a partner in a vital enterprise"[14] whose "determination" and "execution" would belong "to local and State educational authorities."[15]

Despite stated purposes and assurances, this initial breakthrough in federal aid, mostly in the form of remedial instruction to the disadvantaged, effectively plunged the federal government into the total educational enterprise. By the late

1960s, Bailey and Mosher would describe education as a "marble cake, not a 'layer cake' of federalism."[16] Indeed, federal aid to education has since created an uneasy local-state-federal partnership whose collective and conflicting aims have shaped educational priorities for the past two decades.

Broadening the Equality Mandate

Through the mid-1970s, legislative action broadened the scope of federal assistance beyond the effects of poverty. The federal largess was opened to the physically and emotionally handicapped, linguistic minorities, and women. With each additional dollar came greater programmatic specifications and greater federal control. And the societal benefit theory became swallowed up in the rhetoric of equality. Equality of opportunity was no longer a means to a more productive society but an end in itself.

The major thrust of this expansion was twofold. The first was to achieve equity for those populations that had been neglected historically under a system of "states rights" and an anti-urban tradition in state policy making.[17] The new federal grants included categorical restrictions and fiscal controls. The federal government would earmark funds for specific educational services to address identified needs and would thereby force states and localities to meet federally defined goals. Non-supplantation and comparability requirements would prevent school systems from decreasing local educational support as federal aid increased. The second purpose was to stimulate similar legislation at the state level. To that end, federal aid was partly successful as 16 states subsequently enacted compensatory education laws,[18] 21 states provided aid for bilingual instruction,[19] and all states mandated special services to handicapped students between the ages of five and seventeen.[20]

Federal involvement did not stop at financial subsidies. Legislative and executive action granted legal rights and protections to the newly identified target groups. The promise of Title VI of the Civil Rights Acts of 1964 had begun to be realized for racial minorities through administrative enforcement and court orders. Other interest groups followed the lead and pressed for protection legislation for women (Title IX of the Education Amendments of 1972),[21] and the handicapped (§504 of the Rehabilitation Act of 1973).[22] In fact, these statutes are almost identical in language and enforcement proceedings to Title VI. All three prohibit discrimination in federally assisted programs (Title IX is limited to educational institutions and programs) and carry with them the threat of federal fund withdrawal in the case of noncompliance.[23] The vague wording and ambiguous scope of these laws would occupy the federal courts for years to come.

From Negative to Affirmative Entitlements

In the language of legal rights, Title VI, Title IX, and §504 were negative directives. They did not mandate a specific type or level of instructional services but merely prohibited school systems from denying equal educational treatment to students based on group characteristics—race, national origin, gender, or handicap. Spurred on by a growing activism among the federal judiciary and a sympathetic bureaucracy within the former Department of Health, Education, and Welfare,[24] negative directives soon turned into affirmative entitlements.

As the federal courts relaxed procedural requirements for class action suits, litigants could pursue litigation with a potentially broad social impact. The field of public interest law evolved and proved successful in protecting and expanding minority rights. Following the model developed by the NAACP Legal Defense and Education Fund that lead up to *Brown v. Board of Education,* other advocacy groups began to use *planned litigation* as a vehicle for incremental social reform.[25] Women, linguistic minorities, and the handicapped—groups historically underrepresented in the majoritarian political process—began to make an end-run around the legislative branch and carry their claims before the federal courts. This increasingly popular strategy served to legitimize certain concerns and to pull together the requisite interest groups to press for a political solution. Two clear examples are the Education for All Handicapped Children Act (P.L. 94-142)[26] and the linguistic minority provision of the Equal Educational Opportunities Act of 1974.[27] Both were stimulated and shaped by earlier court decisions.

Since the early 1970s, this interplay between Congress and the federal courts has in fact established itself as a distinct pattern of education policymaking. The courts initially determine constitutional guarantees, Congress gives substance to those definitions, and the courts in the next cycle clarify ambiguities[28] and, in certain cases, cast the issues back into the political arena for further congressional fine-tuning. Weaving in and out is the executive branch with its regulatory and enforcement powers.

Judicial Activism and Structural Reform

As recent history makes clear, the substance of *Brown*'s mandate for social reform depends in large measure on congressional and executive support. But the federal judiciary has been the dominant force in giving that mandate scope and momentum. Beginning with school desegregation and more recently with handicapped discrimination issues, civil rights groups have increasingly used the federal courts as mechanisms for social reform. This new model of *public law litigation* has cast judges in an activist role with broad responsibilities for case management and relief implementation.[29] In the abstract, this form of litigation has required revised conceptions about party structure, new norms governing judicial behavior, and new ways of looking at the relationship between rights and remedies. It has emerged from the proliferation of well-organized advocacy groups and the tendency to perceive interests as group interests. In cases of this nature, the role of the judge does not end with the decree but continues through the implementation stage. In the context of education decrees, this often involves the judge in restructuring school systems and reordering local priorities.

Judicial activism in structural reform has generated considerable scholarly debate. Some see this role as not only legitimate but necessary. On a broad scale, the judge is just one voice among many in the public inquiry that gives meaning to the ambiguous and often conflicting values contained in the Constitution, such as the equality principle. Courts need not have the only word or even the last word, but they must be allowed to speak and to speak with some authority.[30] In the more narrow context of the individual case, the court in effect facilitates the process of mutual understanding, communication, and consensus building.[31] On a political level, the court is viewed as a partner in the broader political struggle to make the bureaucracy behave. The court is a necessary actor in the modern administrative state.[32]

On the other hand, the opponents of structural reform through court order have assailed the federal courts for acting as super school boards and expanding the use of discriminatory equitable relief beyond its intended limitations. They maintain that courts have distorted the concept of remedy from compensation for individual wrongs to assuaging the effects of past wrongs.[33] According to this argument, an activist federal judiciary has destroyed the nexus between wrong and remedy. An individual wrong now demands a group remedy.[34] On an institutional level, opponents argue that in trying to create a better society, the courts have lost the respect and trust of the people.[35] In fact, where courts assume power not granted them in order to correct an evil that the people are unready to cure, this smacks of the discarded doctrine that "the end justifies the means."[36]

And down from the abstractness of scholarly dialectics, local communities and school officials have railed against the intrusiveness of court intervention. Not only has the federal government made substantive claims on society's resources in the name of minority interests, they argue, but the federal courts have become actively involved in reallocating local resources to fulfill judicially identified entitlements.

Can We Be Equal and Excellent?

Two sets of dualities have shaped the debate over educational policy in the three decades since *Brown v. Board of Education*. The first is a conflict in underlying values between equality on the one hand, and individual liberty and community preferences on the other. The second is a false dichotomy in policy objectives between equality and excellence.

The Supreme Court's decision in *Brown* was based on a

general consensus that racial discrimination violated our national sense of morality and that segregated schools were bad for society. The Court mandated that government could not treat individuals differently because of their race. The Great Society reformers of the 1960s also perceived a consensus of values among the American population and a common goal to provide equal educational access to all.

But as the equality movement took on a momentum of its own, individual rights evolved into group entitlements and equality for some resulted in a denial of liberty for others. From a society that valued merit and talent, we added to our system of rewards the criteria of need and social neglect. The education debate became centered around questions of adequacy and appropriateness in the inputs of instructional services. Little attention was paid to the outputs of student performance. In the process of meeting that national agenda, individual choice and community preference became all but irrelevant in the wider education policy arena.

As the 1970s drew to a close, America witnessed a groundswell of opposition ostensibly against the equality principle but essentially against the specific reforms it had generated. As the federal government looked to protect the rights of minorities as a matter of justice, a growing backlash began to demand greater deference to the individual rights of the majority in the name of federalism and political tradition. Court-ordered busing to achieve racial balance in the schools, the diversion of local funds to meet federal legal mandates, compensatory and bilingual education programs all caught the blame for a host of educational evils—low student achievement scores, vandalism and crime in the schools, and a rising rate of illiteracy.

This erosion in the quality of public schooling, fueled by economic decline and a lost sense of shared morality and values, elicited a rash of prescriptions for correcting the perceived excesses of the past—more control, tougher standards, more requirements, tighter discipline. The flood of reports and studies inundating American educators in the early 1980s centered new proposals for reform on "excellence" as a remedy for and response to the failures of equality.

There is a "rising tide of mediocrity" imperiling American education, we were told. And if the "threatened disaster" were to be averted, then the federal government must "emphasize the pressing need for a high-quality system of education open to all Americans, regardless of race or economic position." American education, so the argument went, had expected too little of its schools over the previous two decades resulting in "a real emergency."[37]

These reports turned public sentiment around from an obsession in the 1970s with education's shortcomings to a renewed enthusiasm for positive action. However, their general tone and their specific mandates for reform overlay faulty assumptions and contained serious gaps. First of all, implicit in many of these reports was a misconception that excellence has all to do with cognitive performance or the "bottom line" on a set of uniform written tasks guided by a common core curriculum. What was clearly missing was any meaningful discussion of the intrinsic worth of education, the sheer pleasure of learning. Related to the uniformity of prescribed instruction was an erroneous belief that the opportunity to achieve imposed standards for excellence is realistically within everyone's reach regardless of limitations imposed by social class, family influences, handicapping conditions, and racial and sexual prejudice.[38] To believe that disadvantaged students are different from others would be both anti-intellectual and antidemocratic.[39]

It was precisely those individual differences among students that underlay the basic concept of compensatory education. It was a recognition that students come to school with differential abilities, needs, and levels of preparedness and that schools must design curricula, strategies, and learning environments to accommodate those differences. The reform reports recognized in general terms that disadvantaged students have special needs, but they stopped with such generalities and never moved on to specific recommendations. They made little mention of school desegregation; the problems of minorities, the handicapped, and women; the increasing percentage of school dropouts; or the changing racial and ethnic demographics of public schooling in the years to come.[40] The inevitable result would be a quest for superiority—and not excellence—for an elite few.

Excellence has now become the shibboleth of the 1980s. But equality is not necessarily antithetical to excellence. Francis Keppel noted the interrelatedness of those two concepts almost two decades ago. For him, not only is the seeming paradox between the two misleading but the exact opposite holds. We cannot achieve quality education without equality. A complex society such as ours cannot afford to deny equal opportunity to all while affording excellence to an elite few. He urged that equality would not lead inevitably to mediocrity and that freedom and justice are not contradictory but essential to each other. According to Keppel, the solution of this contradiction would form the second and necessary revolution in American education.[41]

Equality's detractors might argue that history has proven Keppel wrong—that a concern for justice and the reforms it has spawned have indeed led to mediocrity and, worst of all, have enervated America's spirit, resources, and strength. But that confuses basic commitments and guiding principles with specific strategies. It also discounts the social benefits brought to us in the name of equal opportunity and overlooks a whole range of intervening political and economic factors that have simultaneously weighed upon the educational enterprise.

Perhaps the most unassailable argument for excellence was advanced by John Gardner on the heels of Sputnik and before the dreams of the Great Society were even articulated. Gardner urged that we avoid a narrow and constricted conception of excellence and that we embrace many kinds of achievements at many levels. He also argued, "It is possible to cultivate the ideal of excellence while retaining the moral values of equality."[42]

That essentially is the thesis of this book—not only that we can, but that we should maintain our commitment to equality while we reevaluate specific strategies in our quest for excellence. But in order to do so, we must first acknowledge and understand the broad range of differences within the student population. The discussion that follows attempts to identify those differences and the goals of two decades of reforms, some more successful than others. By looking at the forces and actors that have shaped federal policy, the reader may better understand the current debate and more ably see beneath the political machinations of policy making to the underlying needs of students.

Chapter 1 begins with the philosophical concept of equality in the framework of distributive justice. It underscores the problems inherent in attempts to transmute sound moral principles into workable public policy. Chapters 2, 3, 4 and 5 look at four distinct populations that have been granted special benefits and protections by the federal government—racial and linguistic minorities, the handicapped, and women. Each chapter analyzes the role played by Congress, the federal courts, executive agencies, and interest groups in developing and mandating specific educational approaches in the name of equality. Chapter 6 continues the discussion of the recent federal retreat under the Reagan Administration and assesses the Administration's overall goals, underlying premises, and specific proposals for reshaping the federal role. Finally, Chapter 7 draws some conclusions from the radical pendulum swings of the past and present—from the well-intentioned but overly ambitious goals of yesterday to the shortsighted backlash of today. It calls for a federal government that is willing to support new strategies for achieving quality education for all while remaining steadfast in its commitment to equalize educational opportunities.

I

Educational Equality: From Moral Precept to Public Policy

It is well understood, although seldom stated, that public policy making operates within a given political ideology and draws from particular moral principles. The federal intervention strategies of the 1960s and 1970s evolved in the context of the liberal welfare state with the equality principle as their guiding force. What began, however, as an ideal of social reform two decades ago has since become encrusted with legal jargon, constitutional limitations, and scientific uncertainty. More significantly, the historical alliance between equality and education has recently given way to competing values of liberty and efficiency. And the political consensus to ensure social and economic equality through the redistribution of educational resources has all but dissipated in the air of more minimalist notions of government.

Equality is not simply nor primarily an educational question but one that interacts with the broader political, social, and economic matrix. At the heart of the equality debate is a perplexing dilemma of how to reconcile the rights of the individual with the collective interests of society. In effect, how may we best define the role of government in a democratic state where resources are limited? On the one end is the modern liberal notion that the purpose of government is to facilitate social progress. The contemporary liberal would argue that society has an obligation to provide some of its own resources to create a common pool of minimum goods. Whether called a *basic floor of opportunity* or a *safety net*, such minimums involve a sense of dignity and self-esteem. From this vantage point, public education is the foundation of individual and social betterment, and of such high importance as to justify government interference. At the other extreme is a position more consistent with a conservative political ideology. From this perspective, government exists as a watchdog merely to preserve the status quo of the natural competitive state and has neither the obligation nor the authority to promote change through social institutions such as education.

The efforts of social reformers to apply the tenets of liberalism to social and economic progress through public schooling reached its peak in the Great Society programs. That movement which has now come under severe scrutiny and attack has in fact taught us that in our legal and constitutional order, equality may operate as more than a mere guaranteed individual protection from unequal government treatment. In fact, equality has come to define affirmative allocational rights to goods and services for certain groups, notably those distinguished by relatively fixed qualities such as race, linguistic origin, gender, or handicap. This break from more pluralistic notions of liberalism with their emphasis on individual rights represents one of the most crucial and controversial issues now facing the political establishment.

The group-oriented, redistributionist conception of equality has evoked animosity in those that are disfavored by the legal status and distributions that government has afforded such collective entities. For equality's detractors, it is often irrelevant as to whether the status quo ante, that is, the disadvantage to be remedied or compensated for, is natural as in the case of the handicapped, governmentally produced as in the case of racial minorities and women, or the product of social interactions and culture as in the particular case of linguistic minorities. In a society such as ours where resources have become increasingly insufficient to meet an expanding list of demands, equality, it is argued, becomes a zero-sum game.

Confronted with these undeniable political and economic realities, the proponents of equality are hard-pressed to defend a concept whose very definition is ambiguous, amorphous, and contextual. When applied to public policy, the equality principle persistently provokes certain challenging questions. What does it mean? How can it be justified? In what relation should it stand with other moral precepts? The following discussion seeks answers in the philosophical and sociological underpinnings of federal intervention strategies. In the end it underscores equality's moral force and operational potential as a basis for public policy reform.

The Ambiguity of the Equality Ideal

Equality as a social ideal has attracted almost universal attention from ancient times to the present. The most consistent justification for equality as a primary moral precept has rested on a belief in the dignity of *humans qua humans*. The Stoics based their egalitarian principles on the natural equality of humans as rational beings with an equal capacity for virtue. The New Testament doctrine of equality of all souls in the sight of God is a religious version of a similar principle.[1] In modern times, the American Declaration of Independence proclaimed as self-evident truths, "that all men are created equal, that they are endowed by their Creator with certain inalienable Rights."

In its purest form, equality enjoys popular appeal among a range of political persuasions. Few would deny that all humans are due equal consideration and respect. Few would deny that individuals should enjoy the opportunity to rise as far as their talents and abilities may carry them. But on other aspects of the equality principle we find a clear lack of consensus. In fact, the vagueness and ambiguity inherent in the concept mask strongly divergent views, only to be uncovered in times of political or economic stress.

Equality as applied to a given circumstance demands clarification on several points. First, there are definitional considerations. We must identify those specific aspects in which allegedly equal things or persons are in fact equal. For example, individuals may be unequal in height or weight, characteristics that are objectively measurable, but they may be equal in talent or in potential, attributes that are more subjectively determined.[2] Related to this distinction between objective and subjective criteria is a second dimension to the equality debate, that is, the conceptual network. What are the logical relations among such expressions as "equal," "identical," "same," and "similar." Finally, there exists the relationship between equality and justice—a recurrent theme in contemporary philosophical writings. A given distribution or policy may in fact be equal but is it also equitable or just?[3]

It is clearly understandable how an idea of such complexity combined with its extraordinary symbolic force has drawn the attention of philosophers over the centuries. From Aristotle's concept of *distributive justice* to the modern-day *difference principle* as conceived by John Rawls,[4] theories abound as to the nature of the equality ideal and its application to the unique and common pressures of societies over time.[5]

Aristotle and Distributive Justice

The deepest roots of contemporary egalitarian arguments lie in Aristotle's *Politics*[6] and *The Nichomachean Ethics*.[7] In these he developed a principle of equality wrapped in distributive justice. For Aristotle, equality meant *equal treatment* but only insofar as individuals share like qualities. He clearly did not suggest *equality of result* for all. In fact, like Plato, Aristotle was instinctively inequalitarian. Both believed that differences among individuals should be reflected in all social and political arrangements. All persons should be subject to the law most appropriate to their natural group—one law for citizens and another for those who are slaves by nature.[8]

Aristotle drew a distinction between two types of equality—*proportional* based on distributive justice and *arithmetical* based on compensatory or rectificatory justice. He also introduced the idea of *relevant criteria*. He maintained that no distinction be made between individuals who are equal in all respects relevant to the type of treatment in question even though they may be unequal in other irrelevant respects. Where individuals are unequal in relevant respects, however, they should be treated in proportion to their relevant inequalities. Proportional equality distributes goods and services on the basis of individual desert as determined by free birth, wealth, or virtue.[9] For Aristotle, as for Plato, proportional equality takes priority over arithmetical.[10] The latter serves a corrective function. Individuals do not have absolute insight into each other's value, and so a certain amount of arithmetical equality serves to compensate for possible injustices in the application of the proportionality principle.[11]

Aristotle's concept of equality as distributive justice has clearly influenced modern-day distributionist theories. Contemporary thought theoretically gives preference to strict arithmetical equality or equal treatment to all by virtue of a commonly shared quality in being human.[12] Nevertheless, the effect is largely the same despite the reordering of preference. Proportional distribution comes into play secondarily, but like Aristotle's view, nonuniform treatment must be justified by relevant criteria. In sum, to act justly is to treat all individuals alike except where there exist relevant differences between them.

Aristotle held a narrow view of relevance based on the predeterminations of birth. The system of relevance that has won most widespread acceptance in our culture is one associated with meritocracy. Fundamental to this construct is the view that human beings should be judged and rewarded on the basis of individual merit. Here achievement and performance run high in the differential distributions of society's resources, i.e., those with the most merit reap the greatest reward. Other contemporary distributionist theories present a more expansive range of relevant criteria including economic disadvantage, physical or emotional disability, or even past societal mistreatment or neglect. Obviously, much depends on what we hold to be most relevant. The implications of and problems inherent in this concept of relevance will come into focus in the discussion of equality of opportunity and political ideologies.

Theories of Rights and of the State

The theme of distributive justice has in fact dominated contemporary discourse on educational equality. Within that framework, education is viewed as a system for distributing certain goods and benefits including skills, information, and life opportunities.[13] Theories of distribution, or to be more accurate, redistribution, draw from the modern liberal ideology of the activist state as compared with more conservative notions of the minimal state. Varying degrees of governmental intervention in the distribution of society's resources, including nonintervention, carry with them certain public policy implications. They raise fundamental philosophical questions concerning the degree to which society's members can make moral demands on one another and ask the state to act as the intermediary in meeting those demands.

Among contemporary distributive theories, the philosopher John Rawls' theory of *justice as fairness* stands out as the most widely debated. Under his *difference principle*, "all social primary goods" must be distributed equally throughout society unless unequal distribution of any of these goods is to the advantage of the least favored class.[14] Similar to the modern liberal view, mere equality of opportunity is not enough because it allows great differences to emerge from the way in which different individuals are able to use the equal opportunities available to them. This position is more egalitarian than more moderate liberal positions because it does not simply provide a guaranteed minimum of social resources. It requires that social arrangements favor those in the most disadvantaged position.

The political philosopher Michael Walzer presents a more moderate view of what distributionist governmental policies should be. His *spheres of justice* represents an argument for a pluralistic concept of equality.[15] Walzer maintains that society may be viewed as comprising separate spheres, each of which is characterized by its own criteria for distributing goods. He defines his spheres of justice according to the different goods or benefits that society distributes among its members. Included among these is education.[16] Once the members of a given society have determined the meaning of a certain good, then the appropriate criteria for its distribution will ineluctably follow.

According to Walzer, justice is a matter of maintaining the separate integrity of each of the spheres. The distribution of goods in one sphere must not affect the distribution of goods in another as when, for example, the possession of money becomes the means of attaining education. Although his system of justice would work toward the general good and meet common needs, it would also provide for the distribution of rewards and punishments on the basis of actual individual desert.

Walzer admits that needs are elusive. Individuals do not have needs; they have priorities and degrees of need that are related not only to human nature but to history and culture. For him, this indefiniteness of need does not diminish its relevance as a distributive criterion but rather casts its determination into the political and not the philosophical arena. Walzer accepts as inevitable and acceptable a needs-based distribution whose limits are arbitrary and temporarily fixed by shifting political coalitions and majorities. This particularistic approach is clearly relevant to justice in the educational sphere where policy decisions must account for the diverse needs of students such as the handicapped, the economically disadvantaged, and linguistic minorities.

Walzer's theory draws its strength from its recognition that justice depends upon spheres of distribution that must not be crossed. By setting his argument in a broader framework, he underscores the most prevalent injustice in commercial society where wealth tends to determine the distribution of other goods. Nevertheless, his theory's weakness lies in the extreme relativism in which he embeds his idea of justice. If justice is culture-bound and dependent on actual consent (as compared with the hypothetical consent of most social contract theories), then Walzer leaves unresolved the problem of unequal access to the means of persuasion or to the media of information such as education. Certain goods then appear to be more fundamental and inequalities in these inevitably lead to inequalities in others.[17]

One of the most noteworthy critics of distributive theories is Robert Nozick who clearly represents a nondistributionist point of view.[18] Nozick questions the widespread philosophical presumption in favor of equality, maintaining that there exists a dearth of arguments supporting that presumption. According to his "entitlement conception of justice," the nonvoluntary redistribution of income to achieve "equality of material condition" is morally impermissible. In fact, he argues that it is morally illegitimate for any government to tax some of its citizens in order to provide food, shelter, medical care or social services for other, less fortunate citizens.

Nozick builds his *minimal state* theory on a foundation of individual rights. For him, governmental functions are limited to the protection of the populace from force, theft, and fraud, to the enforcement of contracts, and to the preservation of basic liberties. Any more extensive theory of the state would violate individual rights to be free from coercion. His minimal state treats each person as an individual who may not be used by others as a means to an end or as a resource. He attacks distributive justice as a non-neutral term. His theory in fact denies that there should be a central authority empowered to make distributional decisions although he agrees that some government intervention is justified to redress the results of past grievous injustices. Nozick assails distributive justice on the ground that it can only be maintained through continued governmental intervention in private attempts to transfer resources. He contrasts such a system with that of a free society, in which distributional decisions are the product of individual choice made by diverse persons who control diverse resources.

Not only does Nozick's theory of the state depend upon his moral theory of individual rights, but his moral theory incorporates a particular theory of personal rights based on natural rights. He believes that the moral basis of rights is founded in the capacity to live a meaningful life. Individuals with that capacity have rights that place constraints on the way others must behave toward them. But Nozick's first premise of individual rights does not demand a noninterventionist theory of the state. In fact, it can be argued that the characteristics of his "meaningful life" might overlap considerably with alternative conceptions of individual rights, including the ability to live a decent and fulfilling life.[19] If so, then Nozick's theory of rights is not inconsistent with distributionist theories. Of course, a redistribution of society's goods and benefits undeniably and unavoidably infringes on the liberty interests of some. Nevertheless, the restrictions on liberty necessary to guarantee what most of us would consider as a meaningful life are not so severe as to prevent the victims of taxation, for example, from leading a meaningful life as well.

A Typology of Equality

In the interests of order and simplicity and at the risk of reductionism, the interrelatedness of distributive justice and theories of the state can be outlined in a three-part typology of equality.[20] The three conceptions of equality and their corresponding political positions are as follows:

		Theories of Justice	
		Distributionist	Nondistributionist
Theories of the State	Activist	1. Social-democratic or left-liberal position— equal apportionment of all kinds, especially economic benefits.	2. Modern liberal position— protection of basic rights, equality of opportunity, and equal apportionment of basic benefits (medical care, basic education, care of the aged).
	Nonactivist		3. Conservative position— protection of basic rights.

The *basic rights* approach represents the traditional conservative position (now considered a libertarian view) whereby the coercive power of government can be used only to enforce basic liberties. It is an individualistic approach founded on the moral view that what we claim from one another or what we ask government to force others to accord us is limited to a certain set of basic rights upon which others may not infringe. It is a system under which individual liberty is given priority over equality as a moral principle. The government may not force redistributions in order to compensate those individuals who are disadvantaged or to provide benefits for the general population.

This conception is generally referred to as *legal equality* or *formal equality.* For the political conservative, *ability, talent,* and *merit* stand out as criteria relevant to the unequal distribution of society's resources through the natural lottery system and not through government intervention strategies. These criteria derive their relevance from the importance that private individuals place upon them and the goods and benefits they bear. As a legal standard, equality before the law was designed to limit governmental power to disadvantage individuals on invidious grounds. As such, it is process-oriented, emphasizing fairness in the decisional process.[21]

The second conception, basic rights, equal opportunity and the equal apportionment of certain basic benefits including education, represent the modern liberal position, in the sense of the Lyndon Johnson-type political liberal and not the John Stuart Mill philosophical liberal. While adherents to this position may differ as to the depth of the floor of opportunity provided, they basically agree that society must protect basic equal rights and provide equal access or opportunity to society's benefits through a guaranteed social minimum of some sort. Society must compensate in some way for the unequal starting points that people occupy both socially and economically.

The content of equality of opportunity has been determined by its history. It was originally formulated as a lever to overthrow formal or legal inequality. In its early form, formal equality of opportunity was presented in negative rather than positive terms—as freedom from restraints rather than as possession of power. It meant that all individuals should have an equal opportunity to develop their talents and that there should be equal rewards for equal talents. This formula can be radically misleading. It is more accurately articulated as equality of opportunity to develop the talents that are highly regarded in a given group. Only those who are superior in the desired qualities have the opportunity to develop them and the gap between the highest and the lowest inevitably widens. While equality of opportunity has been defined as *equal access* to social goods, it can translate into *constructive exclusion* for those individuals who fail to possess certain qualities.[22] An opportunity is an opportunity only for those who may or may not make use of it.[23]

Modern-day liberal proponents of equality of opportunity consider this conception as narrow, coldly artificial, and fundamentally unfair.[24] They condemn it for taking people simply as they are and for judging them without asking why one performs better than the other. True equality of opportunity requires, so they argue, that we modify those aspects of people's circumstances that prevent them from performing up to their natural abilities. For a distributionist such as Michael Walzer, his theory of the activist state emphasizes a needs-based distribution in which need is defined through political means as a function of the goods and benefits to be allocated. This pluralistic conception of equality lends itself particularly well to the educational sphere where equality of educational opportunity takes on a unique operational significance when applied to the whole panoply of individual student needs.

At the most extreme end of distributionist theories would be the socialistic ethic in the Marxist sense. Here class struggle would effectively reduce social and economic inequalities. A theory akin to the social-democratic position yet one that depends upon social cooperation and centers on self-esteem in a free-competitive society is that of John Rawls.[25] Yet his egalitarian difference principle also shares several features in common with the modern liberal approach to equality of opportunity. Both provide for state intervention in redistributing benefits and burdens beyond the protection of basic rights. Both are based on the moral view that the range of life's possibilities is limited by birthright, including the socioeconomic class into which we are born and our genetic makeup. The initial distribution of life's benefits are therefore arbitrary and beyond the individual's control. Both accept *need* and reject *merit* as the sole basis for differential treatment.

However, where the liberal and egalitarian positions part ways, is in the end which the equality principle may legitimately pursue. Equality of opportunity as carried out in public policy has followed two strands in liberal thought. The first focuses on the individual and the personal benefits to be derived from economic and social advancement. The second strand emphasizes the general welfare of society as measured by the good of the majority. If we provide additional resources to the disadvantaged, then society as a whole benefits—less crime, lower unemployment, fewer families on public assistance. Moral claims are here seen as aggregative, that is, each individual's claims are weighed along with everyone else's in the state's determination of overall claims.

As to the egalitarian difference principle, on the other hand, the end is a result-oriented equality that leads to equal status or condition. Equality here is viewed as an end in itself. Adherents to this position would sacrifice the total general welfare to produce greater equality for those at the bottom of the distributive ladder.

Both equality of opportunity and the difference principle have sparked heated debate in recent years. The former has provided the philosophical underpinnings for large-scale government intervention strategies in providing educational services and has produced a major role change for the federal government. The merits and success of that enterprise are still a matter of controversy. The difference principle in its precise terminology and Rawlsian formulation has not been applied overtly to public policy making. However, Rawls' theory of justice as fairness in general, and his difference principle in particular, visibly and systematically represent a new way of talking about equality as a guide for public policy making.

Social Egalitarianism and the Difference Principle

In *A Theory of Justice,* John Rawls attempts to provide a persuasive, coherent, and more egalitarian alternative to prevailing forms of liberalism. The time period in which he developed and refined his work covered crucial years of intense political struggle when the basic tenets of liberalism were widely challenged. In the United States, the civil rights and antiwar movements of the 1960s brought millions of Americans into open conflict with existing political and social institutions. Questions concerning the protection of liberties and the distribution of social goods among social strata were raised far and wide. The fact that Rawls worked on his book throughout this period has led at least one commentator to conclude that the book in fact represents a response to those times.[26]

In the tradition of the social contract theorists, Rawls

begins his theory by establishing his fundamental vision in which he places all individuals in an *original position* prior to the formulation of a hypothetical society.[27] Those in the original position are characterized as equal moral persons, that is, persons who have a conception of the good and a capacity for a sense of justice. Such individuals are forced to choose distributive principles as to the basic structures of society from behind a *veil of ignorance*. Unaware of the positions they will occupy once the society begins to work, they choose on the basis of what would be best for them as far as they can determine.

All individuals in the original position are in a state of primary equality. Rawls tells us that such persons would agree on two principles of justice. The first, which takes priority over the second, states that "each person is to have an equal right to the most extensive basic liberty compatible with a similar liberty for others." The second establishes that "social and economic inequalities" are to be arranged so that they are both (a) to the greatest benefit to the least advantaged and (b) attached to offices and positions open to all under conditions of fair equality of opportunity.[28]

According to his difference principle, "all social primary goods—liberty and opportunity, income and wealth, and the bases of self-respect—are to be distributed equally unless an unequal distribution of any or all of these goods is to the advantage of the least favored."[29] Rawls' principles of justice are lexically ordered; the first (liberty) takes priority over the second (equality), and the second takes priority over the difference principle. As a result, liberty can be restricted only for the sake of liberty and equality of fair opportunity takes precedence over the difference principle. All are lexically prior to the principle of efficiency, that is, maximizing the sum of advantages throughout society.[30]

In a typology similar to the one already laid out, Rawls distinguishes among systems of natural liberty, liberal equality, and his own theory of democratic equality. He applies each of these to the concepts of *positions and offices open to all* and *fair equality of opportunity* as presented in his second principle of justice. The system of natural liberty, as defined by Rawls, claims that a basic social structure that satisfies principles of efficiency and that allows for positions open to all those capable and willing to strive for them *(careers open to talents)* will lead to a just distribution.[31] Such a system requires a formal equality of opportunity in that everyone has at least the same legal rights of access to all advantaged social positions. Rawls criticizes natural liberty for failing to recognize the cumulative effects of prior distributions of natural talents and abilities as they have been favored or disfavored over time by social circumstances. Those with social advantage in reality have more opportunity. According to Rawls, the arbitrariness of such factors from a moral perspective renders such a system unjust.[32]

The liberal interpretation of equality, as Rawls defines it, adds to the requirement of careers open to talents the further condition of the principle of fair equality of opportunity. Positions are not open merely in a formal sense but all individuals at the same level of talent and ability and with the same willingness to use these should have the same chance of success regardless of the economic or social class into which they are born. This interpretation requires that "the school system, whether public or private, should be designed to even out class barriers."[33] Rawls criticizes liberal equality on two counts. First, it permits the distribution of wealth and income to be determined by the natural distribution of abilities and talents. Rawls views this "natural lottery" as equally unjust as the "social lottery" of the natural liberty system. Furthermore, the liberal interpretation only partially mitigates the effects of social conditions and class attitudes that influence the degree to which natural capacities reach fruition. Rawls is primarily concerned here with the effects of the family on the development of abilities and talents.[34]

Rawls views social contingencies and natural chance as equally arbitrary determinants of distributive shares from the moral perspective. He presents his interpretation of *democratic equality* as a more just and stable alternative. He arrives at this conception by combining the concept of fair equality of opportunity as contained in his second principle of justice with the difference principle. These two lexically ordered principles, working in tandem, create a basic social structure whereby the higher expectations of the more fortunate are just if, and only if, they work as part of a scheme that improves the expectations of the least fortunate in society.[35]

For Rawls, the role of education is to enable "a person to enjoy the culture of his society and to take part in its affairs."[36] With self-respect as the primary good in this system, the point of education is to enrich personal and social life even more than to train productive abilities.[37] His theory carries two implications for educational policy. One draws from the *principle of redress* whereby the state is to somehow compensate for inequalities of birth and natural endowment that are undeserved. Rawls notes that the principle of redress is not the sole criterion of justice but is one that must be weighed in the balance with others such as the principle to improve the average standard of life, or to advance the common good. In contrast to the principle of redress, "the difference principle does not require society to try to even out handicaps as if all were expected to compete in the same race. But the difference principle would allocate resources in education, say, so as to improve the long-term expectation of the least favored."[38]

The second implication which the theory holds for educational policy draws from a more general principle that talent should be regarded as a social asset, the fruits of which should be made available to all, especially the less fortunate. This represents a fundamental rationale for a shift in values. Instead of the principle "from each according to ability, to each according to ability," as exemplified in the meritocratic ideal, we now have a prior principle, "from each according to ability, to each according to need" with preference given to meeting the needs of the most disadvantaged where such advantages are beyond their control. What Rawls says about social and economic inequality, and about educational inequality by implication, is that it is justified only if it genuinely serves the least advantaged members of society.

From Equal Treatment to Equal Results

The Supreme Court's opinion in *Brown v. Board of Education* was a monumental decision for race relations in this country. From a mandate for educational equality has grown a radical transformation in our social institutions. But the

Brown mandate was modest in scope, merely calling for "equal treatment of equals" in the sense of respect for the dignity of all human beings. It represented a somewhat conservative view of equality based on the protection of individual basic liberties.

It was not until ten years later with President Lyndon Johnson's War on Poverty that the equality principle was to serve as the basis for broad-scale social reform through the vehicle of public schooling. No longer would equal treatment suffice. Underlying the War on Poverty was a commitment to affirmatively remedy the effects of past discrimination. In his 1965 commencement address at Howard University, President Johnson stated, "We seek not just freedom but opportunity—not just legal equity but ability—not just equality as a right and a theory but *equality as a fact and as a result.*[39] Underlying passage of the Elementary and Secondary Education Act[40] that same year was a renewed faith in the learning potential of all children. As stated by Francis Keppel, "The school must inspire hope, instill desire, and show all our children that they are free to develop their capabilities as far as their ability and ambition will take them."[41]

Indeed these were ambitious goals for public education. Equality meant more than equal treatment or access. Disadvantaged children needed more to win the educational race then mere equal inputs. The hope was that by redistributing society's resources to the economically and educationally disadvantaged at an early age, then real and not merely formal equality of opportunity would be achieved. This was the beginning of a compensatory education approach that would dominate federal policy for the next two decades and engage the government in a major redistribution of society's resources.

These early intervention strategies were based on what Rawls refers to as *liberal equality*. Their greatest significance rested in their rejection of former meritocratic notions of merit, ability, and talent as the sole relevant criteria for differential distribution of social rewards. Equality of opportunity took on a new ring. While the political rhetoric continued to emphasize individual rights and self-esteem, in reality federal programs identified the disadvantaged on the basis of certain group characteristics—race, handicap, language dominance, gender—and targeted these for *more* or *different* treatment. Government would continue to protect basic liberties. but would also provide an apportionment of basic benefits to those in need. Equality of opportunity was also seen as a means to promote the general welfare of society.

But the identification of group rights, the redistribution of society's resources on the basis of need, and the provision of a certain "floor" of basic benefits were still insufficient for some social reformers. It is here that we see a parallel development in certain social theories of that day, particularly those advanced by Coleman and Jencks, and the *democratic equality* ideal espoused by Rawls.[42] In the wake of *Brown* and to provide theoretical substantiation to the Civil Rights Act of 1964, Congress commissioned the U.S. Office of Education to conduct an inquiry into equality of educational opportunity. In 1966, Professor James Coleman of Johns Hopkins University concluded his massive survey of 4,000 schools and 600,000 students and published his findings in a report entitled, *Equality of Educational Opportunity*.[43]

Both the Office of Education and Coleman himself had expected to find gross inequalities in educational resources between predominantly black and white schools and to use these findings as an argument for large-scale spending to redress the imbalance. What the report did find, in fact, was little difference in educational inputs between black and white schools. It also found that a significant gap in achievement scores between black and white children was already present in the first grade and that gap widened appreciably by the end of elementary school. The only consistent variable explaining the differences in achievement within each racial and ethnic group was the educational and economic attainment of the parents. Coleman concluded that family background and peer differences account for much more variation in achievement than do school differences. While the report advanced the cause of school integration, it struck a hard blow at compensatory education.[44]

Segments of academia and the public at large reduced these findings to the conclusion that "schools make no difference." But in the long run, perhaps the more important aspect of the report was less its findings than its major thesis which redefined equality of opportunity. Coleman had been charged to examine the link between educational resources (inputs) and student achievement (outputs), the assumption being that social policy had to equalize the unequal inputs thought to exist among schools. Rather than use inputs as his criterion for measuring equality, Coleman used achievement or results. In effect, he redefined equality of opportunity from "equal access to equal educational resources" to "equal performance on standardized achievement tests." For Coleman, equality was not merely a means to an end but an end in itself.[45] As he stated in an essay that preceded the report, the focus had to shift from "equal schools to equal students."[46]

What Coleman was saying was that inequality runs deeper into our society than unequal educational resources. Family background and social class are the major determinants of educational achievement and these are the variables that must be compensated for to provide equality of educational opportunity. Coleman suggested that Rawls' work presents the possibility of examining the deeper questions of moral philosophy surrounding the existence of inequality in our society.[47]

In the early 1970s, Christopher Jencks and his associates at Harvard University further developed Coleman's thesis. They reviewed a vast bulk of evidence on schooling and family, and published their findings in a book entitled *Inequality*.[48] They argued along with Coleman that since the effects of schooling were essentially trivial, nothing short of a major redistribution of social resources would produce an adequate measure of equality. The aim of social policy must be equality of results rather than equality of opportunity.

A decade later we now realize that neither Rawls' *democratic equality,* nor Coleman's *socialist ethic,* nor Jencks' *equality of educational results for all* ever fully captured America's allegiance. Economic decline, municipal bankruptcy, and the rising costs of meeting legal mandates as to educational services all sounded the death knell for equality of educational results. Besides, as the list of disadvantaged groups began to grow and as assessment techniques became more sophisticated, a broad range of individual differences among students and between groups began to emerge. It became apparent that equality of results is limited by more than social and economic conditions; it is severely limited by individual differences in potential.

When we talk about the education of the poor, we can set ambitious goals of maximizing potential as did the architects of compensatory education programs back in 1965. We can give the poor a "head start" or remedy the effects of an "uneven start" through guaranteed minimal subsidies. But, at the other extreme, when we talk about maximizing the potential of the severely mentally retarded, for example, where the full potential may rest at buttoning one's coat, the cost to society not only diverts funds from other groups but may also be prohibitive. These are certainly hard problems for a *just* society to resolve.

As Coleman himself has pointed out, Rawls' theory runs into some serious stumbling blocks when applied to social policy.[49] *A Theory of Justice* is clearly a book about equality and one can reasonably conclude from it that, with regard to education, equality of opportunity would be the dominant consideration for Rawls. Yet in his lexical ordering of principles, liberty takes priority over equality of opportunity. How would he then resolve the issue of court-ordered busing to promote equal opportunity for racial minorities? School desegregation is a clear case in which individual rights of free association collide head on with minority rights to equal educational access. In fact, Rawls' theory could lead us to acquiesce in voluntary segregation, for when the state demands otherwise, it reduces liberty in order to increase equality and thereby violates Rawls' ordering of principles.[50]

The school desegregation issue points up a related limitation of Rawls' theory in light of educational reforms and legal standards that have evolved in the name of equality over the past several decades. Rawls treats the problem of justice as a problem relating to individuals in their separate personal capacities rather than as members of groups with collective interests. Whether groups should be said to have moral claims is open to argument. Nevertheless, groups identified by characteristics such as race, handicap, linguistic dominance, and gender have in fact demanded and obtained economic entitlements and legal rights in recent years. In the broader social context, affirmative action policies and programs draw from the concept of group rights. In the context of education specifically, government intervention in the racial integration of schools has come to require the proportionate representation of racial groups in both the student body and the faculty without proof of direct harm or injury to the individual beneficiaries. In such cases where status and rights are granted to groups, these inevitably modify the rights of individuals. On the other hand, concern for individual interests limits the rights of groups. Rawls' principles of justice and his priority rules simply fail to envisage this level of group rights and status between the individual and the state. Yet the concept of group rights has developed into a controversial political and legal reality.[51]

Of more general relevance to educational policy is Rawls' difference principle and the serious questions that arise in its application. How do we identify the least favored in our society? What criteria do we use for identification? How do we measure degrees of deprivation? Educational deprivation is a relative term. But what reference group do we use to measure the degree of disparity? In its application would the difference principle result in a regression toward the mean in student performance as scarce resources are diverted from the more advantaged to the least favored?

Rawls himself places certain limits on society's obligation to compensate for inequalities of birth and natural endowment. In his discussion of the *principle of redress,* he states that "society must give more attention to those with fewer native assets and to those born in the less favorable social position." He suggests that, in pursuit of this principle, greater resources might be spent on the education of the "less intelligent." But Rawls realizes that his principle of redress is not the sole criterion of justice. On the contrary, it must be weighed in the balance with other principles—to advance the common good of society.[52] Rawls clearly states that even his difference principle does not require society to even out all social disadvantages. But it would allocate educational resources to "improve the long-term expectation of the least favored."[53] This represents a far more modest goal for education than maximizing potential or achieving absolute equality of results.

Despite its obvious limitations, Rawls' theory of justice represents one of the most significant contributions to political philosophy of this century. Rawls himself did not intend for his theory to serve as a formula for redesigning the just society but rather as a normative standard, an ideal, against which to measure the justice of a given society.

It is true that America has not fully embraced Rawls' concept of *democratic equality*. But his theory has put teeth into equality of opportunity and has helped establish a moral vision for public policy making in the post-*Brown* era. His principle of redress, even with its limitations, and especially his difference principle have provided a philosophical foundation to reinforce certain social concepts of the Great Society— needs-based distribution of resources, compensatory programs, and social responsibility to the disadvantaged. His perspective on the role of education as enhancing "participatory" rights in society's culture and affairs has been argued before the courts on behalf of the poor and linguistic minorities. His shift in focus from inputs to outputs, from the distribution of resources to the distribution of benefits has provided a direction for educational policy making if not a goal. His view of justice as fairness has given moral force to the concept of equity as popularly used, in particular, by school finance reformers seeking to redress the gross disparities in expenditures between rich and poor school districts. Finally, his concern for environmental factors and the influence of the family on motivation and learning is echoed in the writings of social theorists such as James Coleman.

Summary Comments

Over the past several decades, government intervention on behalf of the disadvantaged has clearly demonstrated the connection among political ideology, moral philosophy, and educational policy. The first two mutually reinforce each other and together determine preferences within the third. That is to say, once we set upon a theory of rights, that choice shapes our vision of the relationship between the individual and the state which, in turn, leads us to certain policy alternatives.

Through the 1960s and 1970s, the moral precept dominating public policy in the United States was that of equality as distributive justice. The political vehicle used to breathe life into the equality ideal was the activist welfare state. During those years, the federal government assumed an increasingly affirmative role in redistributing society's resources and redefining rights in order to provide equal educational opportunity for certain groups of children. As a result, the concept of equality incrementally expanded from the *equal treatment* or protection of basic rights notion of *Brown v. Board of Education*, to the *more is equal* economic entitlements of compensatory education programs, and finally to the *equal status or condition* approach of civil rights enforcement. From equal opportunity or access, we slowly reached the goal of equal results.

Throughout this period, political philosophers and social theorists attempted to develop a theory of rights that would either discredit such creeping government interference in the marketplace of voluntary relationships or, in the other direction, draw from it a normative theory of the social order. For a theorist such as Robert Nozick, it was the first. For Michael Walzer and John Rawls, it was the second. From Nozick, we get a conservative argument promoting the minimalist state. From Walzer, we see a pluralistic development of the modern liberal ethic based on diverse needs and rights. From Rawls, we have a more radical attempt to justify affirmative government action on behalf of the disadvantaged.

The equality movement of the past two decades was primarily the brain child of modern liberalism. Nevertheless, the reforms that movement generated were clearly in the mode of more liberal-democratic scholars. In retrospect and without imputing any causal derivation between theory and policy, Rawls' *justice as fairness* provides a particularly useful framework for assessing that effort and for continuing the dialogue on equality. Rawls' theory has in fact underscored the problems that arise when government attempts to satisfy competing claims among the disadvantaged. It has also reaffirmed the inherent and irresolvable tension between equality and liberty interests. Nevertheless, framed as a system of social norms, it presents us with an ideal toward which to strive as a society that values both justice and individual liberty.

The evolution of the equality mandate of *Brown* has clearly presented operational difficulties. But it has also demonstrated the vitality of this precept as a guidepost for public policy making. Far from being an empty or derivative principle,[54] equality has provided standards to the federal courts and to Congress upon which to found substantive educational rights and has aided federal agencies in their enforcement. It is to those legal and political events that we now turn.

II

Race Discrimination: Planting the Seeds of Reform

Since the arrival of the first slave ship on our shores in 1619, the question of race has shaped the course of American history. In 1944 Gunnar Myrdal wrote, "When we say there is a Negro problem in America what we mean is that Americans are worried about it. It is on their minds and on their consciences." Myrdal saw race relations essentially as a moral issue. At its core was a conflict between more general American values of "liberty, equality, justice and fair opportunity for everybody" and more specific values of "individual and group living" dominated by "personal and local interests."[1] Myrdal also recognized two fundamental truths about race relations in this country. Not only have they been shaped by changing conditions and forces in the larger American society, but race itself has played a significant role in forging America's destiny. The race question has been an integral part of our history. No where is it seen more clearly than in the arena of American schools, the microcosm of society.

After two hundred years of ambivalence, conflict, and all too incremental change, we now know that the economic and political interests at stake make the problem far too complex for simple or quick solutions. During the nineteenth century, the struggle to gain equality for blacks was fought on the battlefields. In the twentieth century, the fight shifted to Congress, the federal courts, and neighborhood schools. Desegregation, and later integration, became the strategy and education became its cornerstone.

School desegregation in the post-*Brown* era has presented the three branches of government with difficult questions whose answers appear to lie in indeterminable facts and conflicting values. The debate has centered on the point where law, social science, and public policy intersect. Conclusions drawn from scholarly research have informed the judiciary in identifying harms and establishing remedies and have assisted legislatures and school boards in weighing policy alternatives. Studies have examined the impact of court-ordered busing on "white flight"[2] and the effects of desegregation on black and white student achievement and attitudes.[3] Recent research has also compared the effectiveness of mandatory busing and voluntary strategies such as magnet schools in reducing racial isolation.[4]

Indeed, as urban school systems became increasingly minority in population throughout the 1970s and as the Supreme Court established strict limitations on interdistrict remedies, the busing issue came to dominate desegregation discourse. As we entered the 1980s, desegregation and mandatory busing became caught up and swallowed up in community demands for greater local control and parental discretion. Fueling the fires of discontent were a more conservative political climate, an economic downturn, and a less sympathetic national agenda.

The process of integrating the schools as a means of integrating society has raised fundamental issues concerning the role of courts in establishing public policy, the federal role in shaping educational policy, and the relationship between public schooling and other segments of society. Once the equality mandate of *Brown* was set loose, only radical intervention strategies could sustain the momentum in carrying us to the idealized just society. But the backlash of the 1980s demonstrates how moral consensus can dissipate in the air of perceived political excess. Just how far can the organs of national government override individual and community interests in order to advance the collective good?

Defining the Constitutional Mandate

The history of government involvement with the race question in this country began in 1863 with the Emancipation Proclamation freeing the slaves. Two years later, the Thirteenth Amendment[5] officially ended slavery. Both raised the hopes of the black population that the opportunities incident to a free and democratic society were theirs to enjoy. But optimism was short lived. Racist sentiment in the South continued in the form of Black Codes that restricted blacks from holding office, voting, purchasing land within city limits, or even entering town without a permit.

The limits of the Fourteenth Amendment[6] guaranteeing to all the "equal protection of the laws" and the powers granted to Congress under the Amendment were tested early on in the Supreme Court. In 1883 in the Civil Rights' Cases,[7] the Court declared unconstitutional §1 of the Civil Rights Act of 1875.[8] That law had granted blacks equal access with whites to inns, theaters, and public transportation. Discrimination in these areas, the Court held, was a private matter not protected by the Fourteenth Amendment prohibition against state action. From here, the states took their cue. Between 1887 and 1891 alone, eight states enacted legislation *requiring* railroads to maintain *separate* facilities for whites and blacks.[9]

The issue of *separate but equal* reached the Supreme Court in 1896 in the now infamous case of *Plessy v. Ferguson*.[10] There the Court effectively sanctioned the South's division into two separate societies—one black and one white—a division that would remain legally unassailable for the next fifty-eight years. *Plessy* represented a challenge to Louisiana's Jim Crow Car Act of 1890, a law requiring railway companies to provide equal but separate accommodations for black and white passengers. In fact, only one of the plaintiff's eight great-grandparents was black. But the Court rejected his argument that to be forced to ride in a separate railroad car stamped him with a "badge of inferiority." Justice Harlan, in lone dissent, attacked the Court's decision as redolent with sociological speculation. In memorable language he further noted that ". . . there is in this country no superior, dominant, ruling class of citizens . . . Our Constitution is color-blind, and neither knows nor tolerates classes among citizens . . ."[11]

This judicially sanctioned *separate but equal* concept subsequently emerged as Jim Crow laws throughout the South, requiring the separation of blacks and whites in schools, housing, jobs, public accommodations, cemeteries, hospitals, and labor unions.[12] For that matter, the Court had validated a practice that was already widespread. At the time of the *Plessy* decision, not only southern and border states, but a total of 30 states in the Union, including most of the West as well as Indiana, Kansas, and New York, had *separate but equal* public school statutes.[13]

State enforced segregation of education facilities was to continue well into the twentieth century. Statistics bear evidence to the *separate* aspect overshadowing the *equal*. In 1930, in Alabama, Florida, Georgia, and Mississippi, per capita expenditures for white students were five times those for blacks while in Maryland, North Carolina, Oklahoma, Texas, and Virginia, they were double.[14] It was to this state of affairs that the National Association for the Advancement of Colored People (NAACP) set its sights during that decade.

Originating in the early 1900s, the NAACP had grown to over 400 local organizations and had won three court cases on voting, housing and juries by 1921. Committed to a strategy of litigation, it had hired its first lawyer in 1915. In the late 1930s, the NAACP Legal Defense and Education Fund (LDF) was created and served as the major source of funds for school desegregation litigation. During those years, the NAACP had formulated a strategy to legally challenge segregation. That strategy rested on two major points. First, sue for equal schools on the theory that the cost of maintaining a dual system would prove so prohibitive as to speed the abolition of a segregated system. Second, pursue desegregation on the university level where it was likely to meet the least resistance. Then proceed incrementally to the elementary and secondary level where choice of school is closely tied to choice of residence.[15]

Between 1938 and 1950, the NAACP gradually whittled away at the separate but equal doctrine by challenging it before the Supreme Court in progressively more problematic cases. In the first two, *State of Missouri ex rel. Gaines v.*

Canada,[16] and *Sipuel v. Board of Regents,*[17] the Court mandated that the state provide equal, albeit separate, facilities for blacks and whites. In *Gaines,* the Court rejected the option offered by the state for black applicants to attend unsegregated law schools in neighboring states. In neither *Gaines* nor *Sipuel* did the state provide any in-state legal education for blacks.

Armed with a mandate for tangibly equal facilities, the NAACP set its sights on the intangible inequalities of separate education. In two unanimous decisions handed down on the same day, the Court signaled to the South that *separate but equal* was gasping its last breath. In *Sweatt v. Painter*[18] and *McLaurin v. Oklahoma State Regents for Higher Education*[19] the Court struck down both interschool *(Sweatt)* and intraschool *(McLaurin)* separation of the races based not only on tangible inequalities but intangible as well. Among the qualities noted by the Court in *Sweatt* that are "incapable of objective measurement but which make for greatness in a law school" are "the reputation of the faculty, experience of the administration, position and influence of the alumni, standing in the community, tradition and prestige."[20] While the Court stopped short of expressly nullifying the separate but equal concept, its willingness to consider the sociological and psychological consequences of segregated educational facilities inexorably paved the way for the school desegregation cases to follow.

"Brown" and Its Progeny

Heady with the victory of *Sweatt* and *McLaurin,* the NAACP lawyers under the guidance of Thurgood Marshall were set for a direct constitutional attack on segregated elementary and secondary schools. They carefully initiated litigation in the District of Columbia and in four separate states: Delaware, Kansas (Topeka), South Carolina (Clarendon County), and Virginia (Prince Edward County). In each case, attorneys argued not only that black schools were inferior, but that the separate but equal laws or policies violated the "equal protection of the laws" as guaranteed under the Fourteenth Amendment.[21] The five cases were consolidated on appeal to the Supreme Court as *Brown v. Board of Education.*[22]

In a unanimous opinion whose rationale would generate infinite legal commentary for years to come, the Court ruled that legally compelled segregation by race in public schools does in fact violate the Fourteenth Amendment. The Justices appealed to the moral conscience of the nation in an effort to gather broad-based support for a decision whose potential social impact could prove limitless. Noting the importance of education as "the principal instrument in awakening the child to cultural values, in preparing him for later professional training, and in helping him to adjust normally to his environment,"[23] the Court asserted that to separate children "from others of similar age and qualifications solely because of their race generates a feeling of inferiority as to their status in the community that may effect their minds and hearts in a way unlikely ever to be undone."[24] In its now famous footnote 11, the Court cited social science evidence "amply supported by modern authority"[25] as to the psychological harm suffered by black children attending segregated schools and ruled that "separate is inherently unequal."[26]

But what exactly was the Court saying in *Brown?* The *separate but equal* doctrine of *Plessy* had not been transformed into "separate is inherently unequal" solely by the mechanical application of legal rules. On the contrary, historical periods are dominated by cultural paradigms of accepted social values. Courts frame legal concepts within this fluid social context. What equal protection of the laws meant in the society of 1896 as compared with that of 1954 and as applied to the social understandings, sensibilities, and perspectives of the time apparently had changed in the intervening years.[27]

Legal scholars have since pondered over the precise meaning of *Brown*'s mandate. Was the decision about education or race? The Court's reliance on social science data as evidence of the harmful psychological effects of segregated schools on black children would seem to limit the holding to education. Yet in the years following *Brown,* the Court summarily invalidated a host of other laws requiring segregation in parks,[28] in intrastate[29] and interstate commerce,[30] at public golf courses,[31] and other recreational facilities,[32] in airports,[33] and interstate bus terminals,[34] in libraries,[35] and in the facilities of public buildings[36] and courtrooms.[37] None of these decisions gave any suggestion of psychological effects. Perhaps then

Brown's central statement was not about education at all but about intentional racial segregation, or, as suggested by William Taylor, about the right to be free from legislation implying inferiority.[38]

Exactly what rights flow to black children from the Fourteenth Amendment equal protection clause—to attend integrated schools or merely to be free from state-imposed segregated schooling? Certainly the limits of judicial remedies in desegregation cases hinge on this question. Was the Court's decision in *Brown* based on a *nondiscrimination* or an *integration* model? If the former, then the right involved is that of attending a public school free of official discrimination and the violation is the official classification by race. Segregated schools are perceived as the effect of such violations, not as the violation per se. If the latter, then the right defined is one of attending integrated schools and the duty imposed on school systems is an affirmative one.

This confluence of right, violation, and remedy would occupy the energies of the federal courts for the coming decades. In fact, it was the Supreme Court itself in *Brown II*[39] that left the task of fashioning particularistic remedies to the lower courts. While the Court in *Brown I* sensed the moral readiness of the country to do something about racial inequality, it was also acutely aware of both the political realities of that day and of its own perceived limitations. And so the Justices refrained from an immediate implementation decree and ordered reargument in all five cases the following year. In *Brown II*, the Court bowed to localism while trying to preserve the legitimacy and force of its pronouncement the previous year. As stated by Owen Fiss:

> No one had a road map at the outset. No one had a clear vision of all that would be involved . . . The second *Brown* decision was far from such a vision: it was but a recognition of the magnitude of the task and an attempt to buy time.[40]

In *Brown II*, the Court left the task to the lower courts to direct and oversee the dismantling of segregated school systems but not at once, or even within any specified time, but merely, "with all deliberate speed." It directed the courts to order a "prompt and reasonable start" but recognized that local administrative difficulties might cause delays in implementation.

In the parlance of implementation theory, the Court was resorting, although not consciously, to an organizational development approach. Fearing that it could not force compliance with *Brown I* and that top-down orders from a higher authority would be ignored, the Court set on a strategy that would co-opt those responsible for implementation and give them a voice in its design and execution. Federal district court judges were closer to the pulse of the community and could more effectively fashion particularistic remedies. And local authorities would comply out of a sense of what is "right."[41]

The Court's apparent attempt to instill new values by moral persuasion and to build commitment and consensus within communities across the South was unrealistic. In fact, the desegregation process initially proved to be "a moderate, localized, sporadic, and delay prone struggle to gain token integration."[42] Not only did district court judges face strong local opposition, but they received little further guidance from the Supreme Court, open hostility from the southern congressional leadership, and apathy from the executive branch. The failure of Congress to support the Court and the unwillingness of the Eisenhower Administration to contravene local resistance until the Little Rock crisis "created the vacuum into which massive resistance entered."[43]

Little Rock finally forced the reluctant hand of President Eisenhower in 1957 to federalize the Arkansas National Guard in an effort to reestablish order and allow a federal court desegregation decree to be carried out. In a unanimous decision the following year in *Cooper v. Aaron*,[44] the Court sternly ordered immediate compliance and further underscored that it is "emphatically the province of and duty of the judicial department to say what the law is."[45]

During the first decade following *Brown,* states and local school systems engaged in numerous legal maneuvers and subterfuges to thwart the progress of school desegregation in the South. By 1957, at least 136 new laws and state constitutional amendments had been enacted to delay or prevent the process. By 1964, that number would increase to 200. Local school boards could manipulate school assignment criteria while lengthy and costly state administrative procedures dissuaded blacks from attempting to challenge local decisions. By September 1965, only the District of Columbia had desegregated completely. While West Virginia, Mississippi, Oklahoma, and Kentucky had commenced desegregation efforts in more than fifty percent of their school districts, in some parts of the South there was virtually no movement, with only token efforts in Texas, Arkansas, and Tennessee.[46]

Despite this initial foot-dragging, the desegregation of Southern schools would pick up significant momentum through the 1960s. Armed with strong presidential support from the Kennedy and Johnson Administrations together with the enforcement powers of the Civil Rights Act of 1964, the federal courts during this decade aggressively began to pierce the veil of local delaying tactics throughout the South. In 1964 in *Griffen v. County School Board of Prince Edward County*,[47] the Court struck down the closing of public schools as a means to subvert desegregation and declared the "[t]he time for 'mere deliberate speed' has run out."[48]

With the federal enforcement machinery in its camp, the NAACP was ready for its next victory in 1968 as it unfolded its litigation strategy. In *Green v. County School Board of New Kent County*,[49] the key issue involved a *freedom-of-choice* plan in a rural and residentially integrated Virginia town with only two schools, one for blacks and one for whites. The variance between theory and practice was clear to the Court. In theory, the child's choice was free. In practice, it depended on black initiative, stamina, and fortitude to circumvent the numerous bureaucratic obstacles set in their path. Periods of choice were few and far between. Blacks were often advised that white schools were overcrowded or that school buses did not pass through their part of town."[50] But there existed even more serious inhibitors to true "freedom of choice." As documented in a Civil Rights Commission study cited by the Court, economic dependency, fear of physical retaliation, and actual incidences of violence prevented blacks from seeking to attend white schools.

Yet the Court's decision did not directly rely on these

factual circumstances but merely used the statistical evidence marshaled in *Green* to raise certain negative presumptions about *freedom-of-choice* as an effective desegregation tool.[51] The Court was not looking for a new round of case-by-case litigation. Its tolerance for delay and evasion had been exhausted and it was looking for results. In *Green,* the Court ruled that school boards such as the defendant were ". . . clearly charged with the affirmative duty to take whatever steps necessary to convert to a unitary system in which racial discrimination would be eliminated root and branch."[52] Under such circumstances, school boards had to come forward with a plan that "promises realistically to work now."[53]

Green is a watershed case for several reasons. The Court displayed a skepticism toward *freedom-of-choice* plans, cited statistical evidence, and insisted on results. But most important of all, the Court used an outcome remedy for a constitutional wrong rooted in the decisional process.[54] In fact, it has been argued that *Green* marks a turning point from the constitutional duty to desegregate to a duty to take affirmative steps toward integration.[55] But the Court in *Green* defined neither a unitary system nor the steps necessary to achieve it.

In 1969, the Supreme Court issued a brief opinion that fundamentally changed the pace of desegregation. In *Alexander v. Holmes County Board of Education,*[56] the Court reversed the decision of lower courts that, with urging from the Nixon Administration Justice Department, had granted certain Mississippi school districts additional time to fully implement desegregation plans. Again speaking in a unanimous voice, the Court declared that "the obligation of every school district is to terminate dual school systems at once and to operate now and hereafter only unitary schools."[57] School districts could no longer maintain the status quo while appeals dragged on. It was a matter of "integrate now and litigate later."[58]

Two years later the Court was forced to address the issue of school desegregation in a large urban setting. And it is here in *Swann v. Charlotte Mecklenburg Board of Education*[59] that busing as a means to achieve racial balance entered the debate and framed the public agenda for the next decade. Although the school system had adopted a neighborhood school policy

by 1965 and the Fourth Circuit had upheld the constitutionality of that system the same year, the schools remained segregated. Following the Supreme Court's pronouncement in
Green, the NAACP initiated a new round of litigation in
Swann asking that the school board take affirmative steps to
integrate the schools.

In a unanimous opinion written by Chief Justice Burger,
the Court spelled out the broad remedial powers of district
courts in fashioning desegregation remedies. The Court sanctioned the use of racial quotas as a starting point in shaping a
remedy and the use of systemwide transportation as one tool
of desegregation. The Court further addressed the question of
causation, albeit in a general way, through discussion of
segregated faculties and the impact of segregated schools on
the establishment of segregated neighborhoods. But the Court
realized how deeply entrenched in American political culture
the neighborhood school had become. In a nod to localism,
the Justices left open the door to valid objections to busing
that may arise "when the time or distance of travel is so great
as to risk either the health of the children or significantly
impinge on the educational process" and that limits of time
may vary particularly with the age of students.[60]

Swann did more than merely implement *Green.* It established the framework for all future judicial decisions on
busing. Henceforth, the remedy must fit the violation. The
Court in fact used past discrimination as a "trigger" for a
remedy encompassing the entire segregated system—a trigger
not "for a pistol but for a cannon." Despite its stated rule, the
Court did not even attempt to tailor the remedial order to the
correction of that portion of the discrimination that might
reasonably be attributed to past discrimination. The Court's
attention to past discrimination itself rather than to specific
causal relations can be viewed as an attempt "to preserve the
continuity of *Brown* and to add a moral quality to its decision."[61]

Swann was the Burger Court's first major school desegregation decision and the last unanimous one. It was also
decided in the midst of the Nixon Administration's strong
antibusing program. The Court's apparent discomfort in
working out a rationale for its ultimate decisions would not be

eased in the coming years. Reading between the lines of the *Swann* opinion, we see the key but often conflicting goals of school desegregation crystallize—to remedy the specific constitutional wrong as matter of legal right, to generally eradicate racial inequality as a matter of social justice, and to achieve educational benefits for students—all the while maintaining political legitimacy at the local level. In sum, desegregation orders must balance societal, individual, and community interests.

Owen Fiss has suggested that we totally reject the *tailoring principle of Swann*—that the *remedy must fit the violation*—as too formalistic. He argues that, by suggesting that the violation will be the exclusive source of the remedy, the tailoring principle obscures both the need for choice of remedy and the criteria for choice. In fashioning remedies for structural reform as in desegregation cases, the courts should have available a choice among a host of remedies. Subsidiary considerations might guide that choice, including respect for state autonomy, evenhandedness, effectiveness, and fairness of the remedy. Fiss' argument addresses the pragmatics of local political realities. The courts need to be efficacious lest they expend their political capital. And he suggests that what they actually do in practice, in order the narrow the gap between declaration and actualization, is work backward to tailor the right to fit the most workable remedy under the given circumstances.[62]

The principal question after *Swann* was how to identify a constitutional violation in the context of a northern school district. The answer came in *Keyes v. School District No. 1, Denver, Colorado*.[63] Despite the absence of segregation by state statutory or constitutional law, the Denver school board had utilized a variety of techniques such as manipulation of attendance zones, teacher assignments and school site selection that resulted in both racially and ethnically segregated schools.

The Court in *Keyes* laid down a spatial presumption to be used by lower courts in defining a constitutional violation in such cases. Henceforth, a finding of intentional segregative policy in a substantial portion of the school district would raise the presumption of intentional segregation in the entire district and would shift to school officials the burden of proving that other segregated schools are not the result of the intentional acts. With court-ordered desegregation moving North, the Court felt compelled to clarify the distinction it had drawn in *Swann* between *de jure* and *de facto* segregation. In doing so, it breathed into the Fourteenth Amendment equal protection clause a standard of intent. The Court held that "in the context of school desegregation cases" and in the absence of a history of officially mandated segregation, a necessary element of an equal protection claim was *purpose* or *intent* to segregate."[64] To underscore the applicability of this standard to the North, the Court indicated that segregative intent could be established not only by the existence of segregation sanctioned by state statute or constitutional provision, but also by evidence of race-conscious acts or omissions that approximate the force of law.[65]

The Court in *Keyes* also took note of the rights of national origin minorities in desegregation plans. The Court ruled that Mexican-Americans as well as black students were subject to discrimination and that both groups should be placed in the same category when fashioning desegregation remedies. Those were the days when bilingual education was gaining recognition as a national policy for linguistic minorities. The potential conflicts between the separatism of that methodology and the goals of racial integration were yet to be realized.[66]

The validity and practicality of the Court's de jure/de facto distinction has been a matter of wide debate. Justice Powell, in a separate opinion in *Keyes,* called for an end to the distinction and for uniform remedies to be applied to both North and South.[67] For him, the uniformity would rest in an *effects* and not on *intent* standard to better insure the elimination of even subtle racial discrimination in the decisions of school board officials. A test based on purpose or intent would not only render equal protection claims difficult to prove, but would lead to "fortuitous, unpredictable and even capricious" results.[68] In the same breath, Justice Powell was criticizing busing as a desegregation remedy. Underlying his argument was a basic belief in the neighborhood school as "reflecting the deeply felt desire of citizens for a sense of community in their public education."[69]

In its decisions up to this point, the Court seemed to be waffling between wrong and remedy. The two issues inexorably coalesced when it became clear that systemwide busing alone would not achieve integrated schools in many of the nation's largest cities. A variety of demographic and social factors had left urban public schools to the poor and mostly to minorities. Included among these were the suburbanization of the previous two decades, middle class flight from economically depressed cities, a general public outrage with urban crime, as well as the vandalism and low achievement scores that were fast becoming characteristic of city schools.

But it was not all social and economic flux that was changing the complexion of urban school systems. Government policy had played a major role in creating both cities and suburbs with rigidly segregated neighborhoods and all levels of government had been implicated. Public enforcement of private restrictive covenants, segregative decisions of the Federal Housing Authority in granting mortgage insurance and the Veterans Administration in granting mortgage loans, and the public housing policies on site selection and tenant assignment of the Department of Housing and Urban Development had joined with a variety of local and state discriminatory tactics to create and maintain segregated neighborhoods where the schools were automatically becoming segregated.[70] And so with few white students to achieve racial balance and armed with substantial evidence that deliberate government acts had confined black children to certain schools, proponents of desegregation began to set their sights on the outlying areas.

The first metropolitan desegregation case to reach the Court was *Bradley v. State Board of Education of the Commonwealth of Virginia*.[71] Here in a 4-4 one sentence *per curiam* ruling, with Virginia's Justice Powell not participating, the Court struck down an interdistrict busing plan for the City of Richmond. The following year in *Milliken v. Bradley*,[72] the issue again came before the Court. Here the NAACP was to suffer its first major defeat following a continuous stream of court victories. The key issue was one of constitutional violation and the setting was the City of Detroit.

Chief Justice Burger, writing for a 5-4 majority, held that

"with no showing of significant violation by the 54 outlying school districts and no evidence of any interdistrict violation or effect" an interdistrict remedy was not permissible. Gone was *Green*'s focus on the effectiveness of desegregation plans. Instead, the Court reiterated the legalistic doctrine of *Swann* that "the nature of the violation determines the scope of the remedy." The majority refused to attach any legal significance to evidence that the state had engaged in segregative acts. Driving the Court's bottom line was a "deeply rooted" tradition of local control over education and its importance in maintaining community concern and quality education. This theme of local autonomy would develop into a common thread running through subsequent Court decisions.

But the majority as well as Justice Stewart in a concurring opinion suggested that metropolitan desegregation might be permissible under certain circumstances, that is, (1) where intentional segregation in one district leads to a "significant segregative effect in another district," or (2) where state officials have "contributed to the separation of the races by drawing or redrawing school district lines" or by the "purposeful racially discriminatory use of state housing or zoning laws."[73] In bitter dissent, Justice Marshall accused the majority of taking "a giant step backwards."[74] Aware of the conceptual uneasiness evidenced by the majority and concurring opinions, he concluded that the holding was "more a reflection of a perceived public mood" that the Court had "gone far enough in enforcing the Constitution's guarantee of equal justice" than it was "the product of neutral principles of law."[75]

Although *Milliken* still rests as the Court's final pronouncement on metropolitan desegregation,[76] it did not sound the death knell for continued litigation in this direction. The inconclusive criteria outlined by the Court have left lower courts to flesh out the precise type and weight of evidence necessary to support a *Milliken*-type argument. Decisions now turn on the peculiar facts of each case. Courts now weigh the significance of such evidentiary issues as the impact of public funded housing projects, official regulation of residential patterns and real estate transactions, segregative drawing or maintenance of school district boundaries, cross-district transportation or transfer of students, refusal to accept student transfers, and school site selections. Yet the Supreme Court itself has refused to elaborate on *Milliken* or to validate lower court interpretation of that ruling. The Court has either remanded, affirmed without opinion, or refused to review lower court decrees upholding interdistrict remedies in Louisville, Kentucky;[77] Wilmington, Delaware;[78] Indianapolis, Indiana;[79], Allegheny County, Pennsylvania;[80] and Benton Harbor, Michigan.[81]

In 1977, the Detroit case went back to the Supreme Court in *Milliken II*.[82] The Court expressly recognized that the right to an integrated education may encompass entitlement to relief for academic deprivation and cultural isolation resulting from segregation. In fact, the Court sanctioned the use of supplemental remedies in addition to student assignment and transportation. These included compensatory remedial reading and communication-skills programs, inservice training for teachers and administrators, guidance and counseling services, and revised testing programs. *Milliken II* represented an effort by both the litigants and the Court to broaden the view of desegregation remedies and goals beyond busing to achieve racial balance and look toward the adequacy of the instructional program. The decision in fact provided a healthy respite from the contentious problem of busing and redirected the focus of desegregation efforts from desegregation as an end in itself to desegregation as a means to providing quality education for black children. Equality of educational opportunity contained elements of both equality and excellence to narrow the achievement gap between blacks and whites.

Milliken II further raised the possibility of state financial responsibility for carrying out a desegregation order. In the late 1970s, as court imposed remedies began to prove costly for school districts, and as other groups such as the handicapped began to compete for shrinking local revenues, it became clear that states would be called upon to shoulder some of the desegregation burden. Nevertheless, the Supreme Court has demonstrated a reluctance to voice a position on the issue of state liability. In 1982, the Court affirmed without comment a 1980 Sixth Circuit decision that held the State of Indiana financially liable for desegregating the Indiannapolis public schools.[83] Both the district and the appeals courts had based their rulings on state legislation that had merged the city and surrounding county governments but had failed to consolidate school districts in the area. The Sixth Circuit had ruled similarly the previous year when it found the State of Ohio liable for transportation costs in desegregating Cleveland[84] and Columbus.[85]

In 1984 in a case that has worked its way up and down the federal courts since 1972, *Liddell v. State of Missouri*,[86] the Court refused to review an Eighth Circuit opinion upholding the basic elements of a 1983 settlement plan. That plan called for the state to pay the full cost of city to suburb and suburb to city transfers, magnet school programs in the city schools, and one-half the cost of the quality education programs in the city schools.[87]

To digress in the chronological ordering of events, the Supreme Court's pronouncements on school desegregation must be viewed in the context of related political circumstances. Throughout the 1970s, the busing issue continued to smolder and at times to erupt in the halls of Congress as well as in communities across the country. During that period, a conservative bloc began to form on the Burger Court which, in isolated cases, was able to garner a bare majority to shape a new agenda. That wing of the Court, in both majority and dissent, has continued to define equal educational opportunity within the parameters of local decisionmaking and judicial deference to local autonomy.

In *Milliken I*, Chief Justice Burger writing for the 5-4 majority emphasized our deeply rooted tradition of local control over education.[88] And in *Milliken II*, the Court took note of the district court's having adopted "specific programs proposed by local school authorities, who must be presumed to be familiar with the problems and the needs of a system undergoing desegregation."[89] In 1976, in *Pasadena City Board of Education v. Spangler*,[90] Justice Rehnquist, in a 6-2 majority opinion, maintained that once school authorities have complied with a court-ordered busing plan and achieved a racially neutral student assignment, they are not constitutionally required to make yearly adjustments in busing zones in order to maintain the initial racial mix. *Pasadena* has been viewed as "the light at tunnel's end." It hinted at long-awaited liberation from judicial supervision and a chance to make decisions on a clean racial slate.[91]

The year after *Pasadena*, Justice Rehnquist would again speak for the majority in *Dayton Board of Education v. Brinkman*.[92] Here the Court held that in a system where mandatory segregation by law has long ceased, the courts must look to the incremental segregative effects subsequent violations have had on the present racial distribution and compare that distribution to what it would have been in the absence of those violations. The court must then design the remedy only to redress that difference.[93] As the Court remanded the case, it reaffirmed that "local autonomy of school districts is a vital national tradition."[94]

If *Milliken I, Pasadena,* and *Dayton I* seem to reflect a Court mirroring an anti-busing national mood, that image becomes somewhat obscured by subsequent decisions. Here we see a relatively conservative Court in a growing conservative political environment renewing its commitment to integrated schools. In 1979, in *Columbus Board of Education v. Penick,*[95] and its companion case *Dayton Board of Education v. Brinkman (Dayton II),*[96] the Court ruled that proof of an intentional pre-1954 violation places upon the school board the continuing affirmative duty to disestablish a present-day dual system. Failure to take affirmative steps to integrate would raise the presumption of present intent to discriminate. These two cases reaffirmed the principles enunciated in *Swann* and *Keyes* that where there exists "uncertainty about whether current segregation is the result of official acts or instead the product of extraneous forces," courts should resolve the issue "in favor of desegregation plaintiffs."[97]

After *Columbus* and *Dayton,* the Supreme Court remained silent on the issue of desegregation and busing for three years. In 1982, the Court decided two cases involving the limits states may impose on the use of busing for school desegregation. In *Crawford v. Board of Education of the City of Los Angeles,*[98] the Court upheld as constitutional California's Proposition 1, an antibusing referendum approved by the state's voters in November 1979. This state constitutional amendment prohibits the state courts from ordering busing without proof of intentional segregation on the part of the school district. A busing order had been imposed on the Los Angeles public schools under a state law that required only proof of discriminatory effect. Speaking for the eight member majority, Justice Powell maintained that states should be left free to repeal legislation "that has proven unworkable or harmful when the state was under no obligation to adopt the legislation in the first place. . . ."[99] Having gone beyond the requirements of the Federal Constitution, the state was free to return in part to the standard prevailing throughout the United States.[100]

By contrast, the case of *Washington v. Seattle School District No. 1*[101] found the Court divided 5 to 4 over the constitutionality of Initiative 350, a 1978 voter-adopted initiative prohibiting school boards from ordering busing beyond the school nearest a student's home unless under court order. The initiative was aimed at the voluntary busing plans adopted by the cities of Seattle, Tacoma and Pasco. Speaking for the majority, Justice Blackmun cited *Milliken v. Bradley* and noted that "[n]o single tradition in public education is more deeply rooted than local control over the operation of schools."[102] He further noted that by singling out busing as an issue no longer subject to local decision making, the Washington initiative effected a reallocation of power that imposed "direct and undeniable burdens on minority interests."[103] These two rulings represent the Court's most significant statement on busing since *Penick* and rest on subtle distinctions as to judicial legitimacy and unconstitutional discrimination.

The development of constitutional principles, however, presents only half the picture with regard to desegregation. The major impetus for desegregation in the early days came not from the Supreme Court but from Congress with the enactment of the Civil Rights Act of 1964. It was the broad powers granted the Attorney General to bring desegregation suits and the termination of federal funds as a sanction for non-compliance that ultimately forced racial desegregation in the South in the late 1960s. And it is a retraction of that commitment on the part of the Reagan Administration that has seriously eroded the equality mandate of *Brown* in the 1980s.

Congressional Policy and the Battle over Busing

As is typical of judicial decisions enunciating new goals of public policy, *Brown* mandated a rearrangement of legal rights and obligations, but it did not guarantee nor did it automatically produce behavior in the real world consistent with that arrangement. Using courts to make things happen in the real world ultimately pits the victorious litigant against those who are inclined to resist. In fact, power relationships that exist post-decree can severely restrict the actual impact of the court's decision. The only countervailing force draws from the court's modest coercive resources.[104]

Brown II instructed the lower courts to "retain jurisdiction" through a complex "period of transition," and in effect, to monitor desegregation plans. But with little support from the legislative and executive branches, the federal courts in the early days after *Brown* could do little more than dance around southern resistance. It would take a shift in congressional membership and a change in Presidential leadership to put some "teeth" into the *Brown* mandate.

From the onset, southern congressional leaders pledged themselves "to use all lawful means to bring about a reversal of this decision which is contrary to the Constitution and to prevent the use of force in its implementation."[105] Added to southern opposition was the Eisenhower Administration's less than enthusiastic position on federal intervention in civil rights matters. Nevertheless, during the years immediately following *Brown,* Democratic members of Congress were able to garner sufficient support to enact some preliminary measures. The Civil Rights Acts of 1957, the first major enactment of its kind since Reconstruction, created the United States Commission on Civil Rights.[106] That same year, the Civil Rights Section in the Department of Justice was transformed into a more effective Civil Rights Division, headed by an Assistant Attorney General.[107]

The civil rights picture changed dramatically under Democratic executive leadership in the 1960s. President Kennedy, sensing black restlessness and impatience, proposed expanded civil rights legislation in June of 1963. President Johnson reiterated that request in his first presidential address before Congress in November. Late in June of 1964, following a seventy-five-day filibuster by southern congressional leaders, Congress enacted the Civil Rights Act of 1964,[108] the most comprehensive piece of civil rights legislation in a century.

The Act consisted of eleven parts or titles. Of those, two specifically promoted equal education opportunity: Title IV[109] and Title VI.[110] Title IV authorized the Attorney General to bring desegregation suits against state and local governments upon receipt of a written complaint by aggrieved individuals. In the context of education this provision was to result in litigation against local school systems and state boards of education. Title IV further authorized grants to state and local agencies to assist them in eliminating school segregation.

Title VI of the Act was enacted to assure that federal funds not be used to support racial discrimination. This was particularly significant on a political level to pave the way for a massive infusion of federal aid the following year under the Elementary and Secondary Education Act of 1965. Title VI provided that "no person can be excluded from participation in, be denied the benefits of," or "be subjected to discrimination under any program or activity receiving Federal financial assistance" on the grounds of race, color, or national origin. It further authorized funding agencies such as the former Department of Health, Education, and Welfare (now the Department of Education) to investigate complaints, conduct compliance reviews, and begin enforcement proceedings that might result in the termination of federal aid. Title VI was later to serve as the model for legislation protecting the educational rights of women and the handicapped.

The joint impact of Titles IV and VI helped move the South toward desegregation in the late 1960s. In fact, in the years after passage of the 1964 Civil Rights Act, the federal government made more substantial progress toward that end than had been made by litigation in the ten years following the *Brown* decision.[111] In 1964, only 2.3 percent of southern blacks attended desegregated schools; in 1965 that figure grew to 7.5 percent, and in 1966 to 12.5 percent.[112] Those figures would continue to climb in subsequent years following executive level guidelines and a more firmly articulated commitment on the Supreme Court.

As the courts moved full-steam ahead at the close of the decade, a decided backlash began to develop in Congress, reflecting a more general concern among the public with court-ordered remedies. While the *Brown* decision had successfully built a national consensus around the proposition that segregation by law is morally indefensible, the idea that integration is always legally required had not gained popular support. This became most apparent in the early 1970s as opposition mounted in Congress against court-ordered busing, fueled by the fires of an intellectual debate over white flight[113] and an antibusing mood sweeping the country.[114]

In 1971, the Supreme Court upheld systemwide busing as an acceptable court-ordered remedy in desegregation cases.[115] In apparent response to that decision, Congress moved on specific legislation designed to impede the desegregation process. In 1972, Congress enacted the Emergency School Aid Act (ESAA)[116] which provided federal funds for school systems undergoing desegregation. ESAA stands out as unique in the interplay among the three branches to develop the equality concept. Similar to legislative initiatives on behalf of the handicapped and linguistic minorities, court decisions shaped the context and the direction of the law. But rather than codifying into statutory law substantive rights and procedural protections identified by the courts on a constitutional level, some elements within Congress here set about to pull the reins in on judicial action. ESAA put civil rights groups on the offensive and on the defensive. As they struggled to obtain federal funds to promote desegregation, they also had to fight back congressional forces bent on using the legislation to limit the use of busing to achieve racial balance.

As early as 1970, the Nixon Administration had proposed a desegregation policy that included a federal funding plan to help desegregate the nation's schools. Civil rights leaders and liberals in Congress initially supported that plan until the Administration attached an antibusing provision prohibiting the use of the proposed funds for the transportation of students in order to achieve racial balance. This provision provoked strong resistance in Congress. Senator Jacob Javits (R., NY) was reluctant to introduce the bill. Congressional education leader Carl Perkins (D., KY) argued that the measure would merely duplicate services provided under the Elementary and Secondary Education Act of 1965.[117] When the Administration deleted the antibusing language, conservative leaders maintained that ESAA was not an "emergency program" but a "new permanent program of dubious value" that "would put Congress clearly on the record as favoring a massive, Federally aided school busing program."[118]

It was not until 1972, after considerable congressional negotiation on its specific content, that ESAA was signed into law as part of the Higher Education Act. Funds would be distributed to the states based on the number of minority group children of school age. States would redistribute their allocations to school districts on a competitive basis. The legislation also set aside special funds for pilot compensatory programs, metropolitan area projects such as magnet schools, bilingual education programs, educational television, and projects operated by community agencies other than school districts. The initial legislation did not prohibit the use of ESAA funds for busing.

But two years later when ESAA returned to Congress for reconsideration, the Nixon antibusing provision was enacted into law. This prohibited districts from using such funds "for the transportation of students or teachers (or for the purchase of equipment for such transportation) in order to overcome racial imbalance" or for transportation when the time or distance of travel threatens the health or affects the education of children or, if the educational opportunities at the schools to which they are transported would be "substantially inferior" to the neighborhood school.[119] However, federal funds could still be used to assist plans that involved busing as long as the funds were not used for busing per se. And the strict antidiscrimination criteria combined with federal compliance monitoring attached to the receipt of ESAA funds served as a check on local practices.

ESAA was the first in a series of small victories won by the antibusing forces in the 1970s. By 1974, the Supreme Court had moved desegregation mandates to the North[120] and congressional opposition to court-ordered busing had begun to mount. In 1974 Congress enacted the Equal Educational Opportunities Act,[121] which expressly declared the policy that all public school children "are entitled to equal educational opportunity without regard to race, color, sex or national origin" and further that "the neighborhood is the appropriate basis for determining public school assignments." Various provisions of the Act indicate congressional rejection of racial balance as the goal of desegregation efforts, and movement towards a less activist and interventionist federal role.

The Act clearly states that the failure of a school district to attain a balance of students on the basis of race, color, sex, or national origin does not constitute a denial of equal educational opportunity or equal protection[122] and that desegregation means the assignment of students without regard to race, color, sex, or national origin and not the assignment of students in order to overcome racial imbalance.[123] The Act lists acceptable remedies in order of priority and suggests the assignment to neighborhood schools, the revision of attendance zones, the establishment of magnet schools and finally the implementation of other "educationally sound and administratively feasible" plans, without any reference to busing.[124] Finally, the Act prohibits the federal courts from ordering the transportation of students unless all alternative remedies are found to be inadequate.[125]

Congressional debate concerning student transportation to achieve racial balance reached a peak in 1974 and 1975. Throughout this period, congressional members cited sociologist James Coleman's controversial argument that busing accelerated white flight.[126] In fact, Coleman was the principal witness at Senate hearings on busing and the antibusing forces capitalized on his apparent retreat from a pro-integration stance in the previous decade. Senator Joseph Biden (D., DE), who would later sponsor the first major and the most effective antibusing amendment ever passed by the Senate, voiced those sentiments when he stated, "[t]he architect of the concept now opposes it. Professor Coleman, an educator, first suggested the possible benefits of busing in a 1966 report. Now in 1975 Coleman says, 'Guess what? I was wrong. Busing doesn't accomplish its goal.'"[127]

As part of the Education Amendments of 1974, Congress added a provision to the General Education Provision Act prohibiting the use of federal funds, except certain impact aid payments, for transporting students or teachers to desegregate schools in order to overcome racial imbalance.[128] During that same year, Congress enacted the Esch Amendment which prohibited any federal agency from ordering the implementation of a desegregation plan that required the transportation of students beyond the school "closest or next closest" to their home.[129]

Beginning in 1976 and in subsequent years, Congress has enacted floor amendments to appropriations bills that supersede the Esch Amendment. The Byrd Amendment, passed in 1976 and reenacted in 1977, prohibited the use of federal funds for the "transportation of any student to other than the school which is nearest the student's home and which offers the course of study pursued by such student."[130] The Eagleton-Biden Amendment, enacted in 1978 and subsequent years, added to the Byrd Amendment the clarification that federal funds cannot be used to transport students in order to carry out a pairing, clustering, or grade restructuring plan but can be used for special education and magnet school purposes.[131] The intended effect of this amendment is to prevent the Office for Civil Rights from requiring transportation beyond the school nearest a student's home as a means of achieving Title VI compliance.

In 1980, the District of Columbia Circuit Court of Appeals upheld the constitutionality of the Esch and Eagleton-Biden Amendments in *Brown v. Califano*.[132] According to the court, Title VI offers an alternative means of enforcement by allowing the Justice Department to bring suit and seek busing as a remedy for violations of the law. The court ruled that both amendments were constitutional on their face but left open the possibility of subsequent court challenges to their constitutionality in cases where neither form of federal enforcement has been used effectively.

Some legislators have attempted by amendment to limit the authority of the Justice Department to use appropriated funds in order to bring any sort of action that requires transportation beyond the school nearest home.[133] Originally introduced as an amendment to the Justice Department appropriations bill, the Collins Amendment was reintroduced unsuccessfully each year from 1981 through 1983. In March 1982, the Senate passed by a vote of 58 to 38 the Johnston-Helms Amendment[134] which would have barred the federal courts from ordering that students be bused more than five miles or fifteen minutes from home. The bill would have further barred the Justice Department from initiating suits that seek busing as a remedy and would have allowed the Department to ask the courts to overturn existing busing plans that exceed those limits. The House failed to act on the bill. In October 1983, Senator Helms offered an identical measure as an amendment to the fiscal 1984 Justice Department appropriations bill. This time the Senate, in what turned out to be a largely symbolic gesture, approved the bill by a 52 to 29 vote. After the vote, Senator Helms withdrew his amendment, claiming that he had "made his point . . . that the Senate had displayed a strong majority will against [forced busing]."[135]

The Johnston-Helms Amendment raises several policy issues worth serious consideration. It sets a precedent for restricting the authority of the Executive to enforce constitutional rights, thereby shifting the delicate balance of power among the three branches of government. And by removing the Justice Department from most desegregation cases, it places the primary financial burden of litigation back on those least able to support it—the victims of segregated schooling.[136]

From Diligent to Dilatory Enforcement

When Congress enacted Title VI of the Civil Rights Act of 1964, it built into the law certain enforcement procedures. The Act provided that each federal department could ensure compliance by (1) refusing financial assistance to any recipient found violating the prohibition after a finding on the record and an opportunity for a hearing; or (2) "by any other means authorized by law."[137] HEW regulations adopted the following year specified referral to the Department of Justice as the primary "other means" under the law.[138] Through agreement with other executive departments, HEW assumed responsibility for Title VI enforcement with respect to most federal financial assistance to elementary, secondary, and higher education as well as other specified health and social welfare activities. But it was the Office of Education within HEW that would assume direct responsibility for implementing the law.

The task of desegregating the nation's schools would prove a monumental one for an agency that had developed for almost a century within a deeply entrenched political culture of local control over education. Now fortified with federal fund termination powers, the Office of Education would help turn the wheels of a major social revolution that would gradually change American federalism for the next two decades.

In 1965, HEW promulgated desegregation guidelines to implement Title VI and subsequently adopted official and more general regulations that same year. The guidelines primarily relied on freedom-of-choice plans and the good faith efforts of local officials. But they warned school officials that actual integration and not mere theoretical opportunity for desegregation would be the test of an acceptable plan.[139] The regulations were more formalized and had the force of law behind them. These mandated affirmative action "to overcome the effects of prior discrimination"[140] and permitted such action even in the absence of prior discrimination in order "to overcome the effects of conditions which resulted in limiting participation by persons of a particular race, color, or national origin."[141]

The following year, HEW issued significantly strengthened desegregation guidelines.[142] These new standards, which were applicable across the South, clearly sounded the death knell for freedom-of-choice plans. Free choice had failed to work in many districts, and school officials had to either find a way to make it work or adopt a more effective alternative approach. The 1966 guidelines strengthened the requirements for such plans, and, following the decisions of the federal courts, required specific progress toward faculty desegregation.

The guidelines elicited strong and vocal opposition in the South and sent a chill of fear through the North. According to HEW interpretation, Title VI and its guidelines applied to any school situation, regardless of geographical area, in which there could be found discrimination through public policy.[143] In 1968, reinforced by the Supreme Court's decision in *Green v. County School Board of New Kent County*.[144] HEW issued another set of guidelines that explicitly rejected freedom-of-choice plans that fail to eliminate the vestiges of a dual system.[145]

In 1967, the Office for Civil Rights (OCR) had been created within HEW. Its dedicated staff, recruited largely from among civil rights activists and answerable directly to the Secretary of HEW, would carry the new guidelines into the South. But they could effectively pressure southern school districts into desegregation agreements only as long as the Secretary of HEW supported those efforts.

Between the passage of the Act in 1964 and March 1970, HEW staff aggressively followed the 1965 Title VI regulations and the desegregation guidelines as they developed through subsequent stages. During that period, HEW brought some 600 administrative proceedings against noncomplying school districts. In the first year, the Department's enforcement efforts resulted in movement toward desegregation in every rural school district. In 1966, the agency focused on faculty desegregation and made its first moves beyond token desegregation of students. In 1968, rural southern schools were put on notice that they must complete the desegregation process by the fall of 1969. By the end of 1968, more than 200 fund terminations had been ordered under Title VI, all of these against southern school districts.[146]

The picture of agency action in the North was starkly different. From the onset, HEW staff were uneasy about applying Title VI prohibitions against northern school districts. In the North, segregated schools resulted not from state constitutional or statutory requirements but at times from less easily identifiable local policy. Nevertheless, in 1965 HEW commenced investigation of northern school districts, including Boston, San Francisco, and Chicago. The last would prove an embarrassment for the Department and a setback for desegregation in the North. After much political opposition and maneuvering, HEW entered into an agreement two years later with the Chicago public schools that resulted in only token movement of students and in only one section of town. By the fall of 1968, HEW was not even monitoring Chicago's performance under the plan.[147]

The Chicago fiasco marked a turning point in HEW enforcement activities. It sent HEW into retreat on northern school desegregation, created suspicion of the Department among northern urban Democrats in Congress, and served to reinforce the antibusing position of the Nixon Administration that came into power the following year.

During the Johnson years, the President and Congress

were aligned with the Supreme Court in forging federal deseg-regation policy. Immediately upon taking office, the Nixon Administration started whittling away at the gains made. This decline in presidential support came on the eve of Supreme Court pronouncements on northern school desegregation and heightened anti-busing sentiment throughout the federal ma-chinery.

In 1969, HEW and the Nixon Justice Department an-nounced a new policy. Federal officials would henceforth end reliance on fund withholding and would rely instead upon Justice Department enforcement through litigation. In that year, HEW conducted 28 Title VI compliance reviews. The shift in executive policy resulted in a steady decline over the next five years and by 1974 no reviews were being con-ducted.[148] Between March 1970 and February 1971, HEW brought no enforcement proceedings while at the same time continuing to advance federal funds to schools found in viola-tion of Title VI. In fact, up to 1980, HEW had terminated funds 225 times (only once in the North from the Ferndale, Michigan schools in 1973), deferred funds 70 times, referred 13 cases to the Justice Department, and used voluntary com-pliance 700 times.[149]

This posture of "benign neglect" pitted the Nixon Admin-istration against such advocacy groups as the NAACP and the NAACP Legal Defense and Education Fund (LDF). In the past, these groups had served as "private attorneys general" to initiate and develop legal precedents for the agencies to follow. They had also cooperated with OCR and Justice Department efforts by filing *amicus curiae* briefs in desegrega-tion lawsuits.

In 1970, the LDF brought suit against HEW on behalf of minority school children. Plaintiffs charged that the agency had failed to meet its statutory duty to enforce Title VI. In *Adams v. Richardson,*[150] the Circuit Court for the District of Columbia affirmed the district court's findings and ordered HEW to take enforcement measures in certain neglected southern cases. The district court had found that 113 school districts had backed down on promises to desegregate after HEW had stopped enforcing Title VI in 1969 and that 74 of these were still illegally segregated in 1972. In 1976, in the companion case of *Brown v. Califano*,[151] the court ordered HEW to conclude pending investigations and commence Title VI enforcement proceedings in 46 specified northern and western school districts.

In 1977, the plaintiffs in *Adams* and *Brown* moved for further relief. The Court heard these cases with that of *Women's Equity Action League (WEAL) v. Califano* (a case filed in 1974 as to Title IX enforcement), and entered a consent order pursuant to a settlement negotiated between the parties and HEW. The order established firm deadlines for HEW to resolve complaints.[152] The time frames required OCR to determine within 90 days of receiving a complaint if a violation had occurred, to seek voluntary compliance within 90 additional days, and to launch formal enforcement proceedings to terminate funds within another 30 days.[153]

In 1981, the LDF and the National Women's Law Center (representing WEAL) went back into court in the ongoing *Adams v. Bell and WEAL v. Bell* litigation. They asked the court to find the newly created Department of Education in civil and criminal contempt of the 1977 order and to order that federal funds be impounded as to those school districts where the Department was behind schedule in investigating complaints. Plaintiffs contended that the government had failed in 88 percent of its race discrimination cases to comply with the 1977 enforcement deadlines.[154] During hearings, the LDF further argued that the Department had met the time frames in only three percent of the compliance reviews and 35 percent of complaint investigations.[155] The court found the Department of Education in both cases and the Department of Labor in the *WEAL* case (Labor enforces an executive order requiring affirmative action for women and minorities by most federal contractors) in violation of the 1977 order. But the court was reluctant to find current administration officials in contempt as they had only recently assumed enforcement responsibilities.

The parties failed to reach an agreement by the court designated date of August 15, 1982, and both sides submitted to the court proposed revisions of the 1977 order. The government urged the court to vacate the five-year-old mandate or, in the alternative, to allow the deadlines to be phased out and considerably relaxed. The *Adams* and *WEAL* plaintiffs, on the other hand, suggested that the original time frames be maintained essentially while permitting the Departments of Education and Labor to place 20 percent of their complaints on an extended schedule of no more than 330 days for resolution.[156]

In March 1983, the Court rejected the plaintiffs' request to find the Departments of Education and Labor in contempt of court, but ordered the departments to speed up their standing investigations of race, sex, and handicap claims.[157] According to the revised court deadlines, in those cases where investigations had been completed, the departments had to secure the case or take enforcement action within 90 days of the March 11 order. In those cases where an investigation had not been completed, the agencies had 180 days to settle the case. In a major strengthening of the 1977 order, the court closed a loophole under which the agencies could delay resolving up to 20 percent of the cases indefinitely. The departments must now resolve even the exempt 20 percent within 345 days of receiving a complaint or within 330 days of initiating a compliance review. In addition, the departments must provide the Court twice annually with comprehensive reports on their enforcement activities, thus enabling civil rights groups to more closely monitor compliance with the court order.[158]

The Labor Department asked that the September 7, 1983 deadline to complete investigations be extended. However the Education Department's Office for Civil Rights alleged that it had almost eliminated its backlog of unresolved bias complaints and compliance reviews by that date.[159] The Justice Department appealed the court order to the U.S. Court of Appeals for the District of Columbia. According to Department of Education officials, the 210-day time frames worked against the resolution of complex cases by forcing OCR staff to complete investigations and to take enforcement action on cases that required additional work. In a brief filed in September 1983 with the federal appeals court, the Justice Department challenged the constitutionality of the deadlines, questioned whether they reflected the intent of Congress in civil rights enforcement, and charged that the district court's oversight of the Education and Labor Departments' activities violated the constitutional principle of separation of powers by establishing the district court as the "perpetual supervisor" of the two agencies.[160]

In September 1984, the Court of Appeals remanded the case to the district court for further fact-finding on two counts.[161] The first concerns the *separation of powers* doctrine and questions whether the case had been brought to enforce specific legal obligations or to seek a restructuring of the executive branch apparatus. The second count is related to the first and concerns the *standing* doctrine. Here the district court must determine whether the original plaintffs continue to suffer injury and therefore have standing to prosecute the litigation.

The real issue in the *Adams* litigation is just how far the federal courts can go in determining management priorities for an executive agency that has failed to carry out effectively its enforcement duties under the law. The case has now taken a turn in the appeals court that will have rippling effects far beyond national desegregation policy. The ultimate resolution of the case will have a profound and far-reaching impact on judicial oversight of federal agency activities and on federal civil rights enforcement efforts.

Recent Shifts in National Desegregation Policy

For the first twenty-five years following the Supreme Court's decision in *Brown v. Board of Education*, national desegregation policy traveled a somewhat direct course of expanded protections for students and affirmative duties for school systems. This is not to negate the heated controversy that arose over court-ordered transportation of students to achieve racial balance. But even here, the antibusing forces in Congress achieved only a modicum of success while successive administrations, both Democratic and Republican, enforced legal rights as found in the Constitution and laws by a Supreme Court that consistently evidenced a less than conservative tone on desegregation issues.

The 1980s, however, have witnessed a marked shift in national desegregation policy as formulated within the executive branch. And just as aggressive enforcement following enactment of Title VI of the Civil Rights Act helped to achieve substantial desegregation in the South in the late 1960s, so too, this recent redefinition of federal policy has decidedly slowed the pace and changed the direction of desegregation efforts throughout the country, but particularly in large urban school systems.

This change in policy has been most clearly articulated by Justice Department officials within the Reagan Administration and has been reaffirmed by both action and inaction within the Department's Civil Rights Division. Critics have assailed the Administration for failing "to develop—and implement—cohesive and consistent civil rights policies"[162] and for having "inadequately enforced and otherwise undermined, if not violated outright, settled law in the field of civil rights.[163] The Department has settled cases granting minimal remedies, has refused to support busing as a remedy, has shifted policy in pending litigation, has refused to appeal lower court rulings limiting the federal government's enforcement powers, and has supported congressional efforts to limit the power of the federal courts to order busing remedies. In sum, the Department's policy on desegregation mirrors the Reagan Administration's more general posture toward a minimalist federal role in education policy making and a deference towards local and state control.

Justice Department officials have been particularly vocal in their repudiation of busing remedies. In September 1981, the Assistant Attorney General for Civil Rights William Bradford Reynolds stated that the Department would "refrain from seeking race-conscious remedies, such as court-ordered busing, solely for the purpose of achieving a particular racial balance."[164] Less than a month later, he told a Senate Subcommittee: "Accordingly, the Department will henceforth, on a finding by a court of *de jure* racial segregation, seek a desegregation remedy that emphasizes the following components, rather than court-ordered busing . . . voluntary student transfer programs, magnet schools, enhanced curriculum requirements, faculty incentives, in-service training programs for teachers and administrators, school closings . . ., new construction . . ., and modest adjustments in attendance zones."[165] In a prepared statement released in September 1984 the Assistant Attorney General emphasized a diminished role for the federal judiciary, arguing, "It is time for the federal courts to release their hold on school districts that have long been in compliance with comprehensive desegregation decrees." Again touching on the antibusing theme of the Reagan

Administration, he maintained that "the country appears to have altered its course and returned to the ideals reflected in the *Brown* decisions—where equal education, not transportation, is the predominant theme."[166]

The Justice Department has also refused to avail itself of certain presumptions developed by the courts to more equitably allocate the burden of proof in desegregation cases. In *Keyes v. School District No. 1, Denver, Colo.*,[167] the Supreme Court held that a finding of state-imposed segregation in a substantial portion of a school district creates a rebuttable presumption of intentional segregation in the entire district, thereby requiring a systemwide remedy. According to the new policy, in deciding to initiate litigation, the Department would not make use of the *Keyes* presumption but would "define the violation precisely and seek to limit the remedy only to those schools in which racial imbalance is the product of intentionally segregative acts of state officials."[168]

The cities of Chicago, and Bakersfield, California, represent the clearest examples of the Department's willingness to settle longstanding desegregation cases with minimal compromise by the school districts involved. In the fall of 1980, the Civil Rights Division entered into a consent decree with the Chicago School Board calling for the school district to file a desegregation plan by March 1981 to be implemented the following September. The district failed to meet the deadline but submitted under court order a statement of principles postponing compliance until the fall of 1983 and defining a 70 percent white school as desegregated. In July 1981, the Justice Department voiced doubts concerning that definition and questioned the school board's all-voluntary approach. But just six weeks later, the Department joined the board in arguing before the court that the board's planning was "headed in the right direction" by adopting a voluntary desegregation strategy. In January 1983, a federal district court approved the Chicago plan[169] which was expected to leave approximately 350 of the city's 597 schools with predominantly minority enrollments while 45 schools would remain all black. The Reagan Administration applauded the plan as reaching for desegregation through quality education and not transportation.[170]

The Bakersfield case represented the first desegregation

lawsuit initiated by the Reagan Administration against elementary or secondary schools. At the same time as it filed the complaint, the Justice Department together with the school district proposed a consent decree that was later approved by the federal district court.[171] The plan called for the conversion of the district's four predominantly minority elementary schools into magnet schools that would offer special programs in science, computers, and the arts. The district was given three years to bring these schools within 20 percent of the racial ratio of the district's population. The Assistant Attorney General for Civil Rights hailed the program as a "blueprint for desegregation in the future without relying on mandatory busing, which does not work anywhere in any meaningful way."[172] Previous administrations had also supported the use of magnet schools but insisted that such voluntary strategies be accompanied by mandatory assignments where necessary to accomplish desegregation.

Consistent with its emphasis on local responsibility, the Reagan Justice Department has elected to take the side in litigation of school boards that have long resisted legal compliance with the mandate of *Brown* and it progeny. In August 1982, the Justice Department, in an unprecedented act, asked the Fifth Circuit to delay its review of the district court's student transportation order in *Davis v. East Baton Rouge Parish School Board*[173] until its attorneys could develop an alternative "voluntary" plan.[174] That plan which was submitted to the court the following December would have increased the number of schools dominated by at least 80 percent of one race from 15 to 37. The plan was repudiated by the NAACP Legal Defense and Education Fund and ultimately rejected by the school board itself on the grounds that it would prove costlier than the plan then in effect.

In November of that year, the Department filed a friend-of-the-court brief urging the Supreme Court to overrule the Sixth Circuit in *Kelley v. Metropolitan County School Board of Nashville and Davidson Country*[175] and to reinstate the district court's plan insulating elementary schools from the desegregation order. Justice argued that lower federal court judges had misinterpreted the Court's 1971 ruling in *Swann v. Charlotte-Mecklenburg*.[176] That decision had upheld busing to achieve desegregation. According to the brief, courts must first adequately investigate alternative plans before issuing a mandatory busing order. In January 1983, the Supreme Court refused to review the case. Civil rights advocates hailed the Court's decision as a major victory and one that would blunt the Reagan Administration's effort to seek the dismantling of existing mandatory busing plans.

But the setback was short-lived. In December 1984, the Justice Department took a controversial position on the issue of "white flight." In the Norfolk, Virginia case, Justice argued for the first time that a local school could abolish a complete busing program ordered by a court to achieve desegregation and could return to a neighborhood school policy even if increased racial segregation in the schools would result. In a friend-of-court brief submitted to the Fourth Circuit Court of Appeals, Justice maintained that the school system had been declared fully desegregated by a federal court in 1975. The Department supported the school district's desire to stem white flight and to increase parental involvement in the schools by returning to a neighborhood school plan.[177] A federal district judge had approved the plan the previous July even though it would leave ten of the city's elementary schools more than 90 percent black.

Lawyers for the NAACP Legal Defense and Education Fund labeled the plan "invidious and race-biased," warning that it would lead to resegregation across the country if allowed to stand.[178] In a friend-of-court brief, the Lawyers Committee for Civil Rights Under Law argued that the plan merely catered to "the desires and prejudices of the white parents" who had "created the segregated conditions in the first place."[179] The brief assailed the school district for attempting to justify the inevitable resegregation by providing tangibly equal educational opportunities in racially isolated schools, a concept repudiated by the Supreme Court 30 years ago in *Brown*.[180]

Not only has the Department refused to support busing as an effective remedy, but it has supported efforts in Congress to limit the power of the federal district courts to order busing as a remedy in desegregation suits. Justice Department officials from the Eisenhower, Johnson, Nixon, and Carter Administrations have challenged the constitutionality of such legislation. In a March 1982 letter to members of the Senate Judiciary Committee, four former Attorneys General and three former Solicitors General unanimously assailed congressional efforts to restrict federal court jurisdiction to enforce the *Brown* mandate.[181] Nevertheless, in May of that year the Attorney General endorsed the Johnston-Helms Amendment that would have barred the federal courts from ordering busing more than five miles or fifteen minutes from the student's home.[182] In fact, the Attorney General issued an opinion upholding the constitutionality of that bill.[183]

The Reagan Administration's policies and practices have indicated a decided preference for the neighborhood school and local responsibility for educational decision making. That position has driven Justice Department officials to reject any notion of interdistrict remedies or state liability even in the context of a voluntary plan. Yet it is just this type of collaborative effort that may prove most effective in desegregating urban school systems with high minority populations while enhancing educational quality in both city and surrounding suburbs.

The Department's position in the St. Louis, Missouri, case is a pointed example. In a brief submitted to the Eight Circuit Court of Appeals in *Liddell v. State of Missouri*,[184] the Justice Department supported the state's argument that it should not be forced to pay for a voluntary desegregation plan negotiated by the LDF between the City of St. Louis and 23 outlying suburban school districts. This represented a switch in the Department's position since it had entered the case in 1977. In February 1984, the appeals court upheld the district court order requiring the state to bear the entire cost of student transportation between the city and the suburbs as well as the cost of establishing magnet schools within the city. The Supreme Court denied review to the case in October of that year.

The St. Louis plan can prove to be an effective model for desegregating similar urban schools systems throughout the country. It combines elements of equality, excellence, and choice and offers, through the use of incentives, something of educational value to both city and suburban school children. Black students have the option of transferring to predominantly white suburban schools or attending any one of the newly established magnet schools. These offer both special programs such as visual and performing arts, math, science and technology and more traditional programs with increased resources and lower pupil-teacher ratios. Suburban districts will reap the benefit of additional students to help solve problems with declining enrollments while suburban students may avail themselves of enriched magnet school programs in the city.[185] Unlike the agreement reached between the Justice Department and the Bakersfield, California, schools, the St. Louis agreement is a binding commitment to minimum desegregation goals with the possibility of future court enforcement if the plan fails. The suburban school districts have agreed to recruit approximately 14,000 black students during the first five years, with additional recruits in succeeding years.

Civil rights advocates, traditionally opposed to magnet schools as an alternative to court-ordered busing, have hailed the St. Louis plan as a promising means of avoiding protracted litigation while effectively integrating city and suburban school systems. The Supreme Court's refusal to review the appeals court decision may signal judicial support for such voluntary measures that respect local discretion while shifting part of the financial burden on to the state. The St. Louis plan clearly embodies an equitable balancing and distribution of benefits and burdens to achieve both educational and excellence goals.

Magnet schools have proven a powerful tool for educational change. Research has revealed high levels of motivation among students and faculty, high levels of student achievement, fewer behavioral problems, and successful racial integration within magnet programs.[186] Research findings also indicate that magnet schools alone are relatively ineffective in desegregating school districts in general. But when combined with mandatory strategies, voluntary measures such as magnet programs can prove particularly effective in moving toward racial balance and improving instructional quality.

Large districts that have adopted magnet schools have demonstrated substantially higher levels of desegregation,[187] with the most dramatic effect in districts with less than 30 percent minority enrollment. In such cases, only small portions of whites are required to volunteer in order to effect desegregation.[188] Other studies have indicated that not only are mandatory desegregation plans more effective than voluntary plans in reducing racial isolation, but that mandatory plans do not result in higher rates of "white flight."[189] A most recent study commissioned by the U.S. Department of Education found that the highest level of desegregation is attained in systems that use a variety of methods as part of a total desegregation plan, including magnet schools, pairing, two-way busing, and mandatory assignments.[190]

Summary Comments

The Supreme Court's decision in *Brown v. Board of Education* has played a significant role in advancing desegregation as a matter of public policy. In *Brown,* the Court overruled the *separate but equal* doctrine of *Plessy* and declared that "separate is inherently unequal." Title VI of the Civil Rights Act of 1964 put teeth into the enforcement of the *Brown* mandate. HEW compliance reviews induced southern school districts to begin dismantling segregated systems through the 1960s. Justice Department lawsuits provided the courts with ample opportunity to breathe the spirit of *Brown* into a range of circumstances nationwide and to set the parameters for fashioning judicial remedies and apportioning financial liability.

But judicial commitment to school integration would translate into empty pronouncements without reinforcement from the legislative and executive branches. As court decisions spread from the rural south to northern urban centers in the early 1970s, congressional action constrained the use of busing as a judicial remedy. At the same time, shifts in executive leadership signaled similar shifts in the pace and approach of administrative enforcement.

In recent years, the issue of busing has become entangled in the equality-quality debate. The Justice Department has abandoned mandatory busing in favor of voluntary programs such as magnet schools to improve the quality of instructional services. Research findings indicate that voluntary strategies alone may not prove as effective in achieving racial balance as pairing of schools, rezoning, two-way busing and mandatory assignment. Perhaps the threat of mandatory assignment is critical to making magnet schools "magnetic."

The Assistant Attorney General for Civil Rights has stated that the Justice Department would work to see that black students in segregated schools are assured equal access to resources and staff.[191] This approach could well turn the clock back a century to the *Plessy* doctrine. More is at stake than the potential danger of blacks not getting their allocational due. First, research evidence suggests that racially integrated education not only improves achievement among black students, but better prepares them to function effectively in the larger society.[192] Secondly, in *Brown,* the Supreme Court measured equality by both tangible and intangible factors. It is not only quality of educational resources that must be considered but the public and professional perception of quality as well. Simply stated, segregated schools traditionally have suffered from inferior facilities and resources. That stigma will continue to limit the career and educational opportunities of black students for generations to come, long after schools have theoretically equalized educational services. Integration and quality need not be mutually exclusive. On the contrary, they represent the basic elements of equal educational opportunity for racial minorities.

Quality education is expensive. Desegregation strategies, whether voluntary or involuntary, are also costly. Herein lies the irony in the Reagan Administration's policy. On the one hand, it has emphasized voluntary approaches to desegregation. On the other hand, it merged into the state block grant legislation desegregation funds formerly allocated through the Emergency School Aid[193] and opposed subsequent legislation enacted by Congress to replace that program.[194] The Administration has also failed to support voluntary interdistrict efforts such as in St. Louis where a combination of mandatory and voluntary measures may prove the most effective in achieving both quality and equality for all students. The Administration maintains that "mandatory busing is unacceptable." Without federal funds to stimulate reform and test alternative approaches, that proposition translates into "segregated education is acceptable."

III

Linguistic Minorities: From Equal to Effective Education

Brown v. Board of Education specifically addressed racial policy in this country. But the civil rights movement that grew out of that decision struck even deeper at the heart of American culture. The sudden surge in black awareness and pride raised serious questions concerning the homogeneity in language and culture that had been sold to millions of immigrants as the only legitimate path to Americanization, social respectability, and political power. And as the country struggled to develop national policies that would negate racial differences, linguistic minorities breathed the spirit of *Brown* into national policies that would in effect preserve language and cultural differences.

America was not alone in having to face the language issue during this historic period. In recent years, linguistic rights have become part of a more universal concern for human rights. But the country had never addressed the problem square on and was suddenly under pressure to develop broad-scale language policy that could prove politically explosive.

Language policy is an emotionally charged issue, inter-

78

twined as it is with more fundamental concepts of personal and cultural identity and allegiance. Each country's unique history and national goals shape its linguistic policies. For some, the language question has arisen from colonization and subsequent independence; for others, from immigration. Third world countries such as the recently created African nations are a clear example of the first. Here we see the inherent tension between the desire to develop a national identity for a diverse indigenous population and the need to communicate, trade, and compete with the established world powers. What language should be officially recognized as the language of government, the courts, and the schools—the colonial language or one of the native languages? If the latter, which one? Language planning and policy in this context evolves as a conscious process and is designed to achieve clearly defined national goals.

Questions of language policy also arise in a very different framework through immigration. Advances in transportation technology and mass media have fostered the migration of people across continents and hemispheres in record time. Political revolution and economic instability have made relocation a matter of survival for many—the Greek, Italian, and Turkish "guest workers" in West Germany, the Indians and Pakistanis in England, the Vietnamese and Cambodians spread throughout the western world. In cases such as these, the host country must weigh policy alternatives to assimilate the influx of linguistically diverse newcomers. Typically, the school system is the first governmental agency to address the problem and typically the strategy is one of temporary accommodation.[1]

The United States fits neatly into neither of these two paradigms but is rather an amalgam of elements drawn from both colonization and immigration. Two centuries ago it was a fledgling nation with all the vision and problems that status entails. By the time it gained independence from England, English had become the dominant language of the colonies and was adopted by use as the official national language. But before the country could establish a unique national identity, it was swept up in a westward expansion and an industrial revolution that brought to America's shores wave upon wave of immigrants, most of them non-English speaking. Strict immigration quotas in the early twentieth century stemmed that tide, only to be unleashed in mid-century by political unrest in other parts of the world.

The early vision of America—a nation of individuals working in unison to develop a shared ethos, free from political strife, religious persecution, and economic hardship—has been tested over time. Inherent in this grand scheme is a conflict between the individualistic pioneer spirit and the necessity of working toward common goals. That conflict has come to a head in the bilingual education movement of recent years, a movement that has polarized the education community at all levels.

Language Policy and Public Schooling

The education of linguistic minority children in this country has weathered a stormy history of politics, pedagogical trends, and immigration waves. Movement from western Europe during the late nineteenth and early twentieth centuries stimulated the rapid expansion of public schooling. For educators and government leaders, the public school system was a means to prepare these new arrivals for a growing industrialized economy and to develop in them a national culture and a common core of values. Some immigrant groups, such as the German-Americans in the Midwest, attempted to maintain their language and culture through native language instruction. This practice became increasingly unpopular in the isolationist years following World War I. At that time, the legislatures of seven states made it a criminal offense for teachers to use a language other than English as the medium of instruction except in foreign-language courses. By mid-century, 28 states had enacted laws mandating English as the sole language of public school instruction.[2]

Throughout this period, the public schools developed a policy of apathy at best and open hostility at worst toward the native language and culture of immigrant children. School officials as a whole made little attempt to accommodate their differences or communicate with their parents. The prevailing method of instruction was total submersion into the English language and "American" culture. For immigrants to ask for more would place into serious question their commitment and loyalty to their new homeland.

During these early years, the Supreme Court invalidated several extreme forms of suppressive state legislation. In 1923 in *Meyer v. Nebraska*,[3] the Court declared unconstitutional a state law that prohibited the teaching of foreign languages before the ninth grade. Two years later in *Pierce v. Society of Sisters*,[4] the Court upheld the right of private groups to operate independent schools as an alternative to public education. Courts have subsequently cited both of these cases as affirming the right of parents to educate their children as they choose subject to "reasonable" government regulation. While these decisions theoretically opened the door to the use of foreign languages as the medium of instruction in private schools, they had no initial effect on pedagogical practice or philosophy in the public schools.

The years following World War II witnessed some change in methodological approach. Buoyed by the success of the Army Language Training Schools in developing foreign-language fluency among American military personnel, language educators adopted the audio-lingual method (ALM) to teach foreign languages to elementary and high school students. From there grew the English as a Second Language (ESL) movement that transferred ALM strategies to the teaching of English to non-English speaking students. For the first time it was recognized that such students require special techniques and specially trained personnel. The ESL approach was based on small-group intensive and highly structured instruction in English language skills in linguistically mixed groups where the teacher need have no knowledge of the students' native languages. The underlying philosophy was still all-American and all-English.

The civil rights movement of the 1960s tempered this push toward Americanization. Ethnic awareness and group rights suddenly turned the "melting pot" into a "seething cauldron."Ethnic groups with diffuse political power concentrated their efforts at the national level and demanded their share of the federal largesse. Underlying these demands were concerns not only for educational opportunity for children but also for political power, cultural identity, and economic advancement for the group in general. For linguistic minorities, most notably Hispanics, federal attention would translate into bilingual education.

Throughout the first half of this century, the non-English speaking population was linguistically diverse and representative of various southern and eastern European countries. Since World War II, Hispanics have formed the most critical mass of foreign-language speakers. By the mid-1970s, they totaled more than five million of the fifteen million persons from non-English speaking households and made up 69 percent of the school-age population among that group.[5] Data from the 1980 Census reveal that 5.3 percent of the total United States population are home speakers of Spanish.[6] Nevertheless, the demographic picture and the configuration of the non-English speaking population is again becoming increasingly diverse. In 1980 alone, the United States officially received 808,000 legal immigrants, more than in any year since 1914. Many came from Southeast Asia and Europe as well as from Latin America. In addition to these, the federal government estimates that a total of six million aliens have entered the country illegally.[7]

This new wave of immigration has had a staggering impact on the public schools. Between 1978 and 1982, the number of children aged five to fourteen years who came from homes where the usual spoken language was other than English rose from 3.8 million to 4.5 million. This represented a 27 percent increase. During the same period, the number of children who were actually of limited English proficiency increased from 2 million to 2.4 million, a jump of 20 percent.[8]

These figures reveal that the non-English dominant school population is not only increasing in number, but is bringing to the school setting more diverse language and cultural backgrounds, political allegiances, educational expectations, and group attitudes towards assimilation. The magnitude and complexity of the population to be served demands a rethinking of American schooling and a careful consideration of instructional options. The situation also demands a level and scope of governmental commitment not merely shaped by political tides but one that responds to educational need and recognizes individual potential.

But language policy is not merely an educational issue; it is clearly a political issue as well. Over the past two decades, it has evolved in fits and starts as the legislative and executive branches have intermittently bent to pressure from the left and right. The central issue is not whether linguistic minority children are discriminated against, but rather a profound disagreement over the most effective pedagogical approach to be used. With little support in constitutional doctrine, the courts have been left to the vagaries of the political arena to define legal minimums for the broader expansion of substantive rights.

Constitutional Rights and Functional Exclusion

The constitutional right to equal education opportunity for linguistic minorities carries the analysis beyond mere equal treatment and is distinct from the race discrimination issue for three reasons. First, linguistic minorities form a racially heterogeneous group. While the courts have recognized that ethnic minorities who are also racial minorities are constitutionally protected from unequal treatment at the hands of government officials, many linguistic minorities (Greeks, Italians, Poles, Russians) are not racial minorities and are not considered a suspect class for Fourteenth Amendment equal protection purposes.[9] Second, education is not a right expressly guaranteed by the U.S. Constitution. The Supreme Court has been reluctant to recognize education as a fundamental right implied in other expressly enumerated rights such as the right to free speech or to vote.[10] These two factors have severely undercut the success of broad constitutional litigation on behalf of linguistic minority children. Finally, the significant issue with respect to educating non-English speaking students is whether the Constitution imposes a duty on state officials to treat members of this group differently from and not the same as other students. Here the violation is the *same* and the remedy is *different* treatment, exactly the obverse of racial segregation. This is a knotty problem for courts to address either as a matter of constitutional or statutory right. Exactly what form should that different treatment take? And by what standards should legal compliance be measured?

Constitutional litigation has contributed in the most minimal way, if at all, to the development of language policy in this country. But a minor digression from linguistic rights is in order here so as to explain the initial hopes of constitutional theorists and the unfulfilled potential of Fourteenth Amendment litigation in this area.

The underlying questions relate to both linguistic minorities and the handicapped. Does the state have an affirmative duty under the Constitution to provide such students with special services to offset a personal characteristic that acts as a barrier to their educational progress, even where the government has played no role in the creation of that characteristic? Does the state's failure to do so constitute a violation of the Fourteenth Amendment equal protection clause? This line of analysis and questioning leads to the *right to education* cases. If education is a fundamental right, then the issue becomes whether the educational services provided are so inappropriate to the individual's or group's needs or so ineffective as to effectively exclude them from obtaining an adequate education. This *functional exclusion* theory derives from the Supreme Court's 1973 decision in *San Antonio Independent School District v. Rodriguez*,[11] a school finance case with broad legal and policy implications.

Rodriguez involved a challenge to the Texas school finance system. Plaintiffs argued that the state's reliance on the local property tax as the primary source of education revenues had resulted in gross interdistrict disparities in per pupil expenditures. Simply stated, property-rich school districts raised more tax revenues and were able to spend more money on the education of each child than property-poor districts. Plaintiffs represented the class of students residing in property-poor districts and claimed a denial of equal protection under the Fourteenth Amendment. They maintained that such a scheme, which was commonly used nationwide, discriminated against a *suspect class* of poor children. The Court rejected that proposition on the grounds that there existed an imperfect correlation between property wealth and income wealth in any given district. According to the Court, the discrimination was against a diverse and amorphous class including wealthy students residing in property-poor communities.[12]

The plaintiffs further argued that education is a fundamental right because of its close nexus with the constitutionally protected rights of free speech and voting. The Court rejected this nexus argument and drew an analogy between education and other social welfare services that are not considered fundamental. However, the Court implied that if the financing scheme had resulted in an "absolute" denial of educational opportunities to any children and not merely "relative" deprivation, perhaps such absolute deprivation would constitute denial of a fundamental right.[13] In a 5-4 pivotal decision, the Court demonstrated a reluctance to translate negative constitutional rights against government into a doctrine of affirmative constitutional claims to governmental services. The Court would take a somewhat different posture the following year, in *Lau v. Nichols*,[14] with regard to affirmative rights under statutory provisions shored up by administrative regulations and guidelines.

In the past decade, the *Rodriguez* opinion has provoked a wealth of critical commentary. Some believe that the Court's unwillingness to raise education to the level of a fundamental right entitled to special protection stemmed from a lack of judicially manageable standards. How would the Court determine the content or scope of education that is constitutionally due each child?[15] Others believe that *Rodriguez* was not a decision about the right to education, but rather a federalism decision—a decision about the proper relationship between the federal government and the states.[16] Still others maintain that the majority opinion hinged on judicial legitimacy and capacity. According to this argument, courts have limited remedial tools available to them. They cannot raise revenue themselves and to have overseen the implementation of such a decree would have demanded extraordinary resources. If the state legislature failed to comply with the court order, the judiciary could lose political credibility.[17] Whatever the Court's underlying justifications—probably a combination of all of the above—the decision proved a serious and perhaps fatal setback to the development of federal constitutional rights to education.

It was not until nine years later in *Plyler v. Doe*[18] that the Court again addressed the issue of Fourteenth Amendment educational rights outside of the desegregation context. This time the subject was the education of illegal aliens. In *Plyler,* plaintiffs challenged a Texas statute that withheld from local school districts any state funds for educating children who were not legally admitted to the United States. The Texas law further authorized local districts to deny such students tuition-free enrollment. Writing for a five-member majority, Justice Brennan stated that while education is not a constitutionally guaranteed "right," neither is it merely some governmental "benefit" indistinguishable from other forms of social welfare legislation.[19] The opinion discusses the importance of education in preparing individuals to effectively participate in our open political system and to become self-reliant members of society.

The Court concluded that the Texas law imposed "a lifetime hardship on a discrete class of children not accountable for their disabling status." The Court stated that "in determining (the) rationality (of such a law), we may appropriately take into account its costs to the nation and to the innocent children who are its victims."[20] The state defended the law as administratively justifiable. Texas officials argued that the law was necessary to conserve limited financial resources for children who are citizens and legal residents. They also noted a state interest in stemming the tide of illegal immigration. The Court rejected these goals as not sufficiently substantial to be considered "rational" in the equal protection sense.

The majority opinion in *Plyler* is narrow both in the support it gathered from Court members (only five Justices) and in its scope. The case clearly dealt with the extreme of absolute deprivation where children were completely denied access to a publicly financed educational system. Given this limitation and the Court's reluctance to decide constitutional issues where alternative statutory grounds for relief exist, it is unlikely that federal courts in the future will rely on the *functional exclusion* theory. The two groups to which the theory most directly applies, linguistic minorities and the handicapped, are already protected under a panoply of federal and state laws and regulations. And it is in the area of statutory rights that the education of these children has most successfully advanced.

Establishing a National Policy

National policy concerning equal educational opportunity for linguistic minorities has evolved over the past two decades through a series of congressional acts, court interpretations, and administrative guidelines. The difficult questions raised as to the permissible scope of federal authority over educational decision making, the nature of the equality mandate, the goals of American education, and the essence of American society itself have fueled the continuing policy debate.

Bilingual Education Act of 1968. During the 1960s, several factors coalesced and resulted in the passage of ESEA Title VII, more commonly known as the Bilingual Education Act of 1968.[21] Spurred on by the growing sums of federal education dollars flowing toward racial minorities, most notably in the form of ESEA Title I remedial programs, and educated in interest group politics through their example, Hispanic groups began to press for a share of federal resources. The 1960s also witnessed a growing national awareness as to the low achievement scores, high dropout rates, poor self-image and low family incomes not only of racial minority students but of school-aged Hispanic children as well. For this latter group, orientation classes and pull-out programs in English as a Second Language had apparently failed to fully integrate them into mainstream America. What lay at the root of their problem was not only poverty but their inability to communicate in English. And so the emerging voices of ethnic lobbyists and civil rights advocates in Congress paved the way for federal involvement in linguistic minority education.[22]

Congressional testimony on the proposed bill revealed a social problem that had reached acute proportions. The central focus of concern was on Mexican-American children in particular but on Hispanics in general. The median years of school completed by Mexican-Americans in the southwest was 7.1 years while for Anglos in the same region it was 12.1 years. In California as of 1960, more than 50 percent of the Spanish speaking males and nearly 50 percent of the females fourteen years of age or older had not gone beyond the eighth grade. By contrast, only 27.9 percent of the males and 25 percent of the females over fourteen in the total population of that state had not advanced beyond that point. These appalling figures were attributed to the language barrier faced by Spanish-speaking children when they entered school—a barrier that only grew more insurmountable with each succeeding year of academic failure.[23]

Political arguments on behalf of bilingual education found reinforcement in the research findings of programs in operation. By the early 1960s, several school districts across the country had begun to experiment with instruction through the medium of the native language. In Dade County, Florida, the impetus came from the Cuban community itself. This group represented the educated class of Cuban society, were politically organized and informed, and had migrated with a core of their own trained Spanish-speaking teachers. With seed money from the Ford Foundation, a bilingual program was initiated in the Coral Way School in 1963. In the southwestern states, particularly Texas and New Mexico, university-based researchers in language development and education served as the driving force in the development of experimental techniques to educate the poor and politically powerless Mexican-American students. These early bilingual/bicultural programs met with success and received recognition by such groups as the National Education Association which sponsored a conference in 1966 on educating the Spanish-speaking child.[24] Linguistic minority advocates had found a specific instructional approach to be advanced as the object of federal financial support.

The Bilingual Education Act that emerged in 1968 clearly represented an ambiguous commitment to that approach and reflected the undeveloped state of the art. The intended beneficiaries of the Act were children of limited English-speaking ability (LESA) between the ages of three and eighteen whose families fell within the Title I poverty guidelines. However, unlike Title I funds that are allocated on a formula per capita basis as an entitlement, Title VII funds would be discretionary and allocated on a competitive basis among school districts submitting project proposals. School systems would use these funds to develop exemplary pilot and demonstration projects. According to Senator Ralph Yarborough (D.,TX) who sponsored the original bill in the Senate, the goal of the Act was "transition to the mainstream of American life."

The bilingual education movement reached its apex in 1974. The original 1968 law had failed to define bilingual instruction. The 1974 amendments defined the method as education in the student's native language as well as in English and included a bicultural component. The amendments removed the poverty factor thereby expanding Title VII eligibility to a broader group of linguistic minorities. They also made provision for the voluntary enrollment of English-dominant students and authorized funding for staff development, research, curriculum development, the dissemination of instructional materials, and technical assistance at the state level.

At this point Title VII programs had been in existence for six years but the law's instructional objectives were still unclear and its prescribed methodology was still ambiguous. This lack of focus gave rise to heated controversy over *maintenance* versus *transitional* approaches to bilingual education. The first regards native language instruction and competence as an end in itself and promotes continued instruction in the two languages throughout the curriculum and throughout the student's years of schooling. The transitional approach, on the other hand, views native-language instruction as a means toward the goal of English-language proficiency. Once English-language skills are mastered, instruction through the medium of the native language ceases and the student is mainstreamed into the regular curriculum. The pros and cons of these two competing approaches have been the subject of bitter debate shaped by changing political and economic realities.

In early 1977, just as the Title VII reauthorization process was about to begin, the American Institutes for Research published a scathing critique of 38 Spanish bilingual projects examined in the fall of 1975 as they entered their fourth or fifth year of Title VII funding. Approximately 12,000 students were included in this $1.3 million study that had been commissioned by the U.S. Office of Education.[25] Bilingual proponents believed that the study's interim findings were released at that point as a strategy to weaken support for bilingual education in the reauthorization process.

According to AIR's findings, as compared with a control group of comparable students not instructed bilingually, Title VII students performed better in math but worse in English vocabulary and reading as measured by standardized achievement tests. The study further found that a large number of participating students were not judged by their classroom teachers to be limited in English language ability. The report concluded that perhaps students enrolled in Title VII programs were not in fact the intended beneficiaries of the Title VII legislation.

Educational researchers and bilingual education advocates attacked the study for its methodological flaws and invalid conclusions.[26] The research design failed to take into account differences in purposes, staffing, instructional materials, and teaching methodologies across programs. The study had pretested and posttested students over the span of perhaps six months of instruction without considering the cumulative year after year effects of bilingual education. The study had not accounted for differences among students in previous educational experience, years of bilingual instruction, and years living in this country. While the projects studied were in their fourth or fifth year of funding, not all students enrolled in those programs in 1975 had participated for the full project duration. Given the high rate of mobility in poor communities, it is reasonable to assume that some students were new arrivals to the programs or even to the country while others may have been born in the United States but recently enrolled in the particular school or program studied. In fact, depending on local school perceptions of the program, some students may have been placed in Title VII programs as a remedial measure to afford slow learners more individualized instruction and not to overcome language barriers.

The implications of the AIR interim findings were reinforced by Noel Epstein, the education editor for *The Washington Post,* who published a widely circulated attack on the inappropriateness of federally sponsored programs of "affirmative ethnicity." Epstein argued that the research evidence in support of bilingual education was meager and that the rationale for its continued support was less clear-cut than its advocates maintained. He also pointed to the success of Canadian *immersion* programs as the strongest argument against a need to teach students first in their mother tongue.[27]

Both the AIR report and the Epstein piece raised the ante

of the transitional versus maintenance debate and both fueled the fires of a backlash element beginning to emerge in Congress. The arguments they advanced and the questions they raised set the tone for congressional hearings on the 1978 amendments to the Act. Unlike the original hearings a decade earlier, advocates for bilingual-bicultural education were now on the defensive. The focus of debate had changed from the evils of American ethnocentrism to the educational value of bilingual education. The AIR and Epstein indictments of bilingual education further crystallized the importance of prevailing methodology, research substantiation, and the dissemination and interpretation of information by the mass media as interrelated factors in maintaining a national policy in support of bilingual education.[28]

Senators Edward Kennedy (D.,MA) and Alan Cranston (D.,CA) were the major sponsors of the 1978 amendments. These amendments in effect clarified ambiguities in the law but also addressed some of the abuses that had crept into local implementation of bilingual programs under the Act. The 1968 legislation had defined eligible students as "limited English speaking." The 1978 amendments broadened the target group to include students with "limited English proficiency"—those having difficulty reading, writing, or understanding English. In response to concerns that programs were in fact segregating students, the amendments expressly permitted a maximum participation of 40 percent native English-speaking students. This ceiling prevented programs from operating with a majority of English-competent students from the particular ethnic group. Eligible students within a Title VII district were to be identified as those "children most in need of service" under the law. Non-English dominant students were to be reevaluated every two years to determine the need for continued participation.

Included within the definition of bilingual education was instruction in the native language, but only "to the extent necessary to allow a child to achieve competence in the English language." The amendments further required recipient school districts to demonstrate a gradual assumption of program cost under local funds beginning in the third project year and to assume full funding at the end of the grant period.

Clearly, federal bilingual policy had settled on the transitional and not the maintenance approach and the federal government eschewed any role in long-term funding of bilingual programs. The 1978 amendments did not quiet the controversy over bilingual instruction and the federal role. In fact, on the heels of the amendments came a new Administration and a whole rethinking of federal intervention strategies, among them bilingual education. With the Act due to expire in June 1983, the Reagan Administration proposed amendments in the form of the "Bilingual Education Improvements Act of 1983."[29] These changes addressed a number of issues raised in a 1981 Department of Education report that questioned the continued "federal policy promoting bilingual education without adequate evidence of its effectiveness,"[30] a study whose research methodology and inadequately supported conclusions drew severe criticism.[31] In fact, the report's indictment of bilingual education and its strong support for intensive English language instruction drew heavily on the success of Canadian *immersion* programs.[32] But the report failed to acknowledge the obvious political and sociological distinctions between the educational experience of linguistic minorities in the United States whose language is not that of the dominant group and the experience of Canadian English-speaking students immersed in French instruction by their middle-class parents.[33]

The purpose of Canadian immersion is *enrichment* or *additive* bilingualism in contrast to the *displacement* bilingualism advocated by its proponents in the United States. A critical premise of the approach is that given particular sociocultural conditions, a home-school language switch is possible without harmful consequences for the student's native language proficiency. Another significant principle is that students are able to attain a level of academic achievement commensurate with that of students instructed in their native language.

The emphasis of the immersion approach on second language learning holds an obvious appeal for opponents of bilingual education. The proposed Bilingual Education Improvements Act of 1983 was an effort to use the Canadian successes as a basis for a major turnaround in federal education policy. But the changes reflected a more pervasive

Reagan Administration philosophy that the best federal role in education is to strengthen state and local discretion in educational decision making.

The proposed amendments would have authorized local school districts to adopt a broad range of instructional approaches, not just instruction in the native language, and would have targeted funds to children whose "usual language is not English." This narrow definition of eligibility could have eliminated students who might be able to communicate in English but who still needed special assistance. In fact, it was estimated that the use of the term "usual language" could have artificially reduced from 3.6 million to 700,000 the number of eligible students.[34] Finally, the proposed legislation was geared toward building the capacity of school districts to assume funding under local funds and would have limited federal funding to five years. As noted by Albert Shanker, president of the American Federation of Teachers, the five-year limit overlooked the fact that some school districts build programs for one language minority group only to have an influx of students from another country.[35] But aside from significant changes in substantive provisions, the Administration's proposal would have reduced federal support for bilingual education from $139 million in 1983 to $94.5 million in 1984.

The measure brought sharp criticism from bilingual education advocates. The National Association for Bilingual Education (NABE), the League of United Latin American Citizens (LULAC), the National Council of La Raza, and the Mexican-American Legal Defense and Education Fund (MALDEF) all urged Secretary of Education Terrel Bell to withdraw the bill.[36] According to NABE, H.R. 2682 "would revive discredited education practices which have harmed previous generations of linguistically different Americans."[37]

During this same period, House Education and Labor Committee Chairman Carl Perkins (D., KY) introduced a more moderate measure, H.R. 11, that merely would have reauthorized the Bilingual Education Act for an additional four years. Realizing the need for a more affirmative and strengthened federal commitment to bilingual education, the advocacy groups, led by NABE and La Raza, collaborated with Representatives Dale Kildee (D., MI) and Baltasar Corrada (D., P.R.) to develop an alternative proposal. More than 25 national education, civil rights, and ethnic organizations solicited input from their members and made recommendations to the working group.[38] In March 1984, Representatives Kildee and Corrada introduced H.R. 5231, "The Academic Equity and Excellence Through Bilingual Education Act." From the onset, the bill had more than fifty bipartisan cosponsors, including all members of the Hispanic Congressional Caucus. This was a far stronger mandate than that afforded any previous Title VII legislation.

Congressional hearings on H.R. 11 and H.R. 5231 elicited a decidedly stronger response from a broad base of bilingual supporters than from the opposing camp. The president of the Michigan State Board of Education testified as to the role Title VII had played in building state capacity and the continued need for federal support as, "most states, like Michigan, simply do not have the resources to meet this challenge alone."[39] A representative of the National Association for Vietnamese American Education noted the research evidence on the benefits of bilingual instruction—higher attendance rates, fewer dropouts, increased parent involvement, and higher achievement. He also emphasized the need for native language instruction at the high school level to prevent students from falling behind in the content areas while they master English.[40] In a prepared statement submitted to the subcommittee, the Navajo nation rejected "any changes in Title VII that would dilute or make its application more limited" especially those that "would favor English immersion programs and limit eligible students to those with no English language skills."[41]

Support also came from several national organizations. According to the National Education Association, bilingual education "makes excellent pedagogical sense as a route to excellence and English proficiency."[42] The National School Boards Association, while urging greater local flexibility and an expansion of the federal role beyond mere capacity building, supported the Kildee/Corrada bill as a "step forward from existing law."[43]

The only opposing testimony given at the hearings came

from U.S. English, a nonprofit organization founded in 1983 by former Senator S. I. Hayakawa (R., CA). The group's stated purpose is to counterbalance the pressures for greater government regulation of foreign languages in competition with English.[44] With a membership that now exceeds 30,000, U.S. English has developed into the most vocal and organized force in opposition to bilingual education. The group has lobbied for a constitutional amendment to make English the official language of the United States. It has also lobbied in state legislatures across the country for laws that would stress the use of English in local classrooms. Their efforts are beginning to bear fruit. In January 1985, a bill was introduced in the California legislature providing that "the official language of the state of California shall be English."[45] The California measure is similar to those enacted in recent years in Illinois, Indiana, Kentucky, Nebraska, and Virginia. The Virginia law specifically states that "school boards shall have no obligation to teach the standard curriculum in a language other than English."[46]

For U.S. English, transitional bilingual education that lasts for more than three semesters, at most, could throw this country into a "pattern of ethnic rivalries."[47] Their fear of language and cultural politicization have led them to advocate removal of the bicultural component from existing federal law. Culture, they maintain, is "very much the province of the home, of the family, of the church, of the voluntary associations." The mission of the public schools is "to transmit the shared culture that is the heritage of all Americans."[48]

Throughout the Title VII reauthorization process, U.S. English exercised a tenacious and focused lobbying effort against bilingual-bicultural education. But its impact on congressional decision making was substantially diluted by the organized and carefully strategized work of the entire bilingual education community and the Congressional Hispanic Caucus.[49] After months of negotiation and compromise, the thoroughly revised Bilingual Education Act was enacted into law in October 1984 as Title II of the Education Amendments of 1984, P.L. 98-511.

Congress reauthorized the Act for four years, from October 1, 1984 to September 30, 1988, with a fiscal year 1985 authorization of $176 million. The revisions provide for three new types of programs: Programs of Academic Excellence for projects of proven effectiveness; Developmental Bilingual Education Programs to help school districts establish projects for both English dominant and limited English proficient (LEP) students to master English and a second language while mastering subject matter skills; programs for bilingual preschool, special, and gifted and talented education; and Family English Literacy Programs for the teaching of English to parents and adult relatives of LEP children.

At least 60 percent of funds allocated each year must be reserved for bilingual education programs and at least 75 percent of that figure must be spent on transitional programs. These are defined as projects that first, combine structured English-language instruction with a native-language component and secondly, incorporate the students' cultural heritage into the curriculum. In addition to defining bilingual education in greater detail, the Act sets forth a specific standard goal of instruction—to allow students to meet grade promotion and graduation requirements. The law permits continued funding for training, technical assistance, data collection, evaluation and research. It also establishes a National Advisory Council for Bilingual Education composed of twenty members experienced in educating LEP students and to be appointed by the Secretary of Education.

The most controversial and significant change in the law is a provision setting aside from four to ten percent of overall funds for special alternative instructional programs. School districts can opt to use these funds to explore other methods outside of bilingual-bicultural education, including the various hybrids of structured immersion programs that have cropped up across the country in recent years or even English as a Second Language. This represented a serious and politically unavoidable concession on the part of bilingual education advocates. It was the first time in the sixteen years of legislative reauthorizations that they were forced to recognize the legitimacy of other approaches. For the opposing forces who sought total local discretion on methodology, this was a small victory in real terms, but a major one symbolically. In signing the bill into law, President Reagan noted:

> I am especially pleased that the amendments . . . allow some flexibility for local school districts to use Federal funds for the many proven alternatives to the traditional methods in bilingual education . . . In the future I hope to work with Congress to further expand this much needed flexibility.[50]

Nevertheless, the Bilingual Education Act of 1984 preserves transitional bilingual education as the preferred methodology, at least for the next four years. But the legislation still represents a weak national commitment to bilingual instruction and hardly approaches the magnitude of national language policy. The law merely provides funds on a discretionary and competitive basis to school systems willing to apply for consideration. The law does not allocate funds on an entitlement basis as do Chapter 1 of the Education Consolidation and Improvement Act (remedial programs for the disadvantaged) and the Education for All Handicapped Children Act. In fiscal year 1983, Title VII served more than 216,000 students from 106 language backgrounds.[51] But that figure does not approach the estimated 4.5 million linguistic minority students nationwide. Nor does the Act establish bilingual education as a legal right. The discussion that follows examines alternative measures tested by Congress, the federal courts, and the executive branch to substantively define such legal rights for linguistic minority students.

Title VI of the Civil Rights Act of 1964. The Bilingual Education Act has served up to this point as the carrot approach to promoting bilingual education. Throughout the 1970s, Title VI of the Civil Rights Act of 1964[52] served as the stick prodding school districts into accepting that approach under threat of federal fund termination. In fact, it was within the context of Title VI judicial and administrative interpretation that federal policy on the education of linguistic minorities most fully developed during that decade and where the focus shifted from non-discrimination to affirmative entitlements.

Title VI covers discrimination on the basis of both race and national origin. The first official statement on the implications of the Act for linguistic minorities came in a 1970 HEW policy guideline. Where inability to speak or understand English excluded students from "effective participation" in the education program, school districts had to take "affirmative steps" to rectify the language deficiency.[53] No specific pedagogical approach was officially endorsed. However, the mandate clearly went beyond providing the same services as for other students. Something different or extra had to be done. It was not until four years later that some clarification as to that mandate was provided, first by the Supreme Court and later by HEW.

Lau v. Nichols[54] continues as the only Supreme Court decision to deal squarely with the meaning of equal educational opportunity as applied to linguistic minorities. The case was brought as a class action suit on behalf of non-English-speaking Chinese students. The Court found that the San Francisco school district had violated both the Title VI law and HEW's implementing regulations and guidelines by failing to provide meaningful education to such students. The Court based its decision on the 1970 HEW policy statement as well as the 1965 HEW regulations barring official action that has a discriminatory effect even though no purposeful design is present.[55] The Court stated, "Under these state-imposed standards there is no equality of treatment merely by providing students with the same facilities, textbooks, teachers, and curriculum; for students who do not understand English are effectively foreclosed from any *meaningful* education" (emphasis added).[56] For the Court in *Lau,* the affirmative entitlement implied in the 1970 guidelines translated into *effective participation* and not merely equal treatment. For the first time, the Court focused on the content of instruction as a measure of equal access. But the Justices failed to order any specific remedy and thus left unanswered the question as to which educational approaches were legally permissible or mandated.

Following the *Lau* decision, OCR convened a task force to make recommendations on the enforcement of Title VI compliance. Those recommendations were promulgated in the form of a 1975 memorandum to school districts outlining the *Lau Remedies.*[57] The initial intent was for HEW to apply this document to school districts found in violation of Title VI.

However, in practice, it came to be used as a benchmark against which to measure Title VI compliance in the first instance. The guidelines required school districts with twenty or more other-language students to provide bilingual instruction to elementary school students whose sole or predominant language was other than Endlish. Unless the district could prove that an alternative approach used was at least as effective, English as a Second Language (ESL) alone was not appropriate at the elementary level. Since 1975, approximately 500 school districts have negotiated Title VI compliance agreements with OCR requiring native language instruction based on the *Lau Remedies*. While the legal underpinnings of those Lau plans and decrees began to shift in the 1980s, they continue to form the contours of equal educational opportunity for linguistic minorities in school districts across the country.

HEW had issued the *Lau Remedies* merely in the form of a memorandum. The Department had not followed the required procedures for promulgating administrative regulations, including publication in the *Federal Register* and granting the opportunity for public comment. As a result, school districts argued that the guidelines lacked the force of law. One such challenge brought by an Alaska school district led to a consent decree, *Northwest Arctic School District v. Califano*.[58] Here the government conceded that the guidelines were unenforceable and further agreed to issue official rules for the enforcement of Title VI.

During the closing days of the Carter Administration, the newly formed Department of Education published proposed regulations outlining the rights of linguistic minority students and the responsibilities of school districts under Title VI.[59] Nearly 450 people testified and over 4,500 written comments were submitted during the public comment period that was extended from 60 to 75 days.[60] The debate that ensued brought to center stage the key forces shaping language policy in this country. Such groups as NABE, La Raza, and MALDEF believed the regulations lacked adequate detail to preserve bilingual education as a mandate. Others such as the American Federation of Teachers, and the National Education Association believed the proposal was overly detailed and exerted strong lobbying efforts to bury it.[61] The proposed regulations mandated specific entrance and exit criteria, instructional services, and staffing requirements within the context of bilingual education.

Opponents of bilingual education argued that the regulations overly intruded into decision making and were a violation of the decentralized American educational tradition. Proponents of the concept opposed the regulations as well but on the grounds that the federal government had not gone far enough in mandating services for identified students. In February 1981, in the early days of the Reagan Administration, the Department of Education withdrew the proposed regulations. The justification for their withdrawal was based on their potential cost to local school districts and their prescriptiveness in mandating one specific methodology—bilingual instruction. OCR subsequently reverted to the 1970 HEW guidelines. These merely mandate that school districts take "affirmative steps" without prescribing a particular method of instruction.

Equal Educational Opportunities Act of 1974. The Supreme Court's 1974 opinion in *Lau v. Nichols* shifted the focus from equal to effective participation. Congress adopted that standard as a matter of legislative policy later that same year in the Equal Educational Opportunities Act.[62] The Act is primarily concerned with busing to achieve racial balance. However, it also prohibits the denial of equal educational opportunity by "the failure by an educational agency to take appropriate action to overcome language barriers that impede equal participation by its students in its instructional program." This provision of the Act was not part of the original bill but was proposed as an amendment from the floor of the House after weeks of heated controversy over the Act's busing provisions. As such, it generated minimal debate. Without adequate legislative history as their guide, the courts have struggled to inject meaning into the "appropriate action" requirement for language-minority children.

It is not surprising that the Fifth Circuit Court of Appeals, that architect of the law defining the rights of racial minorities, has had the first and last word on the education rights of linguistic minorities.[63] The fundamental question presented in these cases is whether Congress, in enacting §1703(f) on the heels of the *Lau* decision, intended to go beyond the essential *Lau* requirement that schools merely do something. Does §1703(f) imply, through the use of the term "appropriate action," a more specific obligation on state and local educational agencies?

In *Morales v. Shannon*,[64] the Fifth Circuit observed that "[i]t is now an unlawful educational practice to fail to take appropriate action to overcome language barriers," but did not specify the type of action to be taken. Other federal district courts have not hesitated to add considerable detail to the mandate. In *Cintron v. Brentwood Free School District*,[65] the court noted that "appropriate action" includes specific methods for identifying target children, training programs for bilingual teachers and aides, established procedures for mainstreaming students, and planned opportunities for interaction between non-English- and English-speaking students. Citing *Cintron*, the court in *Rios v. Reed*[66] articulated the position that effective education for linguistic minority students must include instruction in the native language by competent teachers and the use of validated tests to assess English proficiency as exit criteria. However, the court was careful to note that school districts are not "obligated to offer a program of indefinite duration for instruction in Spanish art and culture; the bilingual element is necessary only to enhance the child's learning ability. The purpose is not to establish a bilingual society."[67] The year was 1978 and the bilingual tide had turned from a maintenance to a transitional approach.

Not all courts have agreed that §1703(f) requires bilingual/bicultural education. One of these is the Ninth Circuit, the same court whose decision to deny relief under Title VI and the equal protection clause to the plaintiffs in *Lau v. Nichols* was reversed by the Supreme Court. In *Guadalupe Organization, Inc. v. Tempe Elementary School*,[68] decided just eight weeks after *Rios*, the appeals court held that to interpret "appropriate action" as requiring bilingual/bicultural instructional programs "would distort the relevant statutory language severely. The interpretation of floor amendments unaccompanied by illuminating debate should adhere closely to the ordinary meaning of the amendment's language."[69] It must be noted, however, that the plaintiffs in Guadalupe sought bilingual instruction not as a transitional device but as a permanent educational end in itself. For the court to find such a mandate within §1703(f) without any support in the legislative history would have developed federal policy beyond that established by Congress under ESEA Title VII or outlined in early litigation on the issue.

The *Guadalupe* court was reluctant to second-guess congressional intent. Other federal courts have hesitated to become overly involved in the daily management of school districts. In *Martin Luther King Jr. Elementary School Children v. Ann Arbor School District*,[70] the district court seemed reluctant to use the judicial forum to determine the appropriateness or adequacy of educational programs. The court stated, "It is not for the courts to harmonize conflicting objectives by making judgments involving issues of pedagogy."[71] Instead, the court proposed examining the appropriateness of school district initiatives "in light of information they reasonably could be expected to have and that [their] judgments are rational."[72] The decision is significant on two points. First, the court held that a *de jure* segregated system is not a prerequisite to finding a denial of equal educational opportunity under §1703(f) and second, that "language barrier" as used in the statute includes a child's inability to use standard English effectively even where that inability stems from the use of a non-standard variant such as Black English.

This early litigation under §1703(f) outlined a variety of appropriate measures that schools could initiate to help students overcome language barriers. More recent cases have centered on the proof necessary to establish a violation under §1703(f) and on the expected outcomes after a school system has taken "appropriate action." This redirection from inputs to the instructional process and more recently to outputs parallels the development in federal policy in other policy areas—from equality as a means to equality as an end.

In *United States v. Texas*,[73] a case that represents on-going desegregation litigation spanning more than a decade, the district court held that §1703(f) contains no requirement of proof of intent to discriminate. Thus, the provision "applies to any failure by an educational agency to overcome language barriers, regardless of how the barrier originated or why the agency has neglected to take corrective measures."[74] The court considered the issue of expected results and concluded that "[t]he term 'appropriate action' must necessarily include only those measures which will actually overcome the problem."[75]

In attempting to fashion a remedy, the court noted that bilingual instruction per se is not required by §1703(f) or any other provision of the law. The court's remedy mandating bilingual instruction to all students of limited English proficiency in the Texas public schools, however, was informed by testimony provided by educational experts, including the defendants, that bilingual instruction is "uniquely suited" to meet the needs of the state's Spanish-speaking students.[76] Several months following the district court's ruling, the Texas state legislature enacted a bilingual education law mandating native language instruction through sixth grade where there are twenty or more students of limited English proficiency in any one grade. The law requires only one hour per day of ESL for the secondary schools.[77] In July 1982, the Fifth Circuit overturned the lower court decision, holding that the legislature's 1981 Bilingual and Special Language Programs Act would adequately serve Mexican-American students.

This brings us back to the Fifth Circuit. In 1981 in *Castaneda v. Pickard*,[78] that court reiterated a *whatever works* standard for determining statutory compliance. The court developed a three-tier mode of analysis to be used by federal courts in determining the appropriateness of language remediation programs. First, the court must examine the evidence as to "the soundness of the educational theory upon which the program is based."[79] Second, the court must determine whether the programs and practices used by the school system are "reasonably calculated to implement effectively the educational theory adopted." And finally, the court must determine if the program has produced results indicating that language barriers have been overcome.[80] As to the precise nature of the "appropriate action" mandate, the court stated that "§1703(f) leaves schools free to determine [how] to discharge these obligations . . . so long as schools design programs which are reasonably calculated to enable students to obtain parity of participation in the standard instructional program within a reasonable length of time after they enter school."[81]

The *Castaneda* court clearly rejected any notions of maintenance bilingual education. As interpreted by the Fifth Circuit, the legislative purpose of §1703(f) is to provide whatever instruction is necessary in order to move linguistic minority students into "regular" classrooms as quickly as possible. The goal of special assistance programs, according to this court, is twofold: to develop English language skills and to overcome academic deficiencies. Yet as we read the second point of the *Castaneda* analysis, a thorough inquiry into the quality and appropriateness of a school district's language program is an essential and legitimate part of a §1703 challenge. And one of the key issues for the court was whether the district's so-called bilingual education teachers could actually speak or understand Spanish. This has become a useful point of departure for advocates examining programs in other cities. It has also provided a standard for the federal courts as evidenced in a 1983 decision of the district court in Denver.[82] There the court relied heavily on the Fifth Circuit's reasoning in *Castaneda* and stated clearly that "the key to an effective elementary bilingual classroom is the ability of the teacher to communicate with the children." To assure that understandable instruction is taking place, "there must be assurance that the teacher has the necessary bilingual skills."[83]

Section 1703(f) was enacted almost as an afterthought quietly tacked on to controversial busing legislation. After a decade of slow judicial development, it may soon provide the primary vehicle for effecting educational reform as to the rights of linguistic minorities. As noted earlier, given the availability of statutory means and the broad social and political impact of a *functional exclusion* theory, the courts undoubtedly will demonstrate a reluctance to expand the constitutional rights of linguistic minority students under such a theory. Adverse court interpretations have undercut severely the utility of alternative statutes such as Title VI.[84] What remains is §1703(f) whose scant legislative history lends itself to the broadest and narrowest of interpretations.

Recent court decisions clearly have favored a *results* standard. And the process and outcomes analysis of *Castaneda* is now the only active standard for judicial enforcement efforts. Until the Supreme Court rules otherwise, that decision and its progeny instruct us on two significant points concerning

§1703(f) of the Equal Educational Opportunities Act. First, the law does not require proof of discriminatory intent. Good faith efforts on the part of school districts will not suffice; programs must have the effect of removing barriers that impede educational progress. Second, teachers working with linguistic-minority children must be able to communicate in the language understood by those children in order to be effective. For the proponents of transitional bilingual-bicultural education, the most difficult obstacle to overcome is a growing national trend away from the conventional conception of this method toward alternative approaches that give only ancillary recognition at best, and no recognition at worst, to the child's home language and culture.

Myths and Realities of Bilingual Education

Contemporary discourse on the education of linguistic minority children is fraught with social myths and educational misunderstandings. It is also threaded through with political, economic, and cognitive realities. But the deafening shrill of political rhetoric has prevented the wider population of policy makers, educators, parents, and the general public from understanding the real issues and the reasonable alternatives.

For a country such as the United States, the very notion of a national policy prescribing to local school systems a particular pedagogical approach that includes recognition of a foreign language and culture is a highly volatile one on two counts. First, it defies an entrenched political culture of local control over educational policy making. Historically, education has been the almost exclusive province of state and local governments. The selection of educational method is a clear violation of that tradition. Second, bilingual education as mandated policy cuts across the American ethos—a nation of immigrants striving to develop a common identity and shared sense of values. The United States has placed little value on the enrichment bilingualism that has characterized other countries. In fact, our linguistic and cultural chauvinism has blinded us to the economic, social, and personal benefits of a bilingual society.

In recent years, commentators have noted the political and social dangers of bilingual-bicultural education. This approach, we are told, will hamper the assimilation of new ethnic groups, and delay the acquisition of a common culture and common loyalty.[85] By promoting the notion that the process of Americanization is hopelessly ethnocentric, bilingual education, so the argument goes, has robbed the schools of their traditional integrative function and has stripped us of our faith in a universal American culture that transcends ethnic differences.[86] And so we are instructed that "the standard tongue is the appropriate device for individual and national life in a modern civilization."[87] And federal funds now going to bilingual programs should be redirected to the teaching of English language skills to enable us all "to communicate with one another as fellow citizens."[88]

Some of these fears are a reaction to the rhetorical excesses of the early 1970s. At that time, ethnic awareness in this country reached a feverish pitch and many advocates of bilingual education aggressively advanced the maintenance approach as the most effective method for educating linguistic minority students. Instruction through the medium of both English and the native language should continue throughout the child's educational career, they argued. Naturally, this meant employment opportunities for bilingual teachers.

But as the decade wore on, the economy declined and school systems were forced to lay off senior teachers unable to linguistically and culturally communicate with this growing segment of the school population. At the same time, school officials were forced to hire bilingual classroom teachers under local tax levy funds in order to comply with legal mandates. And in many school systems across the country, Title VII projects brought a cadre of bilingual support personnel into the schools—resource teachers, guidance counselors, family workers, paraprofessionals. As regular programs were crumbling under the strain of high pupil-teacher ratios, limited instructional materials, decreased guidance services, and cutbacks in enrichment courses such as music and art, bilingual programs appeared to be growing by leaps and bounds.

These are the social and economic reasons for the current backlash. But there were also problems inherent in the method and programs it generated. Prior to the late 1960s, the educational establishment had had little acquaintance with bilingual instruction. Except for isolated programs operated in private schools by various ethnic groups, the only experience educators could draw on came from the model projects initiated for Cubans in Florida and the university supported projects for Mexican-Americans in Texas and New Mexico. From the outset, no one was quite certain of what Title VII projects should achieve. The 1968 Bilingual Education Act itself did not even prescribe bilingual instruction.

And so, the early Title VII projects suffered from an ambiguous mission, inadequately trained staff, and a lack of appropriate instructional and testing materials. School administrators were not certain how to identify students or group them by language dominance and grade level. Without evaluation devices, it was difficult to assess language skills in two languages, especially where children appeared to have mixed dominance across language skills. Some students did not even speak a standard variety of either English or the native language. For classroom teachers, the uncertainty of language skills posed the dilemma of language use in the classroom. Should the two languages be separated by subject matter—social studies in the native language and math in English? Or should they be separated by time of day—instruction through one language in the morning and the other in the afternoon, possibly with a native-speaking teacher for each? Bilingual administrators and teachers in those days realized that they were forging new ground by trial and error.

These were the methodological flaws of the movement through the 1970s. But as the federal government increasingly supported materials and test development centers, training programs, and research on bilingual instruction, some of the uncertainty was removed. And as the transitional approach evolved into the politically favored, or more palatable method of bilingual instruction, the goals of instructing linguistic-minority students became more clearly defined.

Nevertheless, there still remain significant contextual differences among bilingual programs and classrooms. Projects still differ as to the use of the two languages for instruction, the stress placed on native language literacy especially in the early years, the cognitive abilities of students and their level of prior education in their native country, the geographic mobility of the student population, and the linguistic and pedagogical skills of classroom teachers. For all these reasons, evaluation studies such as that of the American Institutes for Research and comparative analyses such as the Baker/de Kanter study fail to provide valuable information concerning the merits of transitional bilingual education or any other method.[89]

That is not to dismiss all research on the education of linguistic minority students. Perhaps we simply need to reformulate our questions and refocus our analysis. Two lines of research appear to do just that and may potentially prove more fruitful than previous studies. The first draws from the research on effective schools.[90] Instead of looking at test scores as a measure of programmatic success, this research is designed to identify the instructional features that characterize effective bilingual education classrooms and their consequences for limited English proficient students.

One such attempt, the *Significant Bilingual Instructional Features (SBIF)* study,[91] examined 58 nominated teachers and classrooms and 232 target students (grades K-12) in six nationally representative sites that included different ethnolinguistic groups such as Mexican, Puerto Rican, Cuban, Chinese, and Navajo. The major findings of the study cite five characteristics that effective bilingual classrooms share in common: (1) teachers give students a clear picture of what they want and how to perform tasks competently; (2) teachers communicate high expectations of students; (3) both English and the native language are used, with the latter to clarify meaning during English-language instruction; (4) two approaches are integrated—accommodating instructional language to listeners who are not fully proficient in English and providing activities designed specifically for learning a second language; (5) the student's home and community culture are incorporated into the classroom.

A second line of research is related to the first in that it attempts to identify the specific aspects of bilingual education that may reverse the trend of academic failure among certain populations of students. This research focuses not on the linguistic aspects of bilingual education but rather on the sociocultural context of education.[92] According to the theory of *bicultural ambivalence* advanced by Cummins in particular, minority groups that have tended to perform poorly in school have exhibited a pattern of ambivalence or hostility toward the majority cultural group and insecurity about their own language and culture.[93] This approach explains why some linguistic minority students perform well in school while others do not. It also points to certain techniques that might prove effective in promoting academic achievement, English language skills, and retention among those who fail.[94]

When we look at bilingual education programs, we see certain basic features that help break the cycle of inferior status, both real and perceived, that traditionally have prevented certain groups from "making it" in America—community involvement in shaping its own future and overcoming a sense of powerlessness; the initial use of the native language to help students experience academic success from the onset; and the recognition of the native culture to promote a positive self-concept.

Looked at together, the effective schools and sociocontextual research lead us to a rather startling conclusion. Whatever label we give to the method, perhaps the bicultural is as important, if not more so, than the bilingual aspect in promoting academic success among certain groups of linguistic minority students. If *effective participation* is the legal standard for measuring programmatic compliance, then policy makers should take note of the surrounding sociocultural and political factors when considering alternative approaches for educating diverse populations of students.

Summary Comments

Language policy in this country has developed as a patchwork quilt of federal laws, regulations, guidelines, and court decisions centered around student rights and school district responsibilities. Over the past two decades, governmental institutions have translated *Brown*'s mandate of *equal treatment* for racial minorities into a mandate of *effective participation* for linguistic minorities. For the first group, equality is *same,* for the second it is *different.* The precise nature of that difference has become the focus of policy debate.

This shift in emphasis from inputs to process and outcomes has presented policymakers and educators with a host of yet unresolved problems. Should national policy prescribe one method of instruction as a matter of law? Linguistic groups differ as to their aspirations for their children and goals in coming to this country. For groups such as the Puerto Ricans and Mexicans with high mobility back and forth between here and their native land, bilingual instruction provides the skills necessary to function in two linguistic and cultural environments. For others who are political exiles such as the Haitians or the Cambodians, permanent assimilation into American life and culture is an economic necessity.

Aside from group differences, individual students differ as to pace of learning, modality preferences, and linguistic competence. They also differ in background characteristics—the educational attainment of their parents, the presence of books in the home, the economic security of the family, the political power of their group. How do we determine the causes of underachievement? It usually stems from a complex interaction of social, linguistic, and psychological factors. It is far more complex than linguistic or cultural mismatch. In fact, poverty and discrimination may present equally formidable barriers to academic achievement as language barriers. Intertwined with these pedagogical concerns are political issues concerning the appropriate role of the federal government in maintaining foreign languages and cultures and in determining educational policy for a school system founded on the concept of local control.

Bilingual education as a prescribed methodology has probably seen its heyday. The pendulum has begun to swing back. The question is, "How far?" Hopefully not to the "orientation classes" of the early twentieth century or to the English as a Second Language programs of post World War II. The bilingual education movement has taught us a number of lessons worth remembering. It has forced educators to look at the whole child and to integrate linguistic, cultural, and psychological factors into educational assessment and instruction. It has provided a range of counseling and outreach services to bring the family into the school and the school into the community. It has highlighted the contributions of linguistically and culturally diverse people and portrayed America not as a *melting pot* but as a finely worked *mosaic*. And it has brought to public awareness the bilingual potential of non-English dominant children as a national resource to be developed from an early age.

Bilingual/bicultural education does not have all the answers. But it has raised some significant questions and pointed us in the right direction. What is needed at this point is further studies examining the specific features of effective instructional programs for linguistic minority students. Maintenance programs have fallen into disfavor. But it is undeniable that certain aspects of transitional bilingual education make good common sense. Guidance counselors who understand the student's language and culture, classroom teachers who can effectively communicate with the child and the family, cultural respect to develop a positive self-image, dual language instruction to develop marketable skills and enhance career choices—all these foster academic achievement, individual fulfillment, and group advancement.

Perhaps for the federal government to prescribe a specific methodology does fly in the face of American tradition, But if *effective education* is the equality standard for linguistic minority students, then the federal government should use the power of the purse under Title VII to encourage educationally sound innovation among school districts drawing on, and not ignoring, what we have learned about language and culture in the past twenty years. At the same time, it must use its enforcement powers under Title VI to assure that non-English dominant students are indeed receiving an education that respects their cultural heritage, connects with their family, and nurtures their linguistic potential.

IV

Sex Discrimination: Equal Treatment Within Limits

Inequality of treatment is often based on group characteristics that are irrelevant to the distinctions made.[1] Differential treatment of this sort sometimes stems from economic motives that may go unsaid. It can also draw from unfounded myths concerning the needs, limitations, and abilities of the group in question. Both economic concerns and social misconceptions have constrained opportunities for women who, for the greater part of this country's history, were excluded from the universe of "all men" presumably "created equal."[2]

Natural rights theory, which helped shape the philosophical underpinnings of the American belief system, was itself qualified by remarks such as Rousseau's that "the whole education of women ought to be relative to men."[3] Tocqueville himself, in his travels throughout the United States in the 1830s, was struck by the continued inequality of men and women despite democracy's equalizing effect in other spheres. For Tocqueville, the Americans had carefully divided the duties of men and women "in order that the great work of society may be better carried on." His commentary, in fact, rings of economic determinism and romantic paternalism, one

112

a political ploy and the other a patriarchal view of women's prescribed or expected position in society. Both have denied women equality of consideration. He mistakenly concluded that, despite the American woman's inferior social position, she was held in great respect by men and therefore enjoyed a lofty and superior position in society.[4] In his view, the women of America seemed to "attach a sort of pride to the voluntary surrender of their own will."[5]

Such acquiescence may have been common in the sphere of marital relationships. However, even in the early nineteenth century, the push for educational equality for women had already begun. In 1819, Emma Willard attacked the segregated school system of New York. When the state legislature turned a deaf ear to her, she opened the Troy female seminary in 1821. Oberlin pioneered coeducation at the college level in 1833 and by the late 1800s the elite sister schools had opened their doors to upper class women and had affiliated with their male counterparts in the Ivy League.

But it would take another half century and a complete social upheaval before women would begin to enjoy the full advantages of equal educational access. In fact, it was not until the early 1970s that sex bias in American society finally emerged as a major public policy issue. At that time, an educated generation of "baby boom" women were entering the labor force in record numbers only to face a world of limited employment opportunities and a persistent earnings gap between the sexes. The success of racial minorities had encouraged them as to the possibilities of effecting social reform through legislative and judicial action. Involvement in the antiwar and civil rights movements of the 1960s had trained them in the art of organizing group pressure around political and social issues. Disillusioned by the male dominance of these efforts, female activists gradually formed their own political groups such as the National Organization for Women organized in 1966, and the Women's Equity Action League, formed in 1968.

Through the following decade, women's groups directed their energies toward the elimination of sex bias in critical areas of our society, including education. Initial inquiry into the issue revealed an educational system where sex differences were deeply rooted in traditionally accepted sex roles and where differential treatment of the sexes in academic admissions, instructional offerings, guidance and career counseling, athletics and employment opportunities were commonplace.

Efforts to achieve equality for women have assumed a congruence between civil rights and women's rights. Reliance on the race analogy has pushed litigation and legislation on behalf of women in the direction of equal access to jobs, schools, athletic programs, and other social institutions. Similar to the development of federal policy on race discrimination, early legal action focused on expansion of Fourteenth Amendment equal protection doctrine. With the enactment of statutory protections under Title IX of the Education Amendments of 1972[6] and HEW's 1975 regulations,[7] that law began to serve as the primary tool for defining equal educational opportunity for women students.[8] But the struggle to achieve equality for women has been slow and unsteady. Beneath the surface lie cultural and economic questions that have defied easy resolution. In fact, it has been suggested that the reluctance of women's rights advocates to address the unarticulated social consequences of full equality for women may explain some of the uneasiness courts have demonstrated toward feminist demands.[9]

Constitutional Litigation and Women's Rights

The Intermediate Standard Develops. The Fourteenth Amendment provides in part that no state shall "deny to any person within its jurisdiction the equal protection of the laws." While the Amendment was ratified back in 1868, only within recent years have the courts applied its full force to protect women against discriminatory state action. Even today, the courts are reluctant to examine gender classifications with the heightened judicial scrutiny applied to racial classifications.

Judicial inaction and hesitance essentially stems from a narrow view of women's role in society. Over the years, court decisions have reflected a deeply entrenched paternalistic attitude toward women that has served to limit their sphere of influence and narrow their life choices. One of the most famous cases representing this perspective is *Bradwell v.*

Illinois.[10] In their 1873 decision, the Justices of the Supreme Court upheld the right of the state of Illinois to deny women membership to the bar. In his concurring opinion, Justice Bradley stated:

> Man is, or should be, women's protector and defender . . . the natural proper timidity and delicacy which belong to the female sex evidently unfits it for many of the occupations of civil life . . . the paramount destiny and mission of women are to fulfill the noble and benign offices of wife and mother.[11]

These limited expectations and protective notions have persisted into modern times. In 1966, a Mississippi court upheld a state statute that excluded women from serving on juries. The court stated, "The legislature has the right to exclude women so that they may continue their service as mothers, wives, and homemakers, and so to protect them from the filth, obscenity, and obnoxious atmosphere that so often pervades a courtroom during a jury trial."[12] As recently as 1973, a Connecticut court upheld the exclusion of girls from a high school cross-country running team. According to the court, "Athletic competition builds character in boys. We don't need that kind of character in our girls, the women of tomorrow."[13]

The past decade has witnessed slow and intermittent progress in the development of constitutional rights for women. In the field of education, court involvement has been limited to removing government-imposed barriers and has focused on the provision of equal services. When faced with sex discrimination claims, the courts have clearly deferred from mandating specific instructional approaches or requiring significant reallocation of resources. The courts have not exercised such deference when it comes to the rights of racial and linguistic minorities or the handicapped.

Throughout the 1970s, private foundation support quickened the pace of constitutional litigation on behalf of women. The Ford Foundation was the primary benefactor in this effort. Between 1972 and 1974, Ford grants accounted for at least one-half of the $7 billion in foundation funds disbursed for women's programs. In 1976, Ford made twice as many awards to women's projects than any other foundation.[14] As of 1980, Ford was funding four of the national membership groups litigating sex discrimination cases: The American Civil Liberties Union Women's Rights Project, the NAACP Legal Defense and Education Fund, Inc. (indirect support of ancillary activities such as seminars, workshops, and dissemination related to litigation), the Mexican American Legal Defense and Education Fund (MALDEF) Chicana Rights Projects, and the League of Women Voters. In addition, Ford was giving support to three public interest law firms engaged in sex discrimination cases: The Women's Law Fund in Cleveland; the Center for Law and Social Policy Women's Rights Project in Washington, D.C.; and Public Advocates, Inc. in San Francisco.

These advocacy groups focused on the development of constitutional doctrine and gender-based discrimination in key policy areas, including inequities in the Social Security Act, discrimination in employment policies and practices, and inequality in educational access for women students.[15] What they shared in common, aside from their quest for women's equity, was a long-term strategy of social reform modeled after that developed by the NAACP to promote equality for blacks. They used litigation as their tool and the federal courts as their forum. They tried to piggyback on the success of racial minorities in the courts and attempted to establish sex as analogous to race for Fourteenth Amendment equal protection purposes. If the courts would recognize sex, like race, as a *suspect class* entitled to heightened judicial scrutiny, then the burden of justifying sex classifications would shift to the state to prove that the classification promotes a compelling governmental interest.

The women's advocacy groups also drew from the NAACP strategy in going for the easy wins first, thereby building up a momentum of success. They would then incrementally bring more problematic cases before the courts. First, they attacked federal laws that contained sex distinctions on their face and then moved on to sex-neutral government policies that had a disparate impact on women. This last strategic point was dealt a fatal blow in 1976 when the Supreme Court in *Washington v. Davis*[16] held that discriminatory effect alone is not sufficient to establish a Fourteenth Amendment equal protection violation. Actual discriminatory intent must be proven.

As the advocacy groups implemented their strategy through the 1970s, they made considerable progress in attacking facially discriminatory laws. They never succeeded in gaining the Supreme Court's recognition of sex as a suspect class. Nevertheless, the Court's development and continued use of an intermediate standard of review to be applied to gender classifications reflects a heightened sensitivity to women's concerns on the part of at least a majority of Court members.[17]

The first significant victory came in 1971 in *Reed v. Reed*.[18] Here the Court withdrew from its posture of complete deference to legislative judgments on the rights of women. In *Reed,* the Court unanimously invalidated an Idaho statute that required males to be preferred to females as the administrator of a decedent's estate. The Court appeared to apply the traditional *rational basis* test. However, commentators have noted that the result in *Reed* is difficult to understand without assuming that the Court considered in its analysis some special sensitivity to sex as a classifying factor.[19]

Less than two years later in *Frontiero v. Richardson,* a plurality of four Justices explicitly responded to the undesirability of sex-based classifications.[20] The Court invalidated under the Fifth Amendment federal statutes that recognized spouses of male members of the armed services as dependents for military benefits while spouses of female members had to prove dependency for more than half their support. The Court's plurality rejected administrative convenience as an acceptable governmental purpose and described the effect as "romantic paternalism" that operated to "put women not on a pedestal, but in a cage."[21]

In the next several years, the Court struck down similar laws that prevented or discouraged departures from traditional sex roles.[22] The Court's decision in 1976 in *Craig v. Boren*[23] marks the emergence of a consensus among the Justices on the constitutional standard to be applied to gender classifications. Here the Court invalidated an Oklahoma statute prohibiting the sale of 3.2 percent beer to males but not to females between the ages of eighteen and twenty-one. As the Court stated, "Classifications by gender must serve important governmental objectives and must be substantially related to the achievement of those objectives."[24]

This *intermediate standard* is more rigorous than the conventional equal protection standard of *rational basis* but less rigorous than the heightened scrutiny applied in race discrimination cases. As to race, the state must prove that the classification is related to a compelling and not merely an important governmental interest and that it is strictly necessary and not substantially necessary to promote that interest. However, in developing the intermediate standard, the Court acknowledged that sex classifications should not be automatically rationalized.

Although some of the subsequent cases seem to cast doubt on this standard,[25] the Court's 1982 ruling in *Mississippi University for Women v. Hogan* made clear that *intermediate scrutiny* not only retains majority support, slightly reformulated, but can be applied against gender classifications that discriminate against men and not just women. Here the Court, in a 5-4 decision, invalidated the university's all-female admissions policy to its nursing school.[26] Speaking for the majority, Justice O'Connor articulated an affirmative action rationale of limited applicability to other single-sex admissions policies. In fact, she made clear that the Court would not necessarily strike down a restriction on admissions that was designed to address the effect of past discrimination.[27] For example, the Court might not find an all-female dental or medical school in violation of the Fourteenth Amendment as women were effectively excluded from professional education of this nature until very recent years. In the parlance of equal protection doctrine, a single-sex admissions policy in this case would be substantially related to an important governmental interest in promoting women in the dental and medical professions. Obviously such an affirmative action argument cannot be made in a field such as nursing which women traditionally have dominated.

Educational Exclusion and Gender Classifications. As the Supreme Court has struggled to develop a standard of review to apply to gender discrimination cases, lower federal courts have attempted to apply evolving constitutional principles to a broad array of sex-biased situations awaiting legal resolution. A number of these have involved educational issues.[28]

The only federal constitutional violations found by the lower courts to date have involved total exclusion from schools or programs on the basis of sex. And the remedy for such a violation is admission—similar to the pre-*Brown* university cases litigated by the NAACP. Lower courts have found equal protection violations where girls have been denied access to academically prestigious schools *(Kirstein v. University of Virginia)*[29] and where schools have applied differential admissions standards for male and female applicants *(Berkelman v. San Francisco Independent School District,*[30] *Bray v. Lee).*[31] As for participation in athletics programs, courts have generally found a constitutional violation where girls have been completely excluded from participation, that is, where the school has provided no girls team or program and where the case has involved a noncontact sport *(Reed v. Nebraska School Activities Association*[32]—golf; *Brenden v. Independent School District*[33]—cross-country, skiing, running, and tennis; *Gilpin v. Kansas State High School Activities Association, Inc.*[34]—cross-country.) More recent decisions have found constitutional violations in the case of total exclusion from contact sports as well, but most courts have expressly stated that separate teams could satisfy constitutional requirements *(O'Connor v. Board of Education of School District No. 23*[35]—basketball; *Leffel v. Wisconsin Interscholastic Athletic Association*[36]—baseball; *Hoover v. Mikeljohn*[37]—soccer).

The athletics cases indicate that the *separate but equal* doctrine rejected three decades ago in *Brown* as to race may withstand constitutional challenge as to sex classifications. In 1977, the Supreme Court extended that doctrine to admissions policies in *Vorchheimer v. School District of Philadelphia.*[38] Here the plaintiff challenged the denial of her application to Central High School, the city's elite all-male school and the second-oldest public high school in the country. The school district maintained what it considered to be a comparable academic institution for girls, Girls High School.

Based on findings in the district court in *Vorchheimer,* the

Third Circuit Court of Appeals concluded that the two schools were similar and of equal quality. With the exception of superior scientific offerings at Central, the academic facilities of the two institutions were comparable and students from both gained acceptance into the most prestigious universities. The appeals court expressed concern over the broad policy implications of declaring single-sex schools unconstitutional. Without convincing evidence as to the psychological or academic harms of single-sex education, parents and students should be allowed to exercise their freedom of choice.[39] The Supreme Court split 4 to 4 on the decision, issued no opinion, and set no federal precedent. But the evenly divided vote translated into an automatic affirmance of the Third Circuit's judgment.

The issue litigated in *Vorchheimer* was again addressed in the Pennsylvania state court system in the case of *Newburg v. Board of Public Education, School District of Philadelphia.*[40] In August 1983, the trial court ordered that three female students be admitted to Central High School. The *Newburg* case is significant not only for its novel result, but also for what it reveals about developments in the law since *Vorchheimer* and the present-day limits of state and federal constitutional provisions protecting the rights of women. In *Vorchheimer,* the courts ruled only on the Fourteenth Amendment equal protection claim. At the time of the trial in 1975, the Supreme Court had not yet decided *Craig v. Boren* and had not yet applied the intermediate standard of review to gender classifications. The court merely applied the lesser standard of rational basis and concluded that the separation of students by sex in select high schools was "reasonably" related to the "legitimate" governmental purpose of maintaining educational opportunities for women. The *Newburg* court, however, applied the higher standard of review and found that the scheme served no "important governmental objective" and that the means employed, separation of the sexes, were not "substantially related" to the "vague, unsubstantiated theory" that adolescents may study more effectively in single-sex schools.[41]

As to the state equal rights claim, the court applied the strict scrutiny ordinarily reserved for racial classifications.

Here the court found no "compelling governmental interest" to be promoted and that the means used "belies the proffered, but vague, interest asserted" to provide academic options to improve educational quality.[42] The court compared Central High School with its female counterpart, Girls High School, on a number of indices of educational quality. Included among these were the size of each school's campus as compared to its student body, the number of books in each school's library, the number of faculty members holding Ph.D. degrees, the course offerings in mathematics, and the extracurricular programs at the two schools. Finally, the court noted that students at Girls High constantly achieved lower scores on college entrance examinations and standardized advanced placement tests as compared with students at Central High. The court found a causal relationship between these differences and lower average acceptance rates to colleges for Girls High students (87.8 percent) as compared with Central High students (98.8 percent) for the years 1977 to 1981. The female claimants in the earlier *Vorchheimer* case had failed to introduce many of these distinctions into evidence.

The *Newburg* case is important from a doctrinal perspective. While the record documented significant academic disparities between the two schools, in ruling on the Fourteenth Amendment equal protection claim, the court considered not only *tangible* inequalities but such *intangibles* as prestige of school and reputation of alumni as valid measures to be factored into the equality calculus. The case further underscores the utility of state equal rights amendment provisions in promoting equality for women. In recent years, the federal retreat from sex equity enforcement and the defeat of the Equal Rights Amendment have raised state constitutional and statutory protections to a new level of importance.[43] Women's groups argue that state provisions do not achieve the national policy reform of federal mandates. However, a heightened standard of review applied to sex-based claims under state equal rights protections may serve to invalidate practices and policies upheld under the federal Constitution and statutes.

In sum, the federal courts have deferred from completely extending to women the constitutional protections afforded racial minorities. The Supreme Court has refused to subject gender classifications to the heightened judicial scrutiny of racial classifications. Furthermore, traces of the separate but equal doctrine, long rejected as to race, appear to remain as to sex. Separate educational facilities may well reinforce a myth of male superiority. Perhaps the district court opinion striking down single-sex schools in Philadelphia will set the stage for a new approach to judicial decision making on this issue.

While the doctrine of equal educational opportunity witnessed a gradual shift in focus from inputs to outputs throughout the 1970s for other disadvantaged groups, it remained at the inputs stage for women. In the field of education, the courts have failed to grant women students special affirmative assistance and remedial services as a matter of constitutional right to overcome the effects of past discrimination.[44] Nevertheless, it can be argued that society historically has restricted women's access to educational opportunities and to the political process and therefore courts must closely examine state-imposed gender classificiations.

Sex Equity as National Policy

Similar to other disadvantaged groups, women took their struggle for equal educational opportunity to the federal level only after years of dealing with disinterested and unresponsive local and state school officials, the overwhelming majority of whom were male. Women realized that their concerns were national in scope. They had also learned a few lessons from the school desegregation experience in the years following *Brown v. Board of Education*. They could not rely solely on litigation which is a protracted and costly enterprise. Courts deal with issues and particular facts on a case by case basis and court decrees, particularly in the days prior to receiverships and court-appointed masters, lacked the teeth of enforcement.

The progress made toward desegregating southern schools immediately following passage of the Civil Rights Act of 1964 and its implementing regulations provided women's groups with encouragement and a strategy for reform. And so they launched a two-pronged effort on the federal government with the intent to use not only litigation but legislation as the primary vehicles for rapid and substantial change. Through the 1970s, groups such as NOW and WEAL focused their sights on two outcomes. The first was passage of the Equal Rights Amendment (ERA) to the U.S. Constitution. The second was the administrative enforcement of statutory protections and rights for women in employment and education.[45]

The ERA which had languished in Washington since 1923 provided that "[E]quality of rights under the law shall not be denied or abridged by the United States or by any state on account of sex." Women's rights advocates believed the ERA would achieve for women the level of progress made by racial minorities through Fourteenth Amendment litigation. The NAACP had used the equal protection clause and judicial intervention to advance the economic status and political power of blacks and move us toward a color-blind society. It was hoped that a constitutional amendment granting equal rights to men and women in all spheres of endeavor would similarly lead us toward a gender-blind society where one's sex would be as irrelevant as the color of one's hair.[46]

In the early 1970s, the popularity of the ERA together with the absence of any organized opposition convinced some elements within the movement that the amendment was certain to be added to the Constitution, thereby making any further legislation superfluous.[47] But the decade following congressional ratification in 1972 proved otherwise. By the fall of 1977, 35 of the necessary 38 states had voted for ratification. Within the next year, three of those voted to rescind. A strong STOP-ERA movement had developed, led by right-wing political groups and fundamentalist denominations, using fear tactics and spreading a variety of myths concerning the amendment's potential impact on social life in America.[48] By June 30, 1982, the extended deadline for final ratification, only 34 states had approved the ERA. With that defeat, the piecemeal legislation enacted by Congress over the previous two decades subsequently has gained a renewed importance in the struggle for women's equality as national policy.

Access to Education

One of the primary targets for congressional action has been the widespread discrimination against women in all aspects of education. And so, in 1972, Congress enacted Title IX of the Education Amendments of 1972[49] as part of a larger legislative package that included amendments to Title VII of the Civil Rights Act of 1964[50] (repealing exemption of educational institutions), Title IV of that Act (authorizing the Attorney General to bring suit in sex discrimination cases regarding admissions and allowing Title IV funds to be used to end sex discrimination),[51] and the Equal Pay Act of 1963[52] (repealing exemption of managerial and executive positions). Title IX was largely the product of skilled drafting and bargaining on the part of Representative Edith Green (D., OR) and Senator Birch Bayh (D., IN). Its legislative record leaves scant evidence of either strong political support for the measure, or of organized lobbying on its behalf.[53] The year was 1972 and the controversy surrounding court-ordered busing eclipsed any implications Title IX might have had for reforming American education. In fact, the battles over Title IX did not begin until after the law was enacted and it was time for HEW to draft implementing regulations. Then the friends and foes of Title IX emerged in full force.

Title IX is a succinctly worded statute modeled in language and enforcement scheme after Title VI of the Civil Rights Act of 1964. However, whereas Title VI prohibits race or national origin discrimination in any federally funded program, Title IX's prohibition against sex discrimination is limited to education programs. Similar to educational matters under Title VI, Title IX is enforced by the Office for Civil Rights whose powers include complaint resolution, compliance reviews, and termination of funding in the case of noncompliance.[54] The law further grants to federal agencies that fund education programs the power and duty to issue implementing rules and regulations consistent with congressional intent. Title IX expressly stipulates that its provisions do not require preferential treatment toward members of any one sex.

It is well-known that the legislative process is one of slow compromise. As a bill works its way back and forth between congressional committees and subcommittees and full floor debate, opposing interests are voiced and some must be accommodated. For Title IX, those interests and accommodations are reflected in the statute's express exceptions. Title IX does not apply to religious educational institutions whose tenets are inconsistent with the law[55] nor does it apply to military training schools.[56] The law further exempts the admissions policies of elementary and most secondary school programs, private undergraduate institutions of higher education,[57] and undergraduate public institutions that traditionally and continually from their establishment have had a policy of admitting students of one sex.[58]

Congress included the forgoing exceptions to Title IX coverage in the original 1972 legislation. Two years later, after HEW had issued its proposed Title IX regulations, Congress enacted additional amendments excluding social fraternities and sororities, Boy Scouts, Girl Scouts, YMCA, YWCA, Camp Fire Girls, and other voluntary youth service organizations.[59] In 1976, Congress again amended Title IX to exclude boy or girl conferences,[60] father-son and mother-daughter activities,[61] and scholarships awarded as prizes for beauty pageants.[62]

These postenactment amendments to Title IX were symptomatic of a small but persistent movement within Congress to limit the law's coverage. That movement spurred pro-Title IX groups to organize and pressure HEW for strong implementing regulations. In fact, it was an amendment introduced by Senator John Tower (R., TX) exempting revenue-producing sports from Title IX coverage that prodded HEW into issuing proposed Title IX regulations in June 1974.

At this point, a coalition of women's groups was formed to persuade Congress to ultimately approve the final regulations[63] and to serve as a bulwark against further attempts to amend the statute. This coalition became known as the Education Task Force. It combined educational organizations such as the American Council on Education and the American Association of University Women, lobbying groups such as the National Student Lobby and the Women's Lobby, research organizations such as the Project on Equal Education Rights (PEER) and the Project on the Status and Education of

Women, and mass-membership groups such as the National Student Association and the League of Women Voters.[64] The broad span of interests represented by the Education Task Force allowed it to exercise influence through a variety of channels. This combination of traditional HEW clientele groups and newer untested women's groups would prove too powerful for HEW or Congress to successfully oppose. On the other side of the lobbying effort stood the Title IX opponents represented by the National Collegiate Athletic Association (NCAA) and the American Football Coaches Association. For this group, Title IX coverage of revenue-producing sports had serious economic implications.

HEW did not submit its final Title IX regulations to Congress until June 1975, one year after it had issued its proposed regulations and three years after Congress had enacted the law.[65] Drawing on Title IX's exhaustive legislative history, the agency interpreted the law's mandates and prohibitions to include employment, athletics, admission and financial aid policies,[66] as well as testing,[67] recruitment efforts,[68] counseling,[69] and criteria for selection to sports programs[70] that have a disproportionate "effect" on students of one sex. The regulations support "separate but equal" services in certain areas and apply a flexible standard to determine equal treatment. For example, while Title IX requires that most physical education classes be conducted jointly for students of both sexes and that all such activities be open to students without regard to sex, the regulations permit the separation by sex in physical education classes or activities whose major purpose involves bodily contact[71] as well as the operation of separate teams by sex where selection is based on competitive skill or the activity involves a contact sport.[72] In determining equal opportunity with respect to athletics, such factors as the interests and abilities of both sexes, travel allowances, facilities, scheduling of games and practice time, and opportunities for coaching and academic tutoring are considered. Unequal aggregate expenditures alone do not constitute non-compliance.[73]

The Title IX regulations include provisions to achieve enforcement and compliance. Inherent in the regulations are various mechanisms for determining violations. Each application for federal assistance must be accompanied by an assurance from the applicant that the program will be operated in compliance with the law.[74] In addition, within one year of the effective date of the regulations, each recipient of funds was required to conduct a Title IX self-evaluation to be maintained on file for three years.[75] Title IX incorporates by reference the Title VI procedural provisions[76] whereby OCR may demand compliance reports of federal aid recipients[77] and must be afforded access to the recipient's books, accounts, and records.[78] Finally, OCR determines Title IX violations through periodic compliance reviews[79] and the investigation of individual and class complaints.[80]

Despite these procedural details provided by regulation, the enforcement process has been slow and ineffective. According to a 1978 study, HEW resolved only one out of every five Title IX complaints filed against elementary and secondary schools between June 1972 when the law became effective and October 1976. The number of complaints rose steadily from 129 in 1973 to 424 in 1976. Ninety-six percent of the complaints filed in 1973 were still pending in 1976 without either findings or negotiated remedies. The cases HEW did resolve during that period waited an average of fourteen months for final action. Those complaints still unresolved in June 1976 had been pending an average of sixteen months. During that same period between 1972 and 1976, of the total Title IX complaints filed, 564 related to employment, 351 to athletics, 289 to access to courses, 187 to student rules, and 64 to miscellaneous violations.[81]

In its contempt of court motion against the Department of Education in 1982 in the ongoing *WEAL v. Bell* litigation, the Women's Equity Action League charged that the Department had failed to issue letters of findings on time in 60 percent of the complaints handled between October 1980 and April 1981. In regard to compliance reviews, within the first four months of 1981, the Department had failed to issue any investigatory findings within the court-mandated 90 days.[82] In fiscal year 1979, an average of one year and five months elapsed between receipt and closure of a Title IX complaint.[83] Sixty percent of the cases pending at the beginning of the following fiscal year had been in the agency for more than one year.[84]

Title IX Goes to Court. As the 1970s wore on, it became clear that the promise of Title IX could never be fulfilled through administrative procedures alone. In the face of limited enforcement activities and processing backlogs within the Office for Civil Rights, individuals began to seek private redress in the courts. And even where OCR had carried a complaint to resolution, school systems and institutions threatened with fund termination for noncompliance brought legal action challenging the regulations as an invalid interpretation of the law. These legal skirmishes over preliminary scope and coverage issues in fact slowed down the development of sex equity. By limiting themselves to technical legal issues, these cases never resolved whether doing X, Y, or Z is in fact sex discrimination or what the appropriate remedy should be to end discrimination and make the plaintiffs whole.[85]

The first Title IX case to come before the Supreme Court was *Cannon v. University of Chicago*[86] in which the Court upheld a private right to sue under Title IX. In a later ruling on this case, the Supreme Court refused to review a Seventh Circuit decision that proof of discriminatory effect alone is not sufficient to establish a Title IX violation. The claimant must prove discriminatory intent on the part of the educational institution. In a more recent decision, *North Haven Board of Education v. Bell,*[87] the Court rejected the position taken by many universities and school districts and upheld the validity of Title IX regulations covering employment. In a 6-3 decision, the majority found in the law's legislation and post–enactment history sufficient evidence of congressional intent to extend Title IX's ban against sex discrimination to employees as well as to students.

The *North Haven* decision resolved a decade-long controversy over Title IX and employment discrimination. However, the ruling left open the issue of what constitutes a federally funded "program or activity." In dicta, Justice Blackmun writing for the majority stated that Title IX's provisions are "program specific," implying that Title IX covers only those programs receiving federal financial support. The Justices, however, cautioned that "we do not undertake to define 'program' in this opinion."[88] The issue remained open until the

Court's opinion in *Grove City College v. Bell*[89] two years later.[90]

Following *North Haven,* the Justice Department maintained that the Court's dicta as to "program or activity" in fact limited the Department's scope of enforcement. In those jurisdictions where lower courts had applied a narrow programmatic interpretation, the Department's action and inaction indicated a reversal in federal policy. For example, following the district court's opinion in *Richmond v. Bell,* OCR halted enforcement proceedings against the College of William and Mary which had refused to equalize athletics scholarships for men and women. The Department further let pass the deadline for requesting a rehearing in *Hillsdale College v. HEW* despite urgings of civil rights groups who believed the case was ripe for consideration. One of the judges in the majority had died shortly before the opinion was formally issued.

In its initial brief filed with the Supreme Court in *Grove City,* the Justice Department asked the Court to uphold the Third Circuit ruling that the college was subject to Title IX because its students received federal aid but also urged the Court not to rule on the definition of "program or activity." In a second brief later submitted, the Department contended that Grove City need only comply with Title IX with respect to financial aid because that was the only program in receipt of federal funds. This position ran counter to long-standing federal policy on Title IX enforcement. Since Title IX's enactment in 1972, the Nixon, Ford, and Carter Administrations, and the Reagan Administration in its early days had afforded the law a broad institutional interpretation. When a school or college received any amount of federal aid, the institution itself was deemed the "program or activity" and therefore subject to Title IX. As a result of this turnaround, the case went before the Court in November 1983 with neither side defending the institutional approach to Title IX.

The narrow programmatic interpretation of Title IX angered and alarmed advocates of women's equity. Women's groups requested to participate in oral arguments but the Court refused. More than two dozen civil rights groups and women's organizations and a bipartisan group of 47 representatives and three senators filed friend-of-the-court briefs with the Court arguing that the Administration had seriously misinterpreted the intent of the law. Their position was reasserted in a November 1983 "sense of the House" resolution approved by the House of Representatives by a 414 to 8 vote.[91] The nonbinding resolution reaffirmed Congress' intention that Title IX and the regulations issued under it "should not be amended or altered in any manner which would lessen the comprehensive coverage of such statute in eliminating gender discrimination through the American educational system."

When the *Grove City* case finally came before the Supreme Court, the Justices addressed two separate issues. The first was the definition of "recipient" of federal aid under Title IX. Here the Court unanimously declared that indirect aid, such as federal scholarship grants that go directly to the students, is sufficient to set Title IX in motion. Thus, although the college received funds indirectly, it was nonetheless subject to Title IX mandates. The second part of the opinion, which garnered only a 6-3 majority on the Court, addressed the definition of "program or activity receiving federal financial assistance." Here the Court construed that term narrowly, determining that it was the financial aid program—not the educational program of Grove City as a whole—that received federal funds. Writing for the majority, Justice White stated that there could be found "no persuasive evidence suggesting that Congress intended that the [Education] Department's regulatory authority follow federally aided students from classroom to classroom, building to building, or activity to activity."[92] Justice Brennan, in dissent, called the majority ruling an "absurdity" that "clearly disregards" congressional intent. Specifically, it would permit institutions to discriminate in athletic programs, admissions, and even various academic departments as long as they did not practice sex discrimination in financial aid programs.[93]

Title IX Returns to Congress. Women's organizations and civil rights groups immediately reasserted Justice Brennan's concerns over the reactionary and unreasonable implications of the Court's decision. Such a narrow interpretation of the law, they argued, would take the teeth out of Title IX enforcement, severely limit the law's coverage, and result in an administratively unworkable and absurd system of rights riddled with gaping holes. They feared that athletics programs, which generally do not receive direct federal aid, would no longer be subject to Title IX. And yet, as evidenced by the extensive congressional debate on athletics discrimination that preceded passage of the Act, Congress clearly intended that Title IX cover athletics, where in fact, women have made the greatest gains since its enactment.

On a more pragmatic note, a program-specific interpretation of Title IX would create a situation in any given educational system whereby teachers and students, even in adjacent classrooms, would be protected or unprotected by Title IX depending on the source of funds supporting a program. Carried to the extreme, a school could discriminate with impunity against female students in its regular program as long as it treated evenhandedly those enrolled in its federally funded programs. Unlike female faculty members who have available alternative avenues of relief under both Title VII of the Civil Rights Act of 1964 which bans employment discrimination and the Equal Pay Act,[94] such statutory alternatives do not exist for female students. They would stand to lose the most under a narrow interpretation of Title IX and the administrative and enforcement chaos that would inevitably result.

The issues of "program specificity" and "recipient of funds" are critical to federal civil rights enforcement efforts in general. Title IX forms part of a comprehensive civil rights strategy that uses the power of the federal purse to induce school systems into adopting and maintaining nondiscriminatory policies and practices. Within days of the *Grove City* ruling, the Assistant Attorney General for Civil Rights told reporters that the Administration would apply not only Title IX, but Title VI of the Civil Rights Act of 1964 and §504 of the Rehabilitation Act of 1973 to federally funded programs only.[95] Title VI has served as the engine for desegregating the nation's schools in the past two decades while §504 has granted procedural protections and substantive rights to the handicapped.

The Department of Education has taken a similar position. In July 1984, the Assistant Secretary for Civil Rights issued to OCR regional directors a statement of policy guidelines. According to that memorandum, the Department entertained "no doubt that the Court's decision (in *Grove City*) is applicable to OCR's other statutory authorities which include the phrase 'program or activity receiving Federal financial assistance.' "[96] By June of that year, the Department had relied on the Courts ruling to close 23 civil rights investigations, to narrow the scope of 18 investigations, and to review 31 other cases. While most of these concerned sex discrimination, 9 of the 18 modified investigations and 8 of the 31 under review involved either Title VI or §504.[97] Within a year after *Grove City*, the Department had moved to close, limit, or suspend at least 63 discrimination cases. Forty-four of these had been brought under Title IX, five under Title VI, and 14 under §504.[98]

The Court's decision in *Grove City* indicated that nothing short of new omnibus legislation would clarify the meaning of Title IX and protect Title VI and §504 from narrow interpretation in the courts and the administrative agency. In April 1984, Senator Edward Kennedy (D., MA)[99] and Representative Paul Simon (R., IL)[100] introduced the Civil Rights Act of 1984. The bill would have overturned the *Grove City* decision by replacing Title IX's "program or activity" language with the broad term "recipient." The measure passed overwhelmingly in the House by a vote of 375 to 32 in June of that year but became caught up in ideological turbulence in the Senate. Supporters of the bill such as Senator Kennedy identified the issue as "whether American taxpayers' money is going to be used for discrimination." But for the bill's opponents such as Senator Orrin Hatch (R., UT) the issue was not discrimination, but "federal power." They argued that the term "recipient" was overly broad, beyond the scope of the law's original intent, and would inject "the federal government into state, local and even private affairs."[101] The bill fell victim to political maneuvering and delay tactics and died in the Senate in the closing days of the 98th Congress.

In the opening days of the 99th Congress, a bipartisan group of members of both houses, led by Senator Kennedy and Representative Augustus Hawkins (D., CA), introduced a somewhat revised measure as the Civil Rights Restoration Act of 1985.[102] The proposed legislation removed the controversial term "recipient" from the previous year's bill and amended Title IX, Title VI, §504 and the 1975 Age Discrimination Act to include an interpretation of "program or activity." Those laws would now expressly cover all operations of a "department or agency of a state or of a local government, or the entity of such state or local government that distributes such assistance and such department or agency to which the assistance is extended." The fund termination provision of each statute would also be amended so that the cutoff of federal funds would be limited to the "assistance which supports the discrimination," that is, the so-called *pinpointing* concept would be retained.

Senator Robert Dole (R., KS) introduced a narrower proposal, the Civil Rights Act Amendment,[103] which would restore the institution-wide scope of the four civil rights laws as existed prior to *Grove City,* but only as they relate to education. The Reagan Administration supported this amendment in favor of the more inclusive bills introduced in the House and Senate. In fact, the Assistant Attorney General for Civil Rights, in congressional hearings, assailed the House version, H.R. 700, as "one of the most far-reaching legislative efforts in memory to stretch the tentacles of the federal government to every crevice of public and private-sector activity." The bill, he charged, "uses the extension of the federal dollar as an excuse for opening virtually every entity in this country— public and private—to federal supervision, regulation, intervention, intrusion, and oversight."[104]

The Reagan-controlled U.S. Commission on Civil Rights leveled a similar criticism against both the bills and the Dole amendment. In a statement adopted by a 5-2 vote, the commission maintained that public institutions that are supported by "all citizens in the form of state and local taxes" should be subject to broad coverage under the civil rights statutes while private and especially religiously affiliated institutions should enjoy the maximum freedom. According to the statement, "America is not ready yet—and may never be ready—for a society standardized by the federal bureaucracy, turning out men and women fashioned by a government shaped cookie-cutter."[105]

These and similar statements emerging from both sides of

the debate are far more than mere political rhetoric. They are clear expressions of political ideology. In fact, the *Grove City* decision has served to crystallize an issue lying beneath the surface of much of the current discourse on the federal role and educational policy, namely, just how far and by what legitimate means the federal government may intrude on private and individual choice to promote the collective good.

Summary Comments

More than a decade of women's rights litigation and legislation reveals a national commitment to sex equity that remains vague and indecisive. Part of the difficulty lies in the nature of the issue itself, rooted as it is in centuries of customs and beliefs concerning the differential roles of women and men. To say that justice demands that government treat members of both sexes equally or the same defies deeply entrenched social norms. So for women's equity, the argument can barely move beyond the threshold stage of equal treatment, that is, a formalistic notion of equality. And a society that cannot reach consensus on that basic premise, surely cannot reach the stage of being gender-blind.

The normative questions raised have caused the women's movement to advance at a snail's pace. Even at their civil rights best, the organs of government have not afforded equality for women the same expansive reading as that allowed other groups such as racial minorities and the handicapped. For example, the Supreme Court has given evidence of some sensitivity toward women's rights, but has not applied the same level of scrutiny to sex classifications as applied to racial classifications. Congress has provided the *stick* of statutory prohibitions and enforcement through Title IX, but effectively has limited the *carrot* approach to meagre appropriations under the Women's Educational Equity Act.[106] In fact, WEEA has never been funded above the $10 million level and in recent years has been the target of repeated efforts by the Reagan Administration to eliminate the program through consolidation into a block grant.

Equality of opportunity for women students means not the *more or different is equal* resource allocation for other groups, but *equal treatment* or *equal access* at best. The stability and effectiveness of that standard hinges on Title IX. Since that law's enactment a decade ago, schools and colleges have made significant progress in meeting the sex equity mandate. According to the National Federation of State High School Associations, 1.85 million young women took part in scholastic athletics in 1980–81 as compared with 294,000 in 1970–71, the year Title IX was enacted.[107] The percentage of high school girls participating in varsity sports rose during that period from 7 percent to 35 percent and school athletic budgets for women's programs increased from 2 percent to 16.4 percent. Prior to Title IX, college athletic scholarships for women were nonexistent. Today, colleges and universities offer 10,000 scholarships to women athletes.[108] The law has had an equally pronounced impact on admissions policies particularly at formerly male-only graduate schools. Between 1972 and 1980, the percentage of women medical students rose from 11 percent to 26 percent while women law students increased from 10 percent to 34 percent and doctoral recipients from 16 percent to 30 percent.[109]

Some may argue that Title IX was more an affirmation of evolving social policy than a cause of social reform. However, it cannot be denied that Title IX has provided women's groups with a means of legal redress, has served as a stick to be wielded at noncomplaint school districts, and has heightened the awareness of girls and women as to the life choices traditionally closed to them. Above all, Title IX has drawn considerable national attention to the educational, and ultimately the economic impact of narrowly drawn sex roles in our society. According to a 1983 report published by the Project on Equal Education Rights of the NOW Legal Defense and Education Fund, nine out of ten of today's young women will work for twenty-five to forty-five years and two out of five will be heads of households.[110] Obviously, the life plans our educational system allows female students to design will shape tomorrow's society.

Despite the gains of the past decade, however, society has not fully met the goal of equal educational opportunity for women. As noted by the National Advisory Council on Women's Educational Programs, the position of women and girls in education today resembles a glass that is "half full or half empty, depending on one's outlook." Progress has been tempered by less favorable statistics that demonstrate a continued gender-gap in educational opportunities for girls and women. Although women presently number almost one-third of college athletes, they receive only about one-sixth of college athletic budgets.[111] During 1978-79, only 13.9 percent of students enrolled in traditionally male vocational courses nationally were female.[112] Of the 433,857 women who received bachelor's degrees in 1980–81 only 3 percent majored in traditionally male subjects such as physical sciences, mathematics, and engineering while 23 percent majored in education and 11 percent in nursing and health professions.[113] Yet it is in the technical and scientific fields that we see the greatest job opportunities.

In view of weakened civil rights enforcement at the Executive level and the Court's reluctance to second-guess legislative intent, sex equity now rests with Congress. In the past, civil rights advocates in both houses have successfully fought back attempts to narrow the scope of Title IX through the amendment process. Congress is again called upon to preserve the integrity of Title IX by overturning the Court's decision in *Grove City*.

There is no doubt that *Grove City* is a serious setback to civil rights enforcement. But it has, in fact, had a positive effect in mobilizing the various elements of the civil rights movement. For the first time since that movement took off more than two decades ago, the advocates and beneficiaries of the piecemeal legislation enacted during those years have rallied around a specific legislative proposal. The proposed legislation has bipartisan support in both houses of Congress and has brought the civil rights groups out in full force.

If the Civil Rights Restoration Act of 1985 succeeds to enactment, it will have proven that, despite the visibility and tenacity of the opposing ideological forces, civil rights is still a matter of national concern. It will also have demonstrated that each of us, now or in the future, will reap the benefits of a strong civil rights policy—whether by virtue of sex, race, age, or handicapping condition.

V

The Handicapped: Diverse Needs and Scarce Resources

The history of education for the handicapped is one of gross neglect, insensitivity, misunderstanding, and exclusion. Until recent years, public schools failed to provide educational opportunities, equal or otherwise, to millions of handicapped children both individually and as a class. School systems denied educational services to the severely handicapped pursuant to state law, haphazardly admitted or denied access to students with the same disabilities, left students on endless waiting lists, misclassified them through the use of discriminatory measures, and placed them in dead-end tracks without periodic evaluation. Even where some level of services was provided, these were often inappropriate to the students' needs thereby functionally excluding the handicapped from any meaningful education. From malfeasance and nonfeasance, the problem had reached staggering proportions by the time it came to national awareness. In 1975 when Congress enacted the Education for All Handicapped Children Act (P.L. 94-142),[1] it was estimated that one-half of the nation's

137

eight million handicapped children were not receiving an appropriate education and that another one million were receiving no education at all.

Public and professional apathy toward the needs of the handicapped stemmed from a variety of reasons. Society did not recognize the handicapped as having rights. The unserved handicapped were at the bottom of the legal and political systems—the mentally retarded, the emotionally disturbed, and the economically disadvantaged. Many of these were children and many were racial minorities. Education was viewed in narrow perspective. A widely accepted rigid definition of schooling permitted states and school systems to exclude handicapped children as incapable of benefiting from a traditional program of public instruction. Insufficient understanding of the teaching/learning process and inadequate knowledge of testing and diagnosis also impeded even the most well-intentioned of school systems from adequately serving this population.

It took a series of post-*Brown* lower court decisions to raise public, and more importantly, congressional awareness of the educational deprivation that the handicapped suffered. This judicial action in the early 1970s laid the foundation for federal legislation raising the rights of the handicapped to a legal mandate.[2]

Early Constitutional Litigation

We can trace the principal elements of present legislation protecting the rights of handicapped children through several *right to education* cases. Similar to judicial decrees defining the rights of racial and linguistic minorities and women, these cases derived their constitutional underpinnings from the equal protection and due process clauses of the Fifth and Fourteenth Amendments.[3] The rationale was that education is pivotal to socialization and the inculcation of cultural values. To exclude some children from schools open to the majority or to deny them an educational program commensurate with their needs deprives them of an equal opportunity to participate effectively in the education process and to adapt successfully to society.

The first major judicial breakthrough for handicapped children came in 1971 with *Pennsylvania Association for Retarded Children (PARC) v. Pennsylvania*[4] followed in 1972 by *Mills v. Board of Education*.[5] In *PARC*, plaintiffs challenged a state law that excluded mentally retarded children from the public schools if they had been certified as "uneducable and untrainable" or had not attained the mental age of a normal five-year-old child. Plaintiffs introduced evidence that all mentally retarded persons are capable of benefiting from a program of education and training. The parties entered into a consent agreement that enjoined the state from "deny[ing] to any mentally retarded child *access* to a free public program of education and training *appropriate* to his learning capacities"[6] (emphasis added). The state agreed to locate and identify all school-age persons excluded from public schools.

Unlike *PARC*, *Mills* was not resolved by a consent decree but by a court judgment against the school district. And unlike *PARC*, *Mills* was not limited to the mentally retarded but involved a broad range of handicapped children. Nor was it limited to exclusion from services but included the suspension and expulsion of handicapped students. Like *PARC*, however, *Mills* resulted in a court order whereby handicapped children could not be excluded from a regular school assignment unless provided with "*adequate* alternative educational services suited to [their] needs and a constitutionally adequate prior hearing and periodic review of [their] status, progress, and the *adequacy* of any alternative"[7] (emphasis added). The school board was required to provide each handicapped school-age child a free and suitable publicly supported education regardless of the degree of mental, physical or emotional disability. *Mills* further provided for certain procedural safeguards including notification of parents prior to placement and the right to a hearing before a hearing officer in the case of unsatisfactory placement.

It is noteworthy that in both *PARC* and *Mills*, the courts sidestepped the issue of whether the handicapped constitute a suspect class or whether education is a fundamental right and thereby avoided strict scrutiny analysis.[8] The courts upheld the plaintiff's claims even under the less stringent rational basis test. The denial of educational services was not reasonably related to any legitimate governmental interest, not even the avoidance of undue financial burdens. As the *Mills* court clearly stated, "The District of Columbia's interest in educating the excluded children clearly must outweigh its interest in preserving its financial resources."[9] The court reasoned that handicapped children must not bear a disproportionate burden of limited funds.

It is also noteworthy that neither decision required any particular substantive level of education but merely held that handicapped children must be given access to an appropriate *(PARC)* or adequate *(Mills)* publicly supported education. Ten years later, the Supreme Court picked up this standard of *adequacy* in an effort to define the parameters of the *appropriate education* provisions of federal legislation (*Board of Education of the Hendrick Hudson Central School District v. Rowley*[10]).

During these pre-legislative years of special education case law, a paradoxical variation developed. While plaintiffs in *PARC, Mills* and subsequent *right to education* cases challenged *exclusion* and demanded special services for identified students, a parallel strand of case law began to take shape. In these cases plaintiffs challenged *inclusion* or the placement of racial and ethnic minority students in special education programs based on testing measures of questionable validity. One such case was *Larry P. v. Riles,*[11] a controversial decision that brought to the forefront of national attention the role of federal courts in establishing educational policy. The case began in 1971, and involved a challenge to the use of IQ tests in placing minority students in EMR (educable mentally retarded) classes. The following year, the federal district court granted a preliminary injunction and restrained the state of California from placing black students in EMR classes. The court rejected the use of IQ tests as the primary criterion for placement where the consequence was racial imbalance in the composition of such classes.

With the successful litigation of *PARC* and *Mills,* 36 "right to education" cases were soon filed in 27 jurisdictions. Subsequent federal legislation and administrative regulations reflect the arguments presented in this body of litigation as well as those proffered in the discriminatory testing cases such as *Larry P.* In doing so, federal intervention has attempted to satisfy seemingly contradictory demands for greater access to special educational services and greater restraint on their use.[12]

The Federal Role Takes Shape

Similar to its carrot and stick approach in promoting equal educational opportunities for other disadvantaged groups, Congress has advanced a two-pronged attack in advancing equality for the handicapped. One involves a non-discrimination strategy as embodied in §504 of the Rehabilitation Act of 1973.[13] The other involves the appropriation of federal funds for handicapped services as represented in various education amendments. The Education for All Handicapped Children Act (P.L. 94-142) is an amalgam of both strategies.[14]

Section 504 of the Rehabilitation Act. The roots of a federal antidiscrimination policy covering the handicapped took hold in several early attempts to amend existing legislation. In 1971, Representative Charles Vanik (D., OH) introduced an amendment to Title VI of the Civil Rights Act of 1964, extending its prohibition beyond race and ethnic origin discrimination to discrimination on the basis of handicap.[15] The following year, Senators Hubert Humphrey (D., MN.) and Charles Perry (R., PA.) introduced a similar amendment in the Senate.[16] That fall following the *Mills* decision, the Vanik-Humphrey proposals were added to a bill that became the Rehabilitation Act of 1973. The nondiscrimination proposals became the final section of the Act, §504, which provides that "[n]o otherwise qualified handicapped individual . . . shall solely by reason of his handicap, be excluded from participation in, be denied the benefits of, or be subjected to discrimination under any program or activity receiving Federal financial assistance." Before this final section was added, the Act was limited to employment. Schools continued to interpret the Act in such a way and failed to respond to its broader coverage. The 1974 amendments clarified the definition of handicapped to include "physically or mentally handicapped children who may be denied admission to federally supported school systems on the basis of their handicap."

HEW failed to issue rules and regulations pursuant to §504 until forced to do so by court order.[17] HEW Secretary David

Mathews, with only a few months left in office, refused to sign the final regulations. After Joseph Califano replaced Mathews in January 1977, HEW undertook a process to review the draft regulations. From the beginning, the Carter appointees within the Department strongly supported the basic §504 regulations. But a number of controversial issues had to be ironed out, such as the scope of architectural modifications that would have to be made by schools and colleges. The disability groups were worried over the possibility of any erosion in their position. Their fears were heightened by residual anxiety from Secretary Mathews' long delay in publishing the draft regulations in the first instance. Operating in the background was the usual tendency of advocacy groups to put additional pressure on a "friendly" administration. And so the disability advocates organized sit-ins at HEW's Washington office, its regional offices, and even at Califano's home.

The regulations which became effective in 1977 describe §504 as "a national commitment to end discrimination on the basis of handicap."[18] Section 504 is modeled in statutory language and enforcement procedures after Title VI of the Civil Rights Act of 1964 and Title IX of the Education Amendments of 1972. Similar to its predecessors, it is enforced by the Office for Civil Rights and it provides for termination of federal funding in the case of noncompliance. Section 504 represents the *stick* of federal civil rights policy for the handicapped.

Early Federal Funding for Handicapped Education. Unlike congressional attempts to promote racial equality where the antidiscrimination provisions (Title VI of the Civil Rights Act of 1964) were set in place before the government appropriated federal funds (Elementary and Secondary Education Act of 1965), congressional policy on the handicapped developed in obverse order. In fact, for more than a decade before HEW had fleshed out §504 into regulations, Congress had been appropriating funds for educational services for the handicapped. Under strong advocacy pressure, most notably from the National Association for Retarded Children (NARC) and the Council for Exceptional Children (CEC),[19] Congress had come to recognize the needs of the physically and emotionally disabled. Over a ten-year period beginning in the mid-1960s, Congress incrementally developed a system of handicapped grants to the states. As a result, during those years the federal government played a significant role in stimulating interest in the disabled, encouraging special education, strengthening the special education profession, stimulating state program development, and encouraging parent organization.

In 1965, the year that Congress enacted the Elementary and Secondary Education Act, there were between five and seven million school-aged children in need of special education services. Only about 25 percent of them were enrolled in public or private schools. The 60,000 special education teachers in the nation's public schools and the 11,000 in the private schools would have had to increase to 300,000 in number in order to educate the total estimated number of handicapped children.[20]

Theoretically, the handicapped were eligible for ESEA Title I remedial services. But in practice, that was not the position of staff within the U.S. Office of Education. They maintained that only low-income children were eligible and those low-income handicapped children who happened to attend Title I schools in low-income areas might receive services. In fact, in the early years of Title I, USOE staff had no data system for gathering specific information concerning disabled children served, although they estimated that perhaps one or two percent of the funds might be spent on this sub-population of the disadvantaged.[21] The federal position was mirrored at the local and state levels. The Title I law was not explicitly designed to meet the needs of the handicapped so school districts spread their Title I funds among those educationally deprived children who fell within the norm of learning ability. During ESEA's first year of operation, only 68 of the 484 state applications received were even loosely tied to programs for the handicapped.[22]

This state of affairs underscored the need for more narrowly focused legislation. To this end the advocacy groups directed their lobbying efforts before Congress. In 1966, Congress added Title VI to ESEA[23] and authorized $50 million for fiscal year 1967 and $150 million for fiscal year 1968 to assist states in improving and initiating educational programs for the handicapped. The legislation also established the Bureau of Education for the Handicapped (BEH) within the U.S. Office of Education. This was a major victory for the handicapped. In fact, the Bureau itself stimulated much of the activity in the following years by suggesting legislation directly to Congress.[24]

But the funds actually appropriated under Title VI amounted to only $2.5 million in 1967 and $14.25 million in 1968, that is, two percent and ten percent respectively of the original authorization.[25] The interest groups strengthened their pressure and in 1970, Congress replaced Title VI with the Education of the Handicapped Act.[26] This new legislation authorized the U.S. Office of Education to award grants to institutions of higher education, state and local education agencies, and other public and private educational research agencies for the purpose of research and training in "specific learning disabilities." Congress authorized $94 million to pay for the new program and increased authorizations from the previous law to $630 million through June 30, 1973.

In 1971, BEH articulated a goal of "Education for All Handicapped Children by 1980" which was accepted by then Commissioner of Education Sidney Marland and widely circulated among state officials. The Bureau also secured the support of the Education Commission of the States which led to a series of regional conferences around the nation. BEH used those conferences to introduce state legislators to a model state statute developed under a Bureau grant to the Council for Exceptional Children.

The proponents of special education were well aware of the gap between federal appropriations and annual allocations. They were also aware of the inability and unwillingness of states and local school systems to assume primary responsibility for educating the handicapped. This history of enormous needs, fitful starts, and broken promises provided the backdrop for the litigation in *PARC* and *Mills*.

In 1973, as ESEA of 1965 and the Education of the Handicapped Act were due to expire, the Nixon Administration introduced before Congress its "Better Schools Act."[27] The proposed legislation would have consolidated 32 categorical programs into one block grant covering five broad categories—programs for the educationally disadvantaged, impact aid for school districts enrolling students whose parents live or work on federal facilities, vocational education, handicapped education, and aid for support services. The proposal would have permitted states to transfer up to 30 percent of the funds allocated for vocational and handicapped education and 100 percent of the funds for supporting services to any of the other five areas except impact aid. Advocates for the handicapped were deeply troubled by the Nixon proposal. Special education relies heavily on support services such as transportation and counseling. It was clear that the Administration's proposal would undercut the gains of the previous decade in recognizing the handicapped as a distinct group in need of special services.

The Nixon Administration's efforts at program consolidation failed to garner adequate congressional support. By 1973, programs for the disadvantaged had developed strong community support through Parent Advisory Councils as mandated under ESEA Title I and through the employment of community members as paraprofessionals in Title I classrooms. Programs for the handicapped had also raised public awareness and developed a national constituency.[28] The upshot was passage of the Education Amendments of 1974 which reauthorized ESEA of 1965 and the 1970 Education of the Handicapped Act.

The Education of the Handicapped Amendments of 1974[29] inscribed into statutory law some of the judicial reasoning of the *right to education* cases. The new law further provided financial assistance to states and local school systems in meeting the mandates of §504 of the Rehabilitation Act as enacted the previous year and laid the foundation for the more ambitious legislation that was to follow in P.L. 94-142. The 1974 Amendments required states to submit comprehensive plans for serving all the handicapped. The legislation mandated that state plans include timetables for implementing goals and provisions for due process to all handicapped children and their parents, and that they describe an instructional strategy designed to provide education to all children in the "least restrictive environment."

The Education for All Handicapped Children Act. The law that emerged from Congress the following year, popularly known as P.L. 94-142, was an artful compromise among the interests of the states, local school systems, the Ford Administration, members of Congress, and the handicap interest groups. The most influential among these in shaping the handicapped legislation were the specialized interest groups. The law's detail on administration, goals, and implementation strategies grew out of advocacy distrust of state and local school officials. HEW opposed the proposal on the ground that education of the handicapped was the responsibility of the states and not the federal government. President Ford reluctantly signed the bill into law but warned that "its good intentions could be thwarted by the many unwise provisions it contains."[30]

The centerpiece of the 1975 Act is a grants-in-aid program authorized under Part B. It requires states to provide all handicapped children between the ages of three and twenty-one with a "free, appropriate education" in the "least restrictive environment." The law carries with it a wide range of requirements as to child identification, evaluation and service delivery. State education agencies are responsible for implementation of these requirements, including the monitoring and evaluation of local school districts.

The detailed provisions of the law have made special education services more readily available to handicapped students but have also significantly increased state and local education expenditures. The law requires school systems to develop an individualized education program (IEP) for every child identified as needing special services. The IEP is agreed upon by representatives of the district, a team of specially trained professionals, and the child's parent or guardian.[31] The law gives parents the right to examine all relevant records. Schools must notify parents in writing prior to any change in the IEP and parents have the right to appeal district level decisions to an impartial hearing officer and ultimately to the state Commissioner of Education.[32] School systems are required to provide not just instructional services to the handicapped, but also related services. These include transportation as well as developmental, corrective, and other supportive services such as speech pathology and audiology, psychiatric services, and physical and occupational therapy.[33]

Finally, states and school systems must assure that handicapped children are educated to the maximum extent possible with non-handicapped children.[34] This requirement to educate handicapped students in the "least restrictive environment" has become popularly known as the *mainstreaming* principle and has developed as a major issue in special education.[35]

States and school systems are eligible for assistance under the law only if they comply with its detailed procedural and substantive provisions. Funds are allocated to the state as a percentage of the national average per pupil expenditure (NAPPE) multiplied by the number of handicapped children served by the state. When the law was passed in 1975, Congress authorized the percentage of NAPPE at 5 percent for 1977–78 and 10 percent for 1978–79 with a 10 percent increase each year. The goal was to reach 40 percent with an appropriation of $3.16 billion by 1981-82.[36] As history unfolded, however, funding levels under P.L. 94-142 never reached beyond the 12 percent level allocated in 1980.[37] For 1984, Congress appropriated $1.05 billion under the Act, a considerable drop from the $3.16 billion originally projected.

This apparent retreat from the federal commitment would become especially problematic for urban school systems as handicapped enrollments and per-pupil costs began to skyrocket.[38] In fact, the number of handicapped children reportedly served under P.L. 94-142 grew from 3.48 million in 1976–77, the year after the law was enacted, to 3.9 million in 1980–81, representing a 12 percent increase, or an additional 456,612 children. These figures are even more striking when viewed in the context of declining public school enrollments. During the same period, the overall school-age population in this country decreased by over 6 percent which ordinarily would have resulted in a loss of between 140,000 to 200,000 special education students.[39] And the number of children served keeps growing. Data based on the 1983–84 school year indicated that figure as 4.3 million.[40]

As the number of children served has rapidly expanded, the federal contribution has remained constant at 12 percent of the national average per-pupil expenditure. And as the economic health of the states faltered in the late 1970s, school systems in high cost regions of the country were dealt a particularly severe blow. For example, the U.S. Office of Education computed the NAPPE for 1979–80 at $1,900 for nonhandicapped children and roughly $2,800 for handicapped children. Yet the actual expenditures varied widely among states and cities. According to a 1979 survey of eleven large cities, the average per pupil expenditure was $2,787 while the cost of educating a handicapped child averaged $3,287. For an urban school system such as New York City, that figure was $5,570 in 1978–79, well above the $2,800 used in federal calculations for P.L. 94-142 allocations.[41]

Commonalities and Distinctions Between Section 504 and P.L. 94-142. With respect to the education of elementary and secondary students, §504 and P.L. 94-142 overlap on a variety of points. Section 504 and its implementing regulations clearly require school systems to adopt a zero-reject policy; provide a free, appropriate education to handicapped children regardless of the nature or severity of the handicap; conduct nondiscriminatory testing; place handicapped children in the least restrictive environment; and guarantee due process in placement procedures.

However, there are noteworthy differences between the 94-142 law and the HEW's §504 regulations. While the requirements of §504 are mandatory for all school systems that receive federal funds from any source, P.L. 94-142 is binding only on states and school systems that received funds allocated under the Act. Unlike P.L. 94-142, no federal funds are allocated under §504. The definition of "handicapped children" under P.L. 94-142 includes "mentally retarded, hard of hearing, deaf, speech impaired, visually handicapped, seriously emotionally disturbed, orthopedically impaired, or other health-impaired children with specific learning disabilities, who, by reason thereof require special educaiton and related services."[42] The definition of "handicapped individual" under the §504 regulations is broader, including drug addicts and alcoholics.[43]

Section 504 does not require an individualized educational program (IEP) for each handicapped child as does P.L. 94-142. Both require a "free appropriate public education" but differ

THE HANDICAPPED / 149

as to its definition. Under P.L. 94-142, an appropriate education is defined as special education and related services designed to "meet the unique needs of a handicapped child.[44]
Section 504, on the other hand, defines appropriate education
as "regular or special education and related aids or services
that are . . . designed to meet individual education needs of
handicapped persons as adequately as the needs of non-
handicapped persons are met."[45] It thus appears from the
regulatory language that §504's standard of service delivery
with regard to the handicapped, that is one based on "adequacy," is more rigid than the standard ordinarily applied to
the nonhandicapped. Although §504 is considered to be an
antidiscrimination and not an affirmative action statute as is
P.L. 94-142, in effect the §504 regulations appear to grant
affirmative educational entitlements to the handicapped.

One very significant distinction between the two laws has
in fact permitted one to induce compliance with the other.
States and school systems are subject to P.L. 94-142 prescriptions only if they choose to accept federal funds under that
law. They can therefore avoid compliance simply by refusing
to apply for P.L. 94-142 funds. On the other hand, they must
still meet the §504 non-discrimination mandate as long as they
receive federal funds from any source. In fact, HEW designed
the §504 regulations to parallel the "free appropriate public
education" provisions of the P.L. 94-142 law specifically to
induce complicance with the latter. In other words, if school
systems must comply with §504 or run the risk of losing all
their federal funds, then they might as well accept P.L. 94-142
monies and comply with its similar provisions.[46] The state of
New Mexico, the only state to refuse P.L. 94-142 funds,
learned this lesson through litigation and ultimately state
legislative action.[47]

The Supreme Court Interprets the Law

Initially, advocates believed they could draw on both
pieces of legislation as a comprehensive scheme for promoting
equal educational access for the handicapped. However, recent Court interpretation has set upon P.L. 94-142 as the
primary vehicle for addressing handicap rights in the context

of elementary and secondary schooling. The provisions for "appropriate education" and "related services" within that law have proven the most problematic for educators to operationalize and for courts to interpret. And the failure of Congress to expressly allow for the award of attorney's fees to prevailing parties in P.L. 94-142 litigation severely curtails the law's utility in achieving broad-based educational reform for the handicapped.[48]

Section 504 and the "Davis" Decision. The Court's first statement on educational rights for the handicapped was framed within a university program. Nevertheless,its 1979 unanimous decision in *Southeastern Community College v. Davis*[49] shed some early light on how far the Court would go in ordering institutions to accommodate handicapped students. The Court held that §504 does not require a community college to make fundamental changes in the nature or goals of its program or to lower the program's standards in order to admit a hearing-impaired applicant into its nursing program. According to the Court, an "otherwise qualified person" is one who "is able to meet all of a program's requirements in spite of his handicap"[50] and "neither the language, purpose, or history of §504 reveals an intent to impose an affirmative action obligation on all recipients of federal funds."[51] The Court, however, recognized that "situations may arise where a refusal to modify an existing program might become unreasonable and discriminatory," for example, where handicapped persons could participate "without imposing undue financial and administrative burdens upon the state."[52]

In a more recent decision, the Court seized the opportunity to clarify the *Davis* decision and to respond to some of the critical commentary that opinion generated in the intervening years. In *Alexander v. Choate,*[53] the Court used *Davis* as a starting point for determining cases in which proof of disparate impact would suffice to bring a claim under §504. In such cases, the plaintiff need not prove discriminatory intent. According to the Court in *Choate,* the *Davis* decision "struck a balance between the statutory rights of the handicapped to be integrated into society and the legitimate interests of federal grantees in preserving the integrity of their programs."[54]

The Court further attempted to clarify its rejection in *Davis* of "affirmative action" as a §504 obligation by drawing a distinction between that and a "reasonable accommodation" standard. According to the majority opinion written by Justice Marshall, it is a matter of degree. While "reasonable adjustments in the nature of the benefit offered must at times be made to assure meaningful access"[55] under §504, substantial "changes," "adjustments," or "modifications" to existing programs would constitute affirmative action outside the mandates of §504.[56]

P.L. 94-142 and the Constraints of "Rowley." The Court's decision in *Davis* must be read with an eye to its specific facts. Not only are there distinct differences between the right to education on the university level and the compulsory nature of elementary and secondary schooling, but the facts in *Davis* dealt clearly with exclusion and did not reach the quality of educational services. The Court's most significant and controversial statement on this point came in 1982 not under §504 but under the "appropriate education" provisions of P.L. 94-142.

The case of *Board of Education of the Hendrik Hudson Central School District v. Rowley*[57] arose in connection with the district's refusal to provide the plaintiff, a hearing impaired child, with a sign-language interpreter. The lower courts had ruled in favor of the child, defining a "free appropriate education" as an opportunity to achieve full potential commensurate with the opportunity provided other children. On review the Supreme Court addressed two issues: first, the meaning of a "free appropriate education" as mandated by P.L. 94-142, and second, the role of state and federal courts in exercising their review powers under the Act.

As to the first issue, the Court held that an appropriate education merely obligates the state to provide "personalized instruction . . . with sufficient supportive services to permit a child to benefit from . . . instruction."[58] Such instruction and services must be provided at public expense, meet the state's educational standards, approximate the grade level used in the state's regular education, and comport with the child's IEP. According to the majority opinion written by Justice Rehnquist, the intent of the Act was more to open the door of public education . . . than to guarantee any particular level of education once inside."[59] The Court clearly stated that "[w]hatever Congress meant by an 'appropriate' education, it is clear that it did not envision requiring a state providing special educational services to handicapped children to maximize each child's potential commensurate with the opportunity provided other children."[60] According to the Court, a "free appropriate education" merely requires that "the education to which *access* is provided be sufficient to confer *some* educational *benefit* upon the handicapped child" (emphasis added).[61]

With regard to state and federal court review of the Act's provisions, the Court held that "the primary responsibility for formulating the education to be accorded a handicapped child, and for choosing the educational method most suitable to the child's needs, was left by the Act to state and local educational agencies in cooperation with the parents or guardian of the child."[62] Citing *San Antonio Independent School District v. Rodriguez*,[63] the Court went on to say that courts lack the specialized knowledge and experience necessary to resolve "persistent and difficult questions of educational policy."[64] For the Court, the judicial role stops at determining whether the requirements of the Act have been met.

The initial reaction to *Rowley* within the handicap advocacy community was largely pessimistic.[65] It appeared that the Court had severely restricted the power of lower courts to assess the substantive appropriateness of services provided to handicapped children. In fact, advocates feared that the Court had gutted out of P.L. 94-142 any judicial review of substantive entitlements, leaving parents with little legal recourse beyond the procedural safeguards provided in the law. The worst case envisioned was that after *Rowley*, an appropriate education would vary as a function of the idiosyncratic philosophy and fiscal constraints of states and school districts. But subsequent history has proven otherwise. Lower court decisions have split 50-50 on the power of courts to review the appropriateness of instructional services and the Supreme Court itself in dicta has recognized not only the procedural but the substantive force of P.L. 94-142 as interpreted in *Rowley*.

Related Services under "Tatro." The Court's decision in *Rowley* established broad goals and guidelines for the provision of a free appropriate education to handicapped children. But it still left unresolved a number of more specific interpretive problems under P.L. 94-142. One of these concerned the definition of "related services," particularly those that are considered health related."

According to the law, an "appropriate education" includes "related services . . . as may be required to assist a handicapped child to benefit from special education." These are defined as transportation and other supportive services, including medical and counseling services. However, the law limits the required medical services to those that are for diagnostic and evaluation purposes only.[66] The P.L. 94-142 regulations construe related services to include "school health services," that is, those provided by a qualified school nurse."[67]

In *Irving Independent School District v. Tatro*,[68] the Court was confronted with the issue of whether P.L. 94-142 or §504 requires a school district to provide clean intermittent catheterization (CIC) as a related service. Writing for a unanimous Court, Chief Justice Burger upheld CIC as a related service required under P.L. 94-142 as it was necessary to permit the child to remain in school and thereby "benefit from special education."[69] He also rejected the school district's contention that it was a "medical service" as it did not require the assistance or supervision of a physician but could easily be administered by a nurse or even a trained lay person.[70]

While the Court's decision in *Tatro* gave an expansive reading of the law, the Court noted several limitations that would minimize the burdens feared by school districts. First, only handicapped students are entitled to "related services" under P.L. 94-142. Second, only those services that would aid a handicapped child to benefit from special education must be provided. This would exclude treatments or services that could be administered outside the school day. Third, the law does not require services that can be performed only by a physician. And fourth, the ruling does not require school districts to provide equipment but only services.[71]

The *Tatro* decision has a legal significance that goes beyond related services. This was the first opportunity the Court had taken to dispel some of the more general clouds left hanging by *Rowley*. In response to the school district's contention that *Rowley* had limited judicial review to procedural requirements, the Court in dicta revitalized the substantive aspects of the law that *Rowley* had seemingly enervated. "Judicial review," the Court maintained, "is equally appropriate in this case, which presents the legal questions of a school's substantive obligations under the "related services" requirement . . ."[72]

"Robinson," the Award of Attorney's Fees, and Congressional Action. In *Tatro*, the Court set aside the plaintiff's §504 claim in view of its holding of the same day in *Smith v. Robinson*[73] that §504 is inapplicable when relief is available under P.L. 94-142. In *Robinson*, the Court held that P.L. 94-142 is the exclusive avenue of relief in a claim for a publicly financed special education. The practical application of that ruling is that it forecloses plaintiffs from obtaining attorney's fees under alternate claims brought under the Civil Rights Attorney's Fees Awards Act[74] and §1983[75] or under §504.[76] P.L. 94-142 does not expressly provide for the award of such fees. Congress has in fact authorized attorney's fees in virtually all other civil rights actions brought under federal law. Advocates for the handicapped argue that Congress originally intended to allow such fees under P.L. 94-142 but simply failed to make it clear in the language of the law.

Within weeks of *Robinson*, legislation was introduced in the House and Senate to overturn the Court's decision. Both bills died in committee. Similar legislation was introduced in the 99th Congress by Representative Pat Williams (D., MT.) and Senator Lowell P. Weicker (R., CT.).[77] While the two bills differed slightly, the Handicapped Children's Protection Act of 1985, would essentially amend the Education for All Handicapped Children Act, P.L. 94-142, to allow courts to award attorney's fees to parents of handicapped children who successfully sue school districts. The amendments would permit such fees to be awarded not only for the costs of litigation, but for legal representation in administrative hearings under certain circunstances. The proposed legislation would further require that §504 be carried out in accordance with regulations in effect on the date of the Court's decision in *Robinson*. These last two provisions covering administrative hearings and the §504 regulations have stirred a heated controversy over the proposed legislation.

In House hearings conducted in March 1985, advocates for the handicapped argued that the amendments would have a beneficial effect in reducing litigation. Citing the findings of a study on handicap litigation where only one percent of all children served under P.L. 94-142 had become the subject of a formal dispute,[78] a consortium of 20 advocacy groups maintained that the ability of parents to take their case to court has in fact served as an incentive for school systems to resolve disputes at the administrative level.[79] The National School Boards Association (NSBA), on the other hand, argued that the award of attorney's fees at the administrative level would produce "polarization between parties and an adversarial approach to determining educational issues." NSBA further expressed concern over the burdens that dual jurisdiction could impose on school districts. If parents could simultaneously bring claims under P.L. 94-142 and §504, then both the Department of Education's Office of Special Education and Rehabilitative Services and the Office for Civil Rights could simultaneously investigate the same school district for the same violation.[80] The Department of Education raised similar objections to the proposed amendments.[81]

The Handicapped Children's Protection Act of 1985 was reported out of subcommittee on April 3 of that year. But the controversial impact of its specific provisions forbode a stormy and concession-ridden path to ultimate enactment. The complex issues underlying the proposed amendments not only pitted the advocacy groups against the interests of school systems, but they placed the community of special educators in a particular dilemma. Special education teachers and administrators are committed to the handicapped and have served in the past, notably through the Council for Exceptional Children, as the vanguard of education reform. But they are also sensitive to the formalization of hearings and the questioning of their educational judgement implicit within procedural safeguards and legal action.

As a practical matter, *Robinson* and its congressional aftermath not only unleashed the various forces operating within and without special education, but brought to public attention a new interest group created by P.L. 94-142 itself. The specific interest at stake, the award of attorney's fees, underscored the significant role played in the advocacy arena by the cadre of attorneys who represent parents and their handicapped children. Unless overturned by congressional action, the Court's decision in *Robinson* would have a devastating impact on their legal practice.

As a case study in policymaking, the events surrounding *Robinson* tell us something about law and politics in the 1980s. The *Robinson* decision is yet another instance where the Supreme Court as a body has backed off from interstitial lawmaking when confronted with statutory ambiguity. Where a congressional mandate clearly lacks precision and a judicial determination could prove administratively burdensome or costly for other institutions of government, the Court in recent years has thrown the issue back into the political arena. And the civil rights supporters in Congress, as here, have been quick to pick the ball up and run along with the advocacy groups. But such "second go-rounds" at legislation often reposition the parties at different bargaining points and present both sides with new obstacles to overcome. On the one hand, the advocates now find themselves on the defensive, no longer fortified by the gross statistics of government neglect and unmet social needs, but burdened by the data of implementation problems and local fiscal constraints. On the other hand, state and local interests must now extinguish the inflated expectations created by, in this case, ten years of lower court decisions breathing clarity and life into imprecise congressional mandates.

Unresolved Interpretive Issues

The Supreme Court's apparent reluctance to address the ambiguities inherent in the handicap legislation has left several significant issues unresolved. Included among these are the provisions of an extended school year for handicapped students, the awarding of special diplomas to handicapped students who cannot pass competency tests, and the right of school districts to suspend the handicapped on disciplinary grounds. The absence of a Supreme Court ruling on these questions has precluded a determination of national policy and uniform standards. However, a look at lower court decisions reflects more general trends in judicial interpretation. Especially since *Rowley*, lower federal courts have emphasized procedural flexibility and fairness in order to maintain the substantive individuality of the law. At the same time, they have deferred to local school officials on specific pedagogical determinations and to state agencies on the broader issues of educational policy and goals.

The Extended School Year. P.L. 94-142 guarantees to all handicapped children the right to a "free appropriate public education" which includes special education and related services. The Act defines special education as instruction that "is specially designed to meet the unique needs of a handicapped child."[82] The law's clear emphasis on the individual needs of students raises the issue of whether the handicapped are entitled, as a matter of law, to instruction beyond the usual 180 day a year limit if their educational disabilities so demand. The argument rests on the belief that handicapped students regress more severely than the non-handicapped during periods of noninstruction.

States have varied in their treatment of the 180 day limit for the handicapped. Some such as Pennsylvania and Mississippi have established a policy of categorically limiting special education to 180 days per school year. Other states such as Georgia and Missouri have established a permissive policy, neither mandating nor prohibiting local school systems from providing special education beyond 180 days. All four states have found themselves in litigation over the extended school year question.[83] And in all four cases, the federal appeals courts have balanced the unique needs of the handicapped against limited financial resources and the preservation of local school district autonomy.

Cases decided post-*Rowley* are particularly instructive on the 180-day question. A careful reading of these decisions indicates that *Rowley* cuts both ways. It clearly rejects ambitious goals to maximize the handicapped child's potential. Yet, as stated by the Fifth Circuit in *Crawford v. Pittman*, the Rowley standard of providing "some benefit" to the handicapped also precludes states and school systems from imposing rigid 180-day limitations or from forcing the handicapped to bear a heavier burden of insufficient funds than the nonhandicapped.[84]

For the Eleventh Circuit in *Georgia Association of Retarded Citizens v. McDaniel*, a rigid 180-day policy for the handicapped failed the *Rowley* standard on two counts. Not only did such a policy overlook the individualized assessment procedures of P.L. 94-142, but it prevented school districts from developing IEP's that were reasonably calculated to enable all handicapped children in the state to receive educational benefits.[85]

Nevertheless, while the courts have relied on *Rowley* to strike down blanket state policies, they have also demonstrated a post-*Rowley* reluctance to establish the extended school year as a legal mandate, preferring to leave local school systems free to make that determination on a case by case basis. In *Yaris v. Special School District of St. Louis County*, the Eighth Circuit cited *Rowley* in support of the proposition that P.L. 94-142 does not grant courts "unlimited discretion in determining how to handle these matters."[86] The Sixth Circuit held similarly in *Rettig v. Kent City School District*, concluding that courts "are not free to choose between competing education theories and impose that selection upon the school system."[87]

So while states cannot deny summer instruction to all handicapped students, school districts may still exercise discretion in weighing the benefit to be gained against the risk of regression for each individual child. Given Rowley's pronouncement that handicapped children need not be provided the best education but merely one that is reasonably calculated to provide "some benefit," the right to an extended school year may well be available only in the most extreme cases where a summer vacation would effectively nullify the progress made in the previous school year.[88] Nevertheless, as a practical matter, the prohibition against rigid state policies permits parents the option to press for inclusion of extended instruction into the child's IEP.

Competency Testing and the High School Diploma. Historically, school systems have utilized standardized tests to measure both intelligence and achievement. These tests have come under sharp criticism for being racially and culturally biased as evidenced by the disproportionately low scores achieved by certain minority groups. In recent years, similar attacks have been leveled against the use of statewide competency tests that determine grade promotion or even high school graduation. According to the Education Commission of the States, 38 states have established some form of competency tests. Laws in 20 of those states provide for diploma sanctions, either statewide or as a local option.[89] Other states use such tests to identify students in need of remediation or to target instruction. In some states, the tests are developed by the state education department and administered throughout the state. In other states, school systems are free to choose among a list of suggested standardized tests or to develop their own measure. Most competency tests evaluate achievement in basic skills such as reading and mathematics although some measure more general life skills, such as balancing a checkbook, while others are more narrowly focused on functional literacy.[90]

The rapid extension of the competency testing movement over the past decade has paralleled the expansion of public attention to the rights of the handicapped. Coming on the heels of federal handicap mandates, it was inevitable that competency tests would provoke additional challenges based on the nondiscriminatory testing provisions of P.L. 94-142 and the §504 regulations. For students identified for special services under the law, the critical question has been whether, having met the goals of their IEPs, they should be denied a high school diploma based on failure of minimum competency standards. Courts in general have upheld the authority of states and school districts to condition graduation from high school upon the passing of a comptency test. State education departments and local school systems have a legitimate interest in preserving the value of the high school diploma and maintaining the quality of instruction. The courts have recognized competency tests as a legitimate means for promoting these interests.[91] Two cases that deal directly with the rights of the handicapped reflect this judicial perspective on state and local educational discretion. One concerns a statewide testing program and the other a local competency requirement.

In *Northport-East Northport Union Free School District*

v. Ambach,[92] a New York appeals court reversed a trial court ruling that two handicapped students who had met the goals of their IEPs could not be denied a high school diploma even though they had failed the state's minimum competency test. The appeals court decided the case on both statutory and constitutional grounds. On the §504 claim, the court ruled that neither of the two plaintiff students was an "otherwise qualified handicapped individual" under the Act since neither could pass the basic competency test. They could not meet all the program's requirements in spite of their handicap as §504 mandates.

As for the P.L. 94-142 claim, the court held that the three-year notice provided by the State Education Department was not of such brief duration as to prevent school districts from programming IEPs of all students to enable them to pass the basic competency test required for diploma graduation. Finally, the court took a somewhat unconventional position on the federal and state equal protection clause claims. The court held that the unfortunate disparity between handicapped and nonhandicapped students is based on "immutable mysteries of genetics, accident, disease and illness"[93] not created by the state and therefore not subject to "middle-tier" or intermediate scrutiny. The court applied the lower "rational basis" standard and held that the protection of the integrity of a high school diploma was both a legitimate state interest and one to which the competency testing program was reasonably related. In October 1983, the New York Court of Appeals affirmed the appellate court's ruling concerning the state's authority to deny diplomas to handicapped students who fail the state competency tests. The U.S. Supreme Court refused to review the decision of the New York state court.

Within a month following the *Northport* ruling, the Seventh Circuit Court of Appeals, in *Brookhart v. Illinois State Board of Education*[94] upheld the right of school districts to require handicapped students to pass a minimum competency test as a requirement for a diploma. On the P.L. 94-142 claim, the appeals court followed the lead of the Supreme Court in *Rowley.* The court concluded that the intent of the Act was more to provide access to education to handicapped children on appropriate terms than to guarantee any particular level of education. The appeals court also relied on the Supreme Court's ruling in *Davis* and held that §504 does not require an educational institution to lower its standards to accommodate a handicapped person.[95]

Student Discipline. The Education for All Handicapped Children Act protects the education rights of both the physically and emotionally disabled. Educators have long been aware that both these groups at times exhibit disruptive behavior that may or may not be related to the handicapping condition. In the past, school systems often excluded handicapped children from any education or isolated them in special schools, and so their disciplinary problems did not affect the smooth and safe operation of the general educational program. But with the advent of P.L. 94-142, all handicapped children must be given not only a "free appropriate education," but one in the "least restrictive environment." This *mainstreaming* principle has forced educators to weigh the rights of the handicapped against those of the nonhandicapped. On the issue of student discipline, school systems have acted out of concern for the general school population, arguing that disruptive students should not be afforded greater procedural protections than others and, more importantly, that they may pose a safety threat to the school environment. Courts, on the other hand, have tipped the balance in favor of the handicapped and have emphasized the law's intent that no child be excluded from some form of continued instruction regardless of handicapping condition.

The leading case on this question is *S-1 v. Turlington.*[96] Here the Fifth Circuit affirmed the district court's issuance of a preliminary injunction in favor of the plaintiffs who had been expelled for the remainder of that school year and the entire year following. Specifically, the appeals court held that an expulsion or long-term suspension is a "change in placement" under P.L. 94-142. School districts may make such changes only in accordance with federally prescribed procedures. These include a determination by a trained and knowledgeable team as to whether the misconduct is related to the handicap, consideration by the district placement team of alternative procedures, notice to parents, and an opportunity for the parents to appeal any change in placement to an impartial hearing officer. Where the school district has followed the above procedures, a long-term suspension may be appropriate in some cases. However, the court also noted that complete cessation of educational services, even where the behavior is related to the handicap, violates the law. The school must continue to provide some educational services during the period of expulsion. The Supreme Court refused to hear the case, letting stand the opinion of the Fifth Circuit.

The *Turlington* decision provoked strong opposition from school administrators around the country. The Fifth Circuit's position, they maintained, created a double standard for student conduct—a handicapped student could commit disruptive acts with impunity while a non-handicapped child would be punished for the same behavior. The Sixth Circuit Court of Appeals, in *Kaelin v. Grubbs*,[97] responded to that argument. Under the *Turlington* analysis, stated the court, a school district can expel a handicapped child as long as it has followed the procedural protections of P.L. 94-142. School officials may even suspend the handicapped temporarily without employing P.L. 94-142 procedures, so long as they follow the procedural requirements laid down by the Supreme Court in *Goss v. Lopez*.[98]

The federal district court in Illinois specifically addressed the issue of short-term suspensions in *Board of Education of the City of Peoria School District 150 v. Illinois State Board of Education*.[99] Here the court ruled that schools may suspend handicapped students for short periods without first deciding if the offense is due to their disability or to an improper education placement. The court held that a five-day suspension of a learning disabled high school student was "such a brief period of enforced absence, possibly equivalent to that often caused by a common cold, [and] simply cannot reasonably be described as a change in a handicapped child's placement or termination of educational services."[100] The court distinguished a temporary suspension from expulsion or termination of special education. As the court noted, "there is absolutely no social or other value in assuming that the 'child's' outburst in these circumstances was due to inadequate placement."[101]

Looking at this line of cases, it appears that short-term suspensions of the handicapped are permissible. However, *Turlington* has left unresolved several nagging questions regarding long-term suspensions and expulsions. In such cases, it remains unclear as to how minimal the educational services offered in the changed placement may be and still comply with the law. Moreover, where the parent appeals the change in IEP, the delay in the changed placement may be considerable, leaving the student in the original placement pending administrative and even judicial proceedings. The only alternatives theoretically available in such circumstances are for the school district to exclude the student on an emergency basis as dangerous or for the parent to agree to the exclusion pending appeal. Yet neither of these seems highly practical. Mere disruptive behavior apparently does not constitute danger and most parents will insist on continued instruction while the appeal process grinds on.[102]

Executive Proposals for Deregulation

Over the past decade, the seemingly rapid expansion of legal rights for handicapped students has provoked harsh criticism from many local school officials. Burdened by increasing demands made on their limited resources by the whole panoply of federal mandates and caught up in costly litigation, school systems have pressed for deregulation and greater local autonomy over educational decision making. The Reagan Administration, bent on withdrawing the federal government from the educational enterprise yet clearly underestimating the political clout of the handicapped advocacy movement, developed a deregulation strategy for special education services early in its first Administration.

In August 1982, the Department of Education proposed changes in the P.L. 94-142 regulations.[103] The proposed rules would have eliminated the detailed list of "related services" under the present regulations. They would have required states to submit to the Department of Education, as part of their special education plans, definitions and standards for "related services." States would have had to submit such plans every three years instead of annually as under present regulations. The proposed rules would have no longer required school districts to reevaluate handicapped children every three years but would have permitted them to tailor the extent of testing for each child to the complexity and severity of the handicapping condition. Separate evaluation procedures for children with learning disabilities also would have been eliminated and would have significantly reduced the number of children classified as learning disabled.

One significant provision included in later drafts of the revisions would have allowed school officials to apply "normal disciplinary standards" to handicapped students in cases where a "handicapping condition" did not cause the disruptive behavior. The proposed regulations made no reference to any requirement that schools provide alternative educational services during the period of disciplinary exclusion. As for the placement of a handicapped child, the regulations required only advance parental notice and not consent. In general, the regulations would have narrowed the definitions of "handicapped children," "special education," "related services," and "specific learning disabilities."

The proposed changes drew a record 23,000 comments. Parents and advocates of the handicapped contended that the amendments would have stripped parents of rights, released school systems from obligations, and eroded gains made in the previous decade. What was clearly predictable was that the ambiguity in the proposed rules would have given school officials a free hand in cutting back services to the handicapped.

In September 1982, the Select Education Subcommittee of the House Education and Labor Committee unanimously adopted a resolution disapproving the full set of the proposed regulations. The measure was sent to the House floor but never voted on. In an extremely stormy session of the subcommittee, Secretary of Education Bell refused to drop the entire package but agreed to withdraw six of the proposed regulations, including those reducing the list of health-related services, those weakening the role of parents in determining services for their children, and those permitting schools to exclude handicapped children from regular classrooms based on disruptive behavior. The previous month, the Senate had attached an amendment to the regular fiscal 1982 supplemental appropriations bill that expressed a similar "sense of Congress" statement in opposition to the proposals. That bill was subsequently enacted as P.L. 97-257.[104]

In March 1983, Secretary Bell announced that the Department had set aside the original timetable to publish revised proposed rules by late summer 1983 in order to allow Department staff to analyze comments received on the original proposed rules.[105] In November of that year, the Department made public its decision not to offer any new proposals for revising regulations under P.L. 94-142. Instead, the Department's emphasis would shift from "regulatory review and revision to technical assistance and financial incentives."[106]

Earlier that year, the Reagan Administration had announced that, after consulting with Congress and the handicap community, it had also decided to drop plans to narrow §504 regulations. The most sweeping change under consideration would have permitted federal aid recipients to weigh a handicapped person's "potential contributions to society" against the cost of making necessary adjustments to accommodate the individual. Other provisions in the Administration's proposal, versions of which had been developed by the Office of Management and Budget and the Justice Department, tried to resolve through the regulatory process two crucial civil rights issues that were dividing the lower federal courts.

The proposed regulations would have required individuals bringing claims against federally funded agencies such as school systems to prove that the agency intended to discriminate against them. At the time this proposal was under consideration, the issue of discriminatory intent under Title VI of the Civil Rights Act of 1964 was working its way up to the Supreme Court in the case of *Guardians Association v. Civil Service Commission of the City of New York*.[107] The proposed regulations would have further limited §504's coverage to programs that specifically receive federal aid. The Supreme Court subsequently ruled on such a narrow programmatic definition of "program or activity" under Title IX of the Education Amendments of 1972 in the case of *Grove City College v. Bell*.[108] The Justice Department supported that position in its written brief and oral arguments before the

Court. As already discussed, Title VI, Title IX, and §504 are similarly worded statutes with similar enforcement provisions. Courts have relied on the interpretation given one to lend support to a similar interpretation of the other two. The Reagan Administration's attempt to limit the scope of §504 through the regulatory process was the first step and the *Grove City* case its most significant victory in a predetermined effort to reduce federal interference with local school management.

Summary Comments

Throughout the 1960s when federal officials aggressively directed their attention to the educational access afforded racial minorities, prevailing public sentiment and entrenched educational policy continued to exclude the handicapped under the label of "uneducable." It was not until the 1970s that the education of this special population fully picked up the momentum of *Brown's* mandate.

Lower court litigation and advocacy group pressure served as the catalyst for the detailed federal legislation and regulations that were to follow. These provided standards of appropriateness and outlined steps for assuring due process. They also offered parents the ultimate right to seek redress in the courts. Consequently, parents began to confront school systems unwilling or financially unable to meet the unique and costly needs of their children and litigation on the handicapped began to mushroom.

Even the most well-intentioned of school districts have been caught in a double-bind. The greater their diligence at assessing, evaluating, and placing students, the higher their enrollments have soared. The more meager their success, the greater the likelihood of protracted litigation. In either case, costs have escalated and so has opposition from other segments of the community. These conflicting social demands have engaged all three branches of government in a balancing act, weighing the individual rights of the handicapped against the interests of the non-handicapped and the costs to the larger society. How the scales tip in each case is largely a function of the decisionmaker's view of the federal role.

In the past decade, the courts have been called upon to resolve a number of disputes arising from P.L. 94-142 and §504. Parents have challenged the denial or appropriateness of educational services. School districts have contested the administrative and financial burdens placed upon them. The Supreme Court has deferred to the political process, agreeing to hear but few cases and maintaining a restrained position on state responsibilities and handicapped rights. Financial cost, administrative burdens, and the importance of professional judgment loom large over the Court's decisions. In fact, the Court appears most willing to paint handicapped rights in broad brush strokes and to leave the finer details of individual instructional choices to local school officials.

The executive branch has defined an even narrower role for federal involvement and its unsuccessful attempts at deregulation could have dramatically curtailed the rights of handicapped students. Civil rights groups have hailed the Reagan Administration's withdrawal of plans to amend P.L. 94-142 and the §504 regulations as a victory for the handicap advocacy movement.

The events surrounding the proposed amendments as well as congressional response to the Court's denial of attorney's fees in *Smith v. Robinson* prove several significant points concerning politics and educational policy. It is clear that the handicap advocates in this country comprise a sufficiently broad-based and powerful interest group, cutting across economic, racial, religious and gender lines. They have successfully swayed the congressional vote in support of high-cost educational services in a time of economic retrenchment. It is also clear that Republican as well as Democratic members of Congress are beginning to question the Administration's efforts to withdraw the federal government from the civil rights arena. A growing trend on the Supreme Court toward narrow statutory construction and local control together with the Reagan Administration's retreat from civil rights enforcement have cast the equality ball right back in the congressional court where it was first thrown out two decades ago.

VI

The Recent Federal Retreat: A New Ideology for a New Federalism

Federal initiatives on behalf of the disadvantaged were borne of and nurtured by a liberal consensus whose password was equity.[1] As that loose coalition of interest groups, academic institutions, scholars, and political operatives began to unravel throughout the 1970s, a new and far more conservative ideology gained increased visibility and credibility.[2] Counted among its growing constituency, in fact, were some disaffected old-guard liberals.

Ronald Reagan's ascendancy to the United States presidency in 1980 and his landslide reelection in 1984 were emblematic of this new perspective on government. His reelection in particular was interpreted by social commentators as a mandate for change. In both years, he ran on a platform of limited government and constrained federal spending. More specifically the 1980 Republican platform promised to:

> restore common sense and quality to education . . .
> replace the crazy quilt of wasteful programs with a
> system of block grants . . . support deregulation by the

federal government of public education . . . encourage
the elimination of the Department of Education . . .
restore prayer in public schools . . . halt forced busing
. . . enact tuition tax relief into law.[3]

Upon taking office, Reagan characterized the governmental legacy left to him as intrusive, unmanageable, ineffective, costly, and not accountable. That legacy was written in the language of the Great Society programs whose original stated intent had been to strengthen and preserve state control over education but whose implementation had proven otherwise. Some of those federal initiatives, in effect, had bypassed the states and created a direct interchange between federal and local government. Others, such as Title I of ESEA and the Education for All Handicapped Children Act, had merely supported the state level bureaucracy without giving it much power over local program design and implementation.

Reagan's *new federalism,* in contrast, would do more than give lip service to state authority. At its core was a vision of state government as the pivot of American federalism. Shaping and directing that vision was a conservative political ideology emphasizing the minimal state, local autonomy, and individual liberty. In his second inaugural address in 1985, President Reagan captured the essence of his perspective on the relationship between the individual and the state. He reminded the American people that the origin of our Republic rests in popular sovereignty and that ". . . government . . . [is] not our master. It is our servant; its only power [is] that which we, the people, allow it to have."[4]

Under the new federalism, states would assume increased fiscal responsibility for maintaining social welfare programs in exchange for greater administrative autonomy. For education, this new federal strategy constituted a major shift in the federal-state-local partnership that had developed over the previous two decades. It further tipped the balance of public-private enterprise in providing educational services. What promised to be a federal retreat from educational priority-setting and a recognition of liberty interests, translated on the one hand into a federal disinvestment in public schooling and a retreat from the equality principle. Budget reductions, program consolidation, deregulation, and proposals to aid private school students dramatically reshaped the popular discourse on education in the 1980s and further diverted public interest from the needs of the disadvantaged. On the other hand, the federal retreat itself inadvertently pushed education into the public arena, revitalized national interest in education, and gave momentum to the excellence movement that had been percolating beneath the political rhetoric and public discontent of the 1970s. Despite this unintended and salutary effect, the budgetary changes proposed by the Reagan Administration have had a decidedly negative impact on educational services for the disadvantaged although his broader policy proposals have met with limited success. The discussion that follows examines specific strategies proposed by the Administration, congressional response to those proposals, and their effect on educational policy and practice.

Budget Reductions

The first massive infusion of federal funds into the schools came with the Elementary and Secondary Education Act of 1965. Between that year and 1980–81, federal expenditures for elementary and secondary education grew from $1.9 billion to a high of $8.7 billion. During that same period, the portion of national education revenue drawn from federal sources increased from 7.7 percent to 8.7 percent, having peaked at 9.2 percent in 1979–80. In recent years, that pattern has reversed. The federal share of elementary and secondary education expenses has steadily decreased from 7.4 percent in 1981–82 to 7.0 percent in 1982–83, 6.6 percent in 1983–84, and 6.2 percent in 1984–85.[5] Between 1980 and 1984, federal expenses grew from $7.9 billion to $8 billion. While in current dollars, those figures represent an increase of 1.2 percent, in constant 1980 dollars, they demonstrate a decrease of 20.6 percent.[6]

In 1980, the Department of Education's total budget was $14.1 billion. The Reagan Administration sought reductions of 20 to 25 percent in elementary and secondary programs and sent to Congress a budget proposal of $13.5 billion for 1981–82. This figure was $2.1 billion below the Carter Administration proposal for that year. Congress approved some reductions in programs for the disadvantaged, bilingual, and vocational education students but increased expenditures in other areas, most notably in programs for the handicapped. This interchange between the executive and legislative branches has been repeated each year. The Administration urges reductions in educational spending and Congress acquiesces to a slower growth rate than in previous years but increases overall appropriations. For 1982, the Administration proposed an education budget of $13 billion; Congress appropriated $14.7 billion. For 1983, the Administration submitted a budget proposal for $10 billion; Congress appropriated $15.4 billion. For 1984, the Administration's budget request amounted to $13.5 billion; Congress appropriated $15.4 billion. And in 1985, the Administration proposed an education budget of $15.5 billion; Congress appropriated $17.9 billion. The low point in the Administration's budget cutting plan came in 1983 when it requested $1.9 billion (down from $3.2 billion in 1980) for Chapter 1 (formerly ESEA Title I) remedial programs, $84.5 million (down from $191.5 million in 1980) for bilingual education programs, and $845.7 million (down from $1 billion in 1980) for special education programs.

In 1985, the Administration in fact did a turn around. It submitted to Congress a proposed education budget in excess of the previous year's appropriations. The $15.5 billion request for Education Department programs represented a $100 million increase from the previous year's level of funding. Chapter 2 block grants to the states represented the most significant jump at a proposed $728.9 million, up from the previous year's appropriation of $479.4 million. Chapter 1 remedial programs and special education would have been level-funded while bilingual education would have been reduced from $169.1 million to $139.2 million.[7]

The Administration's 1986 education budget request was a near carbon copy of its proposal for the previous year, falling $2.2 billion short of the congressionally approved 1985 budget. Handicapped grants to the states would again be level funded at $1.16 billion as would Chapter 2 block grants at $500 million. Other programs would be cut or eliminated. Chapter 1 remedial programs would be reduced by $41 million to $3.65 billion, bilingual projects would be reduced by $30 million to $143 million, and training and advisory services under Title

IVA of the Civil Rights Act of 1964 would be cut $8 million to $16 million. Totally eliminated from the 1986 budget request were two programs the Administration has targeted for block grant consolidation from the onset—the Women's Educational Equity Act (WEEA) and the newly established magnet schools program designed to replace the already merged Emergency School Aid Act (ESAA) projects. WEEA was funded at $6 million in 1985, and the magnet schools a $75 million.[8]

In retrospect, the cuts in federal education spending have been staggering. According to a 1984 Congressional Research Service report, between 1980 and 1985 the "actual purchasing power" of Education Department funds would have dropped by 24.7 percent given the Reagan Administration's $15.5 billion proposal for 1985. Between 1980 and 1984, funding declines for specific major programs when adjusted for inflation were as follows: 9.3 percent for state grants for special education, 19.7 percent for compensatory education, 39.8 percent for bilingual education, and 55.8 percent for programs now funded under Chapter 2 block grants.[9]

The Administration's program of reduced educational spending has had a disproportionately severe impact on urban areas. Between 1979–80 and 1982–83, the average decrease in federal funding as a percentage of urban school districts' budgets was four percent.[10] Large city school systems are typically characterized by a high percentage of disadvantaged, linguistic minority, and handicapped students and have relied heavily on federal funds to meet the high-cost needs of this population. According to the Council of the Great City Schools,[11] Department of Education allocations to the 28 largest urban school systems decreased from $968 million in 1980–81 to $827 million in 1981–82, a reduction of 15 percent. The 1981–82 figure represents 12.9 percent of the Department's total elementary and secondary education budget for that year. During the same year, urban school districts received $536,400 for remedial programs under Chapter 1 of the Education Consolidation and Improvement Act of 1981 (ECIA), down from $570,400 the previous year for programs under Title I of the Elementary and Secondary Education Act of 1965 which the ECIA had replaced. The 28 school systems to which this data relates are among the poorest in the nation.

Thirty percent of the five million students enrolled in these districts live below the poverty line and 75 percent are minority.

Yet research indicates that compensatory education has been particularly effective in raising the achievement scores among disadvantaged students.[12] This is not to say that Title I (now Chapter 1) has been the only force operating to raise basic skills achievement over the past two decades. However, its emphasis on intensive remedial instruction undoubtedly has played a central role in this effort, along with racial desegregation, general sensitivity to serving disadvantaged students, competency testing, and the whole "back to basics" movement that swept the country during the 1970s. Despite this apparent success, Chapter 1, which serves only about half of all eligible children, has been targeted for annual decreases in each presidential budget request since 1981.

Underlying federal attempts to reduce spending for education and other social services is the erroneous belief that state and local governments will pick up where the federal government has left off and establish the same funding priorities. The economic roller coaster of the early to mid-1980s has proven otherwise. Initial federal cutbacks came during a period of mounting inflation, economic downturns, and spending limitations that forced many states to cut back on educational programs. As revenues declined, states and local school systems faced with retrenchment reduced the high-cost instructional services required of special student populations and spread their limited budgets more evenly across the board. According to a 1982 report published by the Education Commission of the States, the deteriorating fiscal condition of many states appeared to be reversing a decade-long trend towards equity in school finance.[13] The economic decline of the early 1980s caused collections from income and sales taxes to fall far short of anticipated levels. More than 60 percent of education revenues are derived from these sources and the shortfalls and instability had a major impact on state budgets.

Since the 1970s, beginning with court-induced finance reform in California,[14] more than half the states have attempted to narrow the spending gap between property rich and property poor school districts and to provide localities with additional funds to meet the cost differentials in educating special students.[15] During this period, the percent of education revenue receipts from state sources nationally increased at a fairly steady pace from 40.7 percent in 1972–73 to 49 percent in 1984–85. For that same period, the local share decreased from 51.4 percent to 44.8 percent, reaching a low of 41.8 percent in 1980–81, the same year that the federal share peaked at 9 percent.[16]

Early school finance reform efforts relied heavily on large state surpluses. As these dried up in the depressed economy of the early 1980s, the future of achieving more equitable distribution of state funds through "leveling up" looked bleak. The additional state dollars needed to bring property poor school districts up to the per-pupil expenditure level of the wealthy simply were not available. And any effort to redistribute existing funds from wealthy to poor districts would have proven politically unacceptable.

As the federal government was retreating from educating the disadvantaged at the same time as state revenues were declining, the champions of equity feared a heavier reliance on local support. In fact, the local share of education revenue steadily climbed from 41.8 percent in 1980–81 to 45.1 percent in 1983–84.[17] But local school districts, especially in urban areas, were experiencing their own contraints on spending. The competing demands that other municipal services typically place on large cities, popularly known as "municipal overburden," undercut local efforts to provide quality education. In the early part of the decade, this well-recognized urban dilemma became magnified by voter initiated tax limitations such as Proposition 13 in California[18] and Proposition 2½ in Massachusetts.[19] As one commentator noted at the time, the "new politics of state education finance" had developed into a tug of war between the interests in educational equity of the early reformers and the tax reform interests as manifested in the taxpayer's revolt.[20] Caught in the middle were the special population of students whose needs in the past had been addressed by an equity-conscious federal government.

The economic recovery of the mid-1980s has swelled state coffers and has joined with a resurgence of interest in education nationwide to increase state education budgets.[21] However, there is little evidence that states have increased their own expenditures specifically to compensate for federal losses. A growing number of states are moving to increase spending on education, but more in response to perceptions of diminished education quality than to offset federal reductions. The salient policy issues have shifted and so have funding priorities and goals. The new discourse on education excellence and accountability emphasizes increasing teacher salaries, improving student and teacher performance, and achieving safer school environments through student discipline.[22] Fiscal equity objectives are merely enhanced incidentally as states allocate new spending through their finance equalization formulas. This tends to narrow the gap between low property wealth and high wealth school districts, but it fails to target additional funds directly and categorically to specific student populations within those districts.

Program Consolidation

Along with federal cutbacks in education aid, the consolidation of formerly categorical programs into state block grants has served as the centerpiece of the federal education agenda for the 1980s. The Reagan Administration's original plan was to repeal certain laws including Title I of ESEA, the Education for All Handicapped Children Act (P.L. 94-142), and the Bilingual Education Act and to consolidate these along with other categorical programs. Each of these three had developed strong interest group representation over the years, partially from the parent and community involvement requirements of the laws themselves.

The bilingual programs were the first to be salvaged. Probilingual groups converged on Washington and found a sympathetic ear in an Administration that had garnered 40 percent of the Hispanic vote in the 1980 election.[23] The retention of compensatory and handicapped education as separate categorical programs was achieved later on through congressional compromise. In fact, the Administration's fiscal year 1982 budget proposed consolidating 44 elementary and secondary programs, including Title I and P.L. 94-142 into two packages totaling $4.4 billion.[24] The bill would have abolished most planning and evaluation provisions, fiscal controls, programmatic regulations, and reporting requirements. States would have been authorized to use the funds allocated for any or all of the activities authorized under the existing legislation.

In 1981, Congress enacted into law a less radical block grant scheme as Chapter 2 of the Education Consolidation and Improvement Act (ECIA). The Act consolidated 29 discretionary programs formerly authorized under six separate acts into one block grant to be allocated to the states.[25] The legislative purpose of the consolidation was to improve elementary and secondary education of public and private school students, to reduce administrative and paperwork burdens, to permit the development of programs in accordance with the educational needs and priorities of state (SEAs) and local (LEAs) education agencies, and to vest in local school districts the responsibility for the design and implementation of programs under Chapter 2.[26]

Funds are allocated to the states on a formula basis in proportion to each state's share of the nation's population aged five through seventeen with a guarantee that no state may receive less than 0.5 percent of the funds reserved for state allotments. Each SEA may retain up to 20 percent for its own use and must distribute at least 80 percent to LEA applicants on a formula basis in proportion to their relative student enrollments in public and nonpublic schools. Enrollment figures must be adjusted to provide higher allocations to LEAs with the greatest number or percentage of high-cost students, such as those from low-income families and those residing in sparsely populated or economically depressed areas. Both LEAs and SEAs must assure that private school children participate "equitably" in Chapter 2 programs.

LEAs are permitted to spend block grant funds with complete discretion within any combination of three broad categories, including basic skills development (reading, mathematics, written and oral communication); educational improvement and support services (including library resources, instructional equipment, desegregation assistance, and guidance, counseling and testing); and special projects (including career education, metric education, and vandalism reduction in the schools). SEAs may spend their maximum 20 percent of the funds on any of the above specified purposes as well as for state leadership and support services (including technical assistance to LEAs, dissemination of information, development of instructional materials, teacher training, research and development, parent training and state administration).

Opponents of consolidation have traditionally argued that a block grant system would have a negative impact on federally identified target groups and that the states with a record of greater responsiveness to the educational needs of middle class students, voters, and taxpayers, would assign low priority to the disadvantaged. A look at recent experience in transforming categorical programs into block grants reveals some undesirable consequences. In general, block grants tend to redistribute funds from central cities and highly urbanized states to suburban and small town areas and states. As a result, they tend to decrease services to low-income and minority groups by spreading funds more thinly. While they increase local participation in the policy process, they also create a tension between local priorities and what were defined as national objectives under the original legislation creating the merged categorical programs.[27]

The education block grant legislation may well bear this out. First of all, city school districts must now share their allocations with private schools.[28] The law requires that Chapter 2 funds be spent "equitably" on public and private school students. This provision has resulted in a windfall for some private schools. In Pennsylvania, for example, private schools have received a 139 percent increase in resources, while in Michigan expenditures for private schools have risen from $385,000 to $1.5 million.[29]

The most severe criticism leveled against private school participation is that such schools are receiving large amounts of federal aid without providing the government with assurances that they do not discriminate against racial minorities, women, or the handicapped. In a 1984 survey of 34 large school districts, the American Association of School Administrators found that 14 of those districts failed to ask private schools to sign assurances as to Title VI of the Civil Rights Act of 1964 (race discrimination), 17 did not require proof of compliance with Title IX of the Education Amendments of 1972 (sex discrimination), and 18 did not ask whether recipients provided equal access to the handicapped under §504 of the Rehabilitation Act of 1973.[30] Related to this question of civil rights compliance is the issue of constitutional violations against First Amendment separation of church and state requirements. According to information gathered in a 1984 survey of 21 states, the District of Columbia, and Puerto Rico, six of those states failed to monitor private schools to assure that funds were used only for "secular, neutral, and non-ideological" purposes while four states did not seek assurances that benefits were for children rather than the schools.[31]

Another area in which the education block grant has attracted criticism from the advocacy groups concerns the state allocation of funds. The law requires states to distribute Chapter 2 funds to school districts taking into consideration the numbers of "high-cost" students. However, the typical state distributes only 30 percent of its school district allocations on this basis.[32] In fact, according to the National Committee for Citizens in Education (NCCE), only five states distribute most of their block grant money based on student need. Those states are Alaska, California, Connecticut, Massachusetts, and New Jersey. Mississippi, the poorest state in the country, is the lowest at five percent. Connecticut, one of the wealthiest states, is the highest with 79 percent of its allocation based on low-income and isolated minority group children. In addition, only 17 of the 50 states surveyed are distributing all of their Chapter 2 block grant aid that has been set aside for special needs students to districts that have the greatest numbers of those students.[33] The remaining 33 states appear to be in violation of the block grant's original intent. According to a 1983 congressional conference report, the extra funds allocated by states for special needs students should flow to those school districts "with only the greatest number or percentage of high-cost children" rather than to districts "with any number of such children."[34]

In a letter to Secretary of Education Bell in January 1984, the Council of the Great City Schools and the Lawyers' Committee for Civil Rights Under Law urged the Department to revise its regulations and nonregulatory guidelines to reflect congressional intent and to give guidance on what would be considered adequate targeting.[35] In a later address to the

Council, Secretary Bell indicated his agreement with the Council's position but noted opposition from the Office of Management and Budget.[36] The proposed Chapter 2 regulations issued by the Department in July 1984 reflect the OMB position on maintaining the block grant with few restrictions.[37] The proposed regulations fail to address the targeting of high-cost funds at all.

Both the targeting problem and other factors have in fact redistributed funds away from urban centers. Large city school districts have a disproportionate number of poor students. They were also the most successful competitors for the categorical aid programs merged into the education block grant. Chapter 2 funds which were formerly concentrated in urban areas are now spread out evenly across school districts.[38]

A major source of funds for cities under the previous legislation was the Emergency School Aid Act (ESAA) which assisted school districts involved in voluntary and count-ordered desegregation. School systems could expend ESAA funds on a variety of activities including remedial services, staff training, and curriculum development. Low-income and minority students were the primary beneficiaries of ESAA aid. Grant awards were large and few in number. In 1982, 250 school systems received grants ranging from $30,000 to nearly $7 million. Seventeen large cities received awards of over $1 million each.[39] During that same year, 20 school systems including Atlanta, Buffalo, Boston, Chicago, Denver, Nashville, New York, and St. Louis received approximately $110 million for programs later merged into the Chapter 2 block grant. Sixty-four percent of these funds had been appropriated for ESAA programs. These same cities received only $38 million to support all programs subsequent to consolidation. This figure is 20 percent below what those districts had received under ESAA alone.[40]

In 1981–82, ESAA accounted for $149.2 million or 34 percent of the categorical funds merged into Chapter 2. According to an Education Department informal survey of 32 states and the District of Columbia, school districts in only 12 states planned to expend any Chapter 2 funds on desegregation. In fact, the 33 respondents anticipated that they would spend only $10.6 million or 5.9 percent of the total funds allocated to school districts on desegregation.[41] This figure closely matches the 5.7 percent found in a study by the American Association of School Administrators.[42]

While the Reagan Administration has repeatedly voiced support for voluntary desegregation, it has opposed congressional efforts to revive federal desegregation aid. As noted by Senator Daniel P. Moynihan (D., NY), sponsor of legislation reenacting ESAA, "If Congress and the courts mandate school-desegregation efforts, then we have some level of responsibility to ensure that the resources to accomplish the task are at hand."[43] The Magnet Schools Assistance Program, enacted in October 1984, authorized $75 million for fiscal year 1985 to encourage voluntary desegregation plans and to support magnet school programs.[44] As already noted, the Administration subsequently eliminated the program from its 1986 budget request.

The Reagan Administration has repeatedly tried to eliminate separate funding under the Women's Educational Equity Act (WEEA)[45] and the desegregation training and advisory services provided under Title IV of the Civil Rights Act of 1964.[46] Using the ESAA strategy, the Administration has made unsuccessful attempts to merge these categorical programs into the Chapter 2 block grant. Having failed in the face of advocacy pressure and congressional support, the Administration has tended to eliminate both of these programs from annual budget requests to Congress. Civil rights and women's organizations, mindful of the fate met by desegregation funds under the merger of ESAA into the Chapter 2 block grant, have pressured Congress to maintain categorical funding for these programs.

In 1984, under pressure from education advocacy groups, President Reagan reluctantly signed into law an omnibus bill that reauthorized for five years ten programs including WEEA.[47] WEEA programs together with Title IX of the Education Amendments of 1972 represent a two-pronged federal strategy to promote sex equity. Title IX prohibits sex discrimination while WEEA aims at eliminating sex-stereotyping in educational programs, activities, and materials. In addition to establishing a National Advisory Council on Women's Education Programs, WEEA has supported model projects to enhance sex equity at all levels of education in six basic areas: educational materials development; preservice and inservice training; research and development; guidance and counseling; educational activities to increase opportunities for adult women; and program expansion for women in vocational, career, and physical education, and educational administration.

The program has experienced gradual cuts in funding over the past several years from $10 million in 1979–80 to $8.1 million in 1980–81 to $5.7 million in each subsequent year with a slight increase to $6,000 in 1984–85. While the funding levels to promote sex equity have never reached the proportions allocated other federal interests, the impact that WEEA projects have made on professional awareness, educational services, and Title IX compliance in general cannot be underestimated.[48]Neither can the law's symbolic value. WEEA in fact represents the coming of age of women as a significant interest group. It also signifies the power of the women's lobby to congressionally keep alive a program that has been steadily targeted for extinction by the executive branch.

The Reagan Administration has met similar failure in its efforts to eliminate Title IV desegregation assistance projects either through consolidation or zero funding levels. The Title IV programs have served as a direct support to civil rights enforcement efforts not only with respect to sex but race and national origin desegregation as well. Funds have been awarded mainly to universities to support desegregation assistance centers that provide technical assistance and training to local school districts within a given geographical area. Institutions of higher education have also received awards for training institutes that assist in sex and race desegregation. In addition, funds have been provided directly to school districts and state education agencies to assist in all three areas of desegregation. The program was funded at a high of $45 million in 1979–80 and has been reduced each year from $37 million in 1980–81 to $24 million in each subsequent year.[49] In its 1986 budget request to Congress, the Administration broke its pattern of zero funding for Title IV and proposed $16 million in funding which represents an $8 million decrease from previous congressional appropriations.

Deregulation Through Alternative Systems of Financing Education

As already noted, the Reagan Administration has exerted great effort toward freeing states and local school systems from what are considered by many to be burdensome and intrusive federal mandates. Since taking office, the Administration has withdrawn proposed rules on bilingual education promulgated in the closing days of the Carter Administration, has merged numerous categorical programs into block grants, and has attempted to loosen federal mandates as to educational services for the handicapped. The Administration has further proposed more radical deregulation in the form of tuition tax credits and vouchers. The tax credit proposal dates back to the 1980 Republican platform and was joined by the voucher concept in the party's platform for 1984. On the theory that "competition fosters excellence," both have become key issues in the second Reagan Administration.

There are significant differences between vouchers and tax credits, both in the way they may be administered and in their potential impact on various economic groups. Nevertheless, they share a common goal, that is, to increase parental choice and educational diversity. Strategies for choice such as these are intended to break the public school monopoly. By creating a competitive market for schooling, the state would grant consumers greater influence over schooling and make schools more accountable to their clients.

Opposition to private choice alternatives center around three themes—discrimination, constitutionality, and the budget. Opponents of vouchers and tuition tax credits argue that government support of private schools may lead to greater racial segregation, would violate constitutional prohibitions against establishing a state religion, and would divert scarce education funds from the public schools that will continue to serve the poor and the private schools that are havens for the rich. This last criticism is leveled specifically at tuition tax credit proposals.

The issue of choice in education strikes at the very heart of the American educational experience.[50] The common school notion, on which the public school system was founded, emerged as an attempt to teach a common core of shared values, a consistent language of politics, and a sense of social institutions for a nation that was struggling to develop a shared identity among a diverse population. That common educational experience inevitably conflicted with the freedom enjoyed by citizens in other spheres of our democratic society.

Some of that tension has been alleviated in the past through local community control over education finance and programming. However, public schooling has become increasingly centralized at both state and federal levels over the past fifty years and even *new federalism* policies will not prevent the encroachment of the state upon local autonomy. In fact, the recent reemphasis on state responsibility has drawn both from the equity-based school finance movement and the accountability-based performance movement to promote greater educational homogeneity.

The effect of current state level reforms on public schooling remains to be seen. Actually, the focus on standards, rigor, and quality could stem the exodus from public to private schools. But there is another movement afoot that poses an even more severe threat to public education. The political conservatism of the past decade has been joined by a surge in religious revivalism. Adherents to various religious persuasions have rejected the values of the public schools and chosen to educate their children in religiously affiliated institutions. It is from this sector that the cry for government aid to private schools has risen from a whisper to a din.[51] With roughly 85 percent of American private schools having a religious affiliation, these institutions stand to reap the greatest rewards from increased government aid.[52]

The private educational choice question is quite complex. It is in fact a web of political, legal, economic, social, and ideological issues all intertwined. It is supported by those on the left of the political spectrum who see it as a means of empowering the poor. It is advanced by those on the political right as a way to control the values embodied in the educational experience.

Among the wider American public, there seems to be no strong consensus. According to Gallup poll data, when asked their opinion on government aid to parochial schools, 48 percent of the respondents favored such aid in 1970 while only 40 percent were in favor in 1981, a decrease of 8 percent.

However, when asked their opinion on a voucher system that would permit parents to choose among public, parochial, or private schools, the results showed a different trend. In 1971, only 38 percent responded favorably while that figure rose to 43 percent in 1981 and 51 percent in 1983. These data indicate an erosion of support for government aid to parochial schools over the past decade on the one hand, and an increasing support for government sponsored choice on the other.[53]

This distinction between parochiaid and choice may determine the political acceptability of various proposals now in the wind. The permutations are many. Choice can come from federal or state government aid in the form of tax credits, tax deductions, or vouchers. It need not include the private sector but may permit parents to choose among educational programs within a public school, school district, or across district lines. It need not encompass the entire educational experience, but may be limited to remedial services, enrichment activities, or other segments of the instructional program. It need not be offered to the entire student population but may be targeted at specific groups such as the handicapped, the educationally disadvantaged, or the gifted.

The discussion that follows focuses on two proposals advanced by the Reagan Administration—a system of federal tuition tax credits and a voucher system for Chapter 1 remedial programs. Each of these has separate and distinct policy implications for the education of disadvantaged children.

Tuition Tax Credits

Tuition tax credits have been part of the Reagan Administration agenda from the very beginning. While similar proposals for tax credits and deductions had been floating around state legislatures for years, the approach had never been successfully attempted at the federal level. Viewed essentially as parochiaid and specifically as aid to the Roman Catholic church, tax subsidies to private school students has never garnered sufficient support in Congress. However, as education has become increasingly privatized in the past decade, the class of potential beneficiaries has broadened and the likelihood of congressional approval has increased.

The Administration's first major statement on the topic

came in the form of a Department of Education sponsored report in 1982.[54] Here the Advisory Panel on Financing Elementary and Secondary Education maintained that tuition tax credits along with vouchers would liberate parents from the constraints of public education by providing "freedom of choice." The report went on to say that the increased competition fostered through such a system would have a salutary effect on the overall quality of education provided by the public schools.

Armed with these recommendations, the Administration in both 1982 and 1983 sent to Congress a tuition tax credit measure for parents who send their children to nonpublic elementary and secondary schools. The proposal would have provided a credit of up to half the tuition paid for each child with a maximum credit of $100 in 1983, $200 in 1984, and $300 in 1985. The full credit would have been available to parents with an adjusted gross income of $40,000 a year. Families earning more than $60,000 would not be eligible for a credit.

In April 1983, the Senate Finance Committee held hearings on the Administration's proposal, S. 528.[55] The plan got a hostile reception from its opponents and criticism from some of its supporters. Even Senator Daniel P. Moynihan (D., NY), a longtime parochiaid advocate, questioned the Administration's "overblown claims" that competition produces excellence in public education.[56] The following November, the Senate voted 59 to 38 to scuttle the Administration's tuition tax credit bill. Twenty-four Republicans, including majority leader Howard Baker, joined 34 Democrats to table the parochiaid measure.

Tuition tax credits raise some serious equity issues. According to a congressionally mandated report prepared by the School Finance Project of the National Institute of Education, approximately 9.2 percent of students currently attending public schools would be "very likely" to transfer if a tuition tax credit of $250 were available.[57] Based on current private school enrollments, the Administration has estimated the loss in federal revenue in the first year at $229 million with a maximum yearly loss of $703 million by the fiscal year ending September 30, 1986.[58] That cost would become inflated as the tax credit itself begins to stimulate additional transfers to the private school sector.

If federal losses from tuition tax credits were compensated by reducing aid to public schools, then federal aid would be reduced by 15 percent. Parents of private school students would receive 31 percent more in tax benefits than the average parent of a public school student.[59] These figures indicate that a tuition tax credit could significantly diminish political and financial support for public schooling in America. Not only would it lead to an exodus of the more fortunate from the public schools, particularly in urban areas, but it would further dilute existing federal funds for education in a time of cutbacks and reduced federal commitment.

A tuition tax credit would clearly place greater constraints on the participation of poor and minority parents. These constraints result from several externalities. First, many poor families would be unable to meet the additional costs of private school attendance beyond the $300 maximum tax credit, such as the additional cost of tuition, fees, books, and transportation. Secondly, poor families have limited or no tax liability and may therefore prove ineligible for a tax credit. Nationwide data reveal that families with incomes below $10,000 pay relatively little in taxes and families with incomes below $5,000 pay no taxes. Ineligibility for minority families is most striking. Nearly 15 percent of Hispanics and over 22 percent of blacks have no tax liability. This figure is only six percent for white families.[60]

Another factor to be considered is the constitutionality of a tuition tax credit plan.[61] Opponents argue that aid to parochial schools violates the First Amendment to the U.S. Constitution which states that, "Congress shall make no law respecting an establishment of religion or prohibiting the free exercise thereof." Over the past decade, the Supreme Court has developed a series of standards and tests against which to measure the constitutionality of various types of government aid. Those decisions have dealt primarily with state legislative attempts to provide services, materials, and direct aid to private schools. In the early 1970s, the Burger Court followed a path of "benevolent neutrality" neither advancing nor burdening religious exercise. As the decade wore on, the Court took on a more conservative bent and appeared to adopt a more *accommodationist* approach to religious freedom and diversity.[62]

The Court's 1983 decision in *Mueller v. Allen*[63] upholding a tuition tax deduction law in Minnesota added fuel to the tax credit debate. In a 5-4 ruling, the Court upheld the Minnesota law on all elements of the three-part test applied in challenges under the First Amendment establishment clause. According to the majority opinion, the Minnesota law had a "secular purpose" of ensuring a well educated citizenry. It had a "primary effect" of neither advancing nor inhibiting religion as the deduction is available to parents of both public and nonpublic school students. And finally, it did not foster an "excessive government entanglement" with religion. According to a strongly worded dissent written by Justice Marshall, however, the Minnesota law had a direct and immediate effect of advancing religion as over 90 percent of the eligible taxpayers in Minnesota send their children to religious schools.[64]

Opponents of tuition tax credits were quick to draw distinctions between the Minnesota law as upheld by the Court and the Reagan Administration's proposal. Aside from allowing a tax credit rather than a tax deduction as in Minnesota, the proposed tax credit is limited to parents of nonpublic school students. This narrower scope may not pass constitutional muster under the second part of the test as to "primary effect."

A broader tax credit that includes the parents of public school students may garner Supreme Court support from the narrow majority of *Mueller*. However, constitutionality does not always translate into sound public policy. And research evidence as well as plain common sense indicate that a federal tuition tax credit may only serve to rob the public schools of their ablest students and their most politically vocal advocates, divert dwindling federal funds from the disadvantaged, and leave public education to the poor and politically powerless, all in the name of "freedom of choice." The question is, "Choice for whom?"

Chapter 1 Voucher Plan

While tax credits have drawn support primarily from politically conservative and organized religious groups, the voucher concept has enjoyed a broader constituency ranging from the political left to the right. All share in common a distrust of government, bureaucracy, and bigness. But the proponents at either political pole differ markedly in their goals and programmatic ideas. On the left, vouchers represent a new institutional means by which government can exercise its responsibilities to the poor while empowering them with the same freedom of choice as the rich now enjoy.[65] On the right, vouchers support a free-market economy to promote competition and enhance educational quality. In operational terms, the chief difference between the two views is whether vouchers should be basic or total, that is, whether upper-income families should have the right to supplement vouchers with their own money.

The pros and cons of voucher plans have been debated for the past two decades. The concept is generally attributed to the economist Milton Friedman whose "pure voucher" scheme would have granted a government subsidy to every elementary and secondary school student equal to average per pupil expenditures. His system would have been unregulated and schools could charge whatever tuition the market could bear.[66] The voucher idea was picked up in the early 1970s by social reformers such as Christopher Jencks and his colleagues at Harvard as well as by the architects of state school finance reform, John Coons and Stephen Sugarman.[67] Both of these groups looked to vouchers as a means of advancing educational equity for the poor.

The Alum Rock, California experiment in the 1970s, carried out under Jencks and the Center for Public Policy in Cambridge, provides the only direct evidence available on schooling under a voucher plan.[68] Sponsored by the U.S. Office of Economic Opportunity and later by the National Institute of Education, the project met with widespread opposition from the onset. Not only did school districts reject the plan, but the very intended beneficiaries—the nation's poor and ethnic minorities—never rallied around the idea. In fact, the local NAACP chapters actively opposed it. As a result of planning difficulties, the project ended up as a limited voucher plan in one school district with only public and not private schools participating.

The limitations of the Alum Rock study leave us with little evidence as to the potential of voucher plans to advance equity goals. Nevertheless, evaluations of the project give some information on the question of family choice. When asked the most important criterion for school selection, a majority of Alum Rock parents responded that "nearness to home" and not "curriculum or instructional methods" was the most significant factor. And as expected, socially advantaged parents were more aware of program alternatives and were more likely to choose "innovative" programs.[69] Other research has highlighted the inadequacies of information delivery systems for the poor and disadvantaged.[70] Minority populations, particularly bilinguals, utilize different channels of information than do majority populations and the cost of effective information flow to a widely diverse public could place an inordinate financial burden on school systems. Finally, the cost of transporting students beyond the neighborhood school to receive services of their choice, especially beyond district bounds, must not be overlooked.[71]

The voucher plan first unveiled by the Reagan Administration in March 1983 is aimed at low-income parents. The intent is to allow parents to purchase Chapter 1 compensatory education services for their children at the public or private school of their choice. The voucher proposal entitled, "Equal Educational Opportunity Act of 1983" (H.R. 2397) was introduced in the House the following month. The plan would allow states to mandate Chapter 1 vouchers statewide. If a state decided not to opt for vouchers, local school systems could still choose to offer them districtwide. In April 1983, the House Subcommittee on Elementary and Secondary Education held hearings on the proposed plan which stimulated only mild support in Congress. The Administration again included a request for congressional authorization to distribute Title I funds on a voucher basis in its 1985 budget.

Public education groups and Chapter 1 advocates have assailed the concept as unworkable and ill-conceived. The plan would not only impose costly and complicated administrative burdens on local school districts, but would dilute the program's widely acknowledged effectiveness in raising the achievement levels of disadvantaged students. Given the increased administrative, information, and transportation costs entailed, a Chapter 1 voucher plan would merely serve to dilute already inadequate funds. The proposal has even met with opposition from the private school community. According to the U.S. Catholic Conference, a group strongly in support of tuition tax credits, there exist too many uncertainties in the plan to merit the organization's support.[72] Parochial and private schools now receive substantial aid through Chapter 1 and are fearful of placing their programs in jeopardy.

Without support from the public or private school community, the political prognosis for the Administration's voucher plan indeed looks unfavorable. However, the voucher concept is still very much alive. In fact, it is now attracting former opponents such as Albert Shanker, president of the American Federation of Teachers, who see vouchers as a free choice option that would strengthen the case against tuition tax credits if limited to the public schools. Public school advocates also see it as a means to professionalize teaching and promote the idea that children are not captives of the schools.

In May 1985, the Colorado legislature adopted a public school voucher program for dropouts.[73] With voucher plans under consideration in other legislatures, the political climate appears ripe for testing the voucher concept.[74] If limited to the public schools, vouchers may prove that equity and free choice are compatible policy goals.[75]

Summary Comments

When it came to office in 1980, the Reagan Administration set about to dramatically reshape and reduce the federal role in education. That goal was founded on a political ideology of limited government and increased privatization. Using the rhetoric of state and local control and individual freedom, the Administration advanced an attack on numerous fronts—budget reductions, deregulation, program consolidation, tuition tax credits, and even the dismantling of the newly created Department of Education. This ambitious agenda promised to turn education on its head. That promise has not been fully realized.

New federalism reforms have decreased the size of the federal role but have barely touched its contours. The Administration's biggest and perhaps only success has been the

Chapter 2 education block grant. Nevertheless, when viewed in broadscope, that victory was a minor one. The three major programs in compensatory, special, and bilingual education were salvaged as categorical aid through advocacy pressure and congressional action. The one large program that was initially consolidated, the ESAA desegregation aid, was returned to categorical status by subsequent congressional action. In terms of dollars allocated, Chapter 2, in fact, represents a rather modest achievement in subordinating former equal educational opportunity concerns to state and local decisionmaking.

The administration's efforts to erode equity-based programs for special student populations were stymied in Congress. Executive proposals to drastically reduce budget allocations proved unsuccessful. So did efforts at deregulation. The Administration pulled back the Carter Administration's proposed bilingual regulations, but was unable to formally replace these with less restrictive guidelines or to significantly alter Title VII's emphasis on bilingual methodology. Proposals to deregulate P.L. 94-142 and §504, the handicapped legislation, met with similar failure. The Administration's attempt to use the budget process to eliminate programs in sex equity and desegregation assistance proved equally unsuccessful. And its plan to provide federal aid to private education through tuition tax credits and vouchers met with embarrassing defeat and disinterest in Congress.

The past several years have seen a lot of shaking but very little movement in dramatically refashioning the federal role. The Department of Education continues to exist. Federal programs still remain primarily categorical with most of the constrictions they started out with. Programs for the disadvantaged remain, albeit at reduced funding levels. The Administration's National Commission on Education and Excellence, in fact, has refocused attention on federal responsibility. And while it appears that the Administration has changed the discourse on education, that has been accomplished more by changing public opinion than by changing federal programs. What the Reagan agenda has achieved, nevertheless, is a rethinking of old strategies for aiding the disadvantaged and a revitalization of advocacy group support that had begun to grow satisfied with its hard won battles.

Why has the Reagan Administration's grand federal pull-out gone awry? The answer to that question is best left to political historians. To venture a preliminary assessment, we would have to look at the big picture of the 1980s. A safe guess is that the Administration has become a victim of its own ideology. It has invested so much energy and political capital in controversial issues such as school prayer that appeal to a narrow constituency, that it has had little left to advance its broader education agenda. Having exercised too much ideological fervor and not enough political foresight, the Administration has apparently missed its opportunity to significantly reshape the federal role in education. But that does not save equity-based programs from further budget-reductions—the inevitable consequence of a rising national debt and an Administration that places education low on its policy agenda.

VII

Moral Vision, Federal Policy, and Educational Rights

In the post-*Brown* era, the ideal of equality has served as the guiding principle for a groundswell of federal initiatives in public education. During these years, federal intervention in educational decision making has expanded, not by a comprehensive set of planned policies but by segmented accretion. As we look back over the past thirty years, we see several themes running through this incremental and unsteady process—the interplay among the three branches of government, the role of interest groups in shaping public policy, and the tension between equality and diversity as policy objectives.

The Supreme Court's decision in *Brown v. Board of Education* drew the landscape on which future political actors were to operate. By 1954, race as the irresolvable American dilemma had become a national moral disaster. But it was not until a decade later that strong executive leadership combined with firm congressional support to translate *Brown*'s legal mandate into an agenda for social reform. During that decade, the three branches worked hand in hand to eliminate race discrimination and overcome the effects of poverty. Equality, the dominant theme, was built on the idea of human dignity, political participation, and individual choice.[1] Social policy was formulated in the context of welfare state goals; public funds would be redistributed to raise needy individuals to a minimum educational level. The costs would be borne by an amorphous government and not by individual taxpayers.[2] The major piece of educational legislation of that period, the Elementary and Secondary Education Act of 1965, was essentially an executive branch creation. Facing presidential determination and lopsided congressional power, the major interest groups made concessions that they might have fought bitterly in other circumstances.[3]

But the 1970s brought dramatic changes in executive leadership and at least nominal changes in Supreme Court membership.[4] It also brought changes in the political dynamic of federal policy making. What had started out in *Brown* as equality premised on respect for the individual began to evolve as a manifestation of group consciousness and group rights. During that decade, the conflict between individual autonomy and social justice, between diversity and equality, came to the fore of the policy debate. By mid-decade, a Republican executive had locked horns with a Democratic legislature on such issues as busing to achieve racial balance, the educational rights of the handicapped, and the preferred approach to federal financing of educational services. And by the end of the decade, demands for parental choice and federal aid to nonpublic education became louder and more organized than ever.

Throughout this period, special interest groups mobilized to shape legislative proposals, stave off unfavorable amendments, monitor enforcement, and support litigation. These groups had little in common with the traditional education lobby which was dominated by the educational establishment. On the contrary, they were suspicious of public schools and their officials and sought to have written into federal law and regulations detailed procedural protections and substantive guarantees. Federal handicapped statutes such as P.L. 94-142 and the §504 regulations as well as the proposed "Lau Regulations" of the Carter Administration are clear examples of this advocacy approach.

As the equality movement gained momentum, it became

clear that not only is equality for all expensive, but equality for some may intrude on the liberty interests of others. And so equality competed with local autonomy and individual choice as values underlying the policy making process. And when resources declined and costs escalated throughout the 1970s, equality began to give way to diversity—diversity of needs and of tasts. Mandatory busing to achieve racial balance had moved north, striking at housing patterns and neighborhood schools and prompting calls for freedom of association. The education of the handicapped was diverting scarce local and state funds from other groups and individuals. Bilingual education as a prescribed methodology for linguistic minority students had struck at the essence of America's identity and was taking jobs away from monolingual teachers. The *melting pot* had become a *seething cauldron* of ethnic group demands. Sex equity had laid bare traditional values and expectations and was threatening wide-ranging consequences for society.

Federal *assistance,* many believed, had evolved into *coercion,* as the government threatened to withdraw federal funds from school systems found in noncompliance with civil rights statutes. School desegregation and special education cases had taken on the characteristics of *public law litigation*—polycentric controversies, with multiple parties and issues entailing prolonged judicial involvement and detailed and continuing remedies.[5] Not only did this drain local finances but it appeared that federal judges were in fact running the public schools and becoming an "imperial judiciary."[6] America's strong political culture of local control over education was besieged from all sides. And so public sentiment turned against the concept of group rights in favor of individual liberty.

It was against this backdrop of political confusion, economic retrenchment, and moral despair that Ronald Reagan approached the 1980 Presidential election. His Administration promised a federal retreat from educational priority-setting that has in fact translated into a disinvestment in public schooling and a retreat from the equality principle. Budget reductions, consolidation of programs into state block grants, deregulation, and weakened enforcement efforts have indicated a marked departure at the executive level from long-standing national policies. Repeated policy shifts among Justice Department officials in pending litigation have signaled a flagrant defiance of the rule of law. The Administration has refused to recognize the continued importance of civil rights and has hidden behind the veil of simplistic solutions to an intractable problem. If permitted full reign, the Administration's policies could lead to a system whereby equal access to education for all children would be defined by local good will and fiscal constraints, advocacy group pressure, and the persistence of individual parents.

But the Administration's ambitious agenda has met political roadblocks along the way. From the onset, advocacy groups and civil rights organizations dramatically reduced initial designs on program consolidation. Bipartisan congressional support for public education has stymied efforts to reduce educational spending or to move on tax credit and voucher proposals. With the ideologues of the political right polarizing the country, Congress has struggled to find the soul of America. In the ideological flux of the 1980s, national consensus on a variety of policy issues has become elusive and the political parties have ended up at war with themselves and with each other. For the civil rights forces, the best that can be done is to stem the tide of creeping regression.

This uncertainty on the moral sense of the nation has also reached the Supreme Court. Throughout the 1970s, the Burger Court demonstrated a continuity with the Warren Court and, in fact, expanded those precedents in the area of educational rights. However, as the decade wore on, the Court began to place greater weight on values of local autonomy and individual choice. As the equality issues became more complex and morally ambiguous and public consensus on social reform grew more ambivalent, the Court became increasingly reluctant to second-guess congressional intent or to make some difficult value choices.

As the country moved into the 1980s, the Court's decisions began to take on a more conservative tone and to reflect a perceived public mood that perhaps the federal courts were going too far beyond the national consensus. The Court, in recent years, has hesitated to validate and put teeth into the ambitious but ambiguous language of civil rights legislation of the previous decade. And so the Justices have cast back into the political arena several civil rights questions with far-reaching implications. Notable among these are the scope of Title IX sex discrimination coverage and the goals of education for the handicapped under P.L. 94-142.

Where does this all leave the equality mandate of *Brown* three decades down the road? Obviously, not to the racial hostility and blatant segregative policies of the 1950s. Nevertheless, with federal commitment on the downside, equality of educational opportunity has assumed a different contour for different groups. For racial minorities, there are indicators of a return to pre-*Brown separate but equal* programs and facilities. For linguistic minorities, *equal* means *effective* as measured against a *whatever works* standard. More than a decade of controversy surrounding proper goals and methodology has brought us full circle back to assimilation as the end, English language instruction as the means, and achievement test scores as the measure of success for children whose dominant language is not English. Cultural pluralism, maintenance programs, and affective development are now vague memories of a not so distant past. As for handicapped students, equal education translates merely into the provision of *some* benefit—a sharp departure from the *maximization of potential* goals of the 1970s. For all these groups, recent federal policies define equality of educational opportunity not as *equal* nor necessarily *more is equal,* but *different* treatment that is circumscribed by considerations of financial cost and administrative burden. As for women, equality had never gone beyond equal treatment per se—there has been no affirmative action for female students. However, weakened enforcement, narrow court rulings, and limited financial resources pose the threat of regression to *less than equal* services and a perpetuation of gender-defined roles.

As history demonstrates, policy innovations are sometimes shaped by presidential leadership—Lyndon Johnson's "war on poverty" led to passage of the Elementary and Secondary Education Act of 1965 and a host of other antipoverty legislation. Richard Nixon's "war on busing" led to passage of the Emergency School Aid Act to promote voluntary desegregation strategies. Ronald Reagan's "war on federal involvement" has resulted in modest changes in federal school finance through consolidation, deregulation, and budget cuts and potentially far-reaching changes in civil rights enforcement. History also proves that policy changes can be stimulated and formed by interest group politics. Bilingual and special education as well as sex equity programs are clear examples of this approach.

Innovations in public policy can also grow out of national crisis or powerful waves of public opinion. The recent push for quality education is one example. The major reports published in the early 1980s leveled severe criticism against the American school system and jarred the educational establishment, the federal government, and the American public into action. It cannot be denied that such broad-based issues as personnel recruitment, curriculum reform, and standards for excellence demand serious consideration. But we must take heed that *quality* education does not merely replace *equality* as the slogan of the decade.

When we cut through the rhetoric, we see two perspectives dominating the equality/quality debate. First, there are those who see a causal link between the civil rights reforms of the past two decades and the decline in educational excellence. Underlying this view is the mistaken belief that equality and excellence are mutually exclusive, that by allocating resources to meet the needs of the disadvantaged we have neglected the needs of the larger population. In reality, the problems plaguing public education in America stem from a far more complex set of social, political, and economic factors.

Then there is the general feeling that quality education must be our primary concern, and that if quality is ensured, then equality will automatically follow. This persuasive political argument rings hollow when played out on the state and local levels, however. It assumes that the needs of all children, including the disadvantaged, would be afforded equal concern and at least equal resources in the policy making process at these levels. History has proven otherwise.

The equality/quality debate actually has little merit. It has proven to be a mental exercise at best and diversionary at worst. In practice, equality and quality are mutually supportive. Both focus on the educational process and provide substantive criteria for the provision of an appropriate education based on individual needs. In fact, discourse on equality has provided the terminology and established the perspective for the current dialogue on excellence. Over the past twenty years, a substantial body of case and statutory law has developed under legal norms that use equality language. Terms used by the federal courts and Congress—"appropriate," "adequate," and "meaningful" education—have focused our attention away from futile attempts to equalize inputs (resources) or outputs (test scores) and toward the process of teaching and learning between those two points. As we have become concerned with providing for the diverse needs of diverse student populations, the right to an equal education has developed as a statement of substantive values and not merely as a procedural guarantee of fair process in administrative decision making and resource allocation. Equality means more than governmental evenhandedness.

It cannot be denied that equality demands making choices among individuals and programs. It demands ordering priorities and developing criteria for distributing goods and services. It is also true that separation of powers, federalism, and a tradition of local educational control will continue to loom above the policy making process. But if the progress made in the past three decades toward reaching a more just society is not to be lost, then we must strike a careful balance between need and merit and between justice and individualism in redistributing society's scarce resources. This is no easy task for a nation whose brief history is both tainted by institutionalized injustice and built on individual freedom and dignity.

Returning to the task at hand, how might we carve out an agenda for policy reform that values the equality principle while responding to current social and economic needs and political pressures? First of all, we must justify why inequalities are intolerable. And secondly, we must leap beyond equality as a relative norm to its underlying substantive right.

On the point of justification, equality is not only morally necessary, but it is economically and socially prudent. This harkens back to the Great Society reformers who persuasively spoke of education's benefits to the individual and to society.

The goal of federal involvement was not only to improve the life chances of disadvantaged children, but to promote the economic well-being and ultimate survival of the nation. This argument on behalf of education as "investment in human capital" draws continued support from recent statistics. Not only does the educational performance of disadvantaged students continue to lag behind that of their more advantaged counterparts, but this segment of the population is growing at a far more rapid rate and with greater linguistic diversity than the larger population.

Dropout rates among hispanics, blacks, and other non-white groups as well as whites from low-income backgrounds are considerably higher than the average for the remainder of the student population.[7] The disadvantaged further demonstrate poorer school performance as measured by achievement scores than do more socioeconomically advantaged students. These differences appear at school entry and widen as students move through the educational system.[8] So while federal compensatory programs have narrowed the achievement gap between white and non-white students, they have far from closed it.[9]

Furthermore, higher birth rates and immigration are rapidly increasing the proportion of disadvantaged school-age children. Over the period of 1970 to 1980, public school enrollments from pre-school to grade 12 declined overall from approximately 46 million to 41 million while minority enrollments rose from about 9.5 million to 11 million, that is, from 21 percent to 27 percent of the population.[10] Included within this group is an increasing proportion of non-English speaking immigrant children from the poorest Latin American and Asian countries. These are sobering figures for a nation concerned about its general welfare and economic future.

Having laid the moral and economic foundation for a continued federal role based on the equality ideal, we now move to the level of legal rights and substantive norms. It is here that the advocates for equality have encountered their highest hurdles. Part of the problem lies in the equality movement having grown out of *Brown v. Board of Education,* a decision based on the black population's right to be treated with equal dignity and respect. The *Brown* decision, with its framework set in the "equal protection of the laws", has continued to shape not only judicial decisions but legislative policy programs. As a result, we have maintained the moral discourse in the language of equality while legislating and adjudicating more and more in the context of substantive rights or entitlements. But our inability to translate those rights into a norm of social policy has stymied out efforts to develop a legally justifiable and politically acceptable educational agenda.

The Great Society programs spoke of equal educational opportunity as the means to overcome social and economic disadvantages. They defined this new federal responsibility as one of providing some "minimum floor" of opportunity. Twenty years ago, this concept appeared to mean a minimal level of inputs through financial resources. Experience with the federal programs that evolved from that mandate now permits us to look beyond dollar inputs and into the types of services those dollars can buy to meet the diverse needs of an increasingly diverse student population. Experience has also taught us that government resources are limited and subject to a host of competing public demands. Those constraints must be factored into any responsible and politically feasible agenda for social reform.

Then how can we define the basic right underlying equal educational opportunity? In effect, it is an amalgam of the 1960s' concept of "minimal floor" of basic services, combined with the process-oriented reforms of the early 1970s, tempered by the economic realities and political concerns of more recent years. As the country moves toward the end of this decade, we should recognize that each child has a right to a minimally adequate education that is appropriate to its needs. Rather than merely asking "How much education?", we should ask, "What type of education?" is necessary to permit the individual to participate effectively in the democratic process and to enjoy the personal benefits that learning brings, within limits set by individual potential.

As a substantive right underlying the equality ideal, this definition shifts the focus of policy reform and debate from group characteristics (a notion that has attracted increasing criticism) to the specific needs of individual students (a notion more closely akin to the spirit of *Brown*). In doing so, we disengage the notion of affirmative government responsibility in the context of education services from the increasingly unpopular concept of affirmative action in the admissions and employment contexts. The former addresses present-day disadvantages while the latter seeks to overcome the effects of past discrimination based on group membership. By introducing the language of "appropriateness" and "minimal levels" of educational services into the new discourse on educational reform, we consider a broad range of disadvantages that impede educational achievement—economic, social, physical, emotional—without unduly sacrificing the needs of the more advantaged. More importantly, by framing the right in individual and not group terms, we avoid the trap of pigeonholing "high risk" children as negatively disadvantaged without considering their more positive talents and potential.

This is not to say that we totally abandon the concept of group disadvantage. Group-oriented language has helped policymakers and educators to identify instructional needs and prescribe particular services. It has also proven useful as a legal norm for identifying the failure of government to provide equal opportunity to certain members of society. In that sense, courts may continue to draw on the history of group discrimination to more carefully scrutinize governmental action or inaction. In other words, the concept of groups remains useful in identifying violations and fashioning relief without locking us into a legal standard of group rights and remedies.

Our struggle to operationalize the equality mandate of *Brown* has taught us that the road between moral precept and public policy is rough and winding. It has also taught us that political consensus eventually evaporates in the air of rhetorical excess to the right or the left. Nevertheless, we must not be immobilized by equality's limitations but rather energized by its substantive force. We now know that equality as a policy goal in itself is unrealistic. Equality of results is limited by economic conditions and by differences in individual potential. But we also know that equal treatment alone often does not suffice. In fact, justice demands a pluralistic perspective on equality whereby *equality for all* means *different or more is equal* for some. We may never achieve the equality ideal, but it must continue to serve as a guiding principle and legal norm that we use to define educational rights. This conception of equality as a direction for educational policy making is a moral and economic necessity.

With the lessons of the past thirty years behind us, we are now better informed than ever, pedagogically and politically, to permit everyone, not just the most advantaged, the freedom to seek a meaningful life. And with fairness and justice as our overarching theme, we should strive to reshape a federal role in education based on far less radical ideology and far more progressive pragmatism than the current climate appears to dictate. Only then will the federal government truly work in partnership with the states to put substantive force into *Brown's* mandate of equal educational opportunity based on individual freedom and dignity.

Notes

Introduction

1. Werner Jaeger, *Paideia: The Ideals of Greek Culture*, 2nd ed. (New York: Oxford University Press, 1945) as quoted in Francis Keppel, *The Necessary Revolution in American Education* (New York: Harper & Row, 1966), pp. 1–2.

2. See National Institute of Education, *State Legal Standards for the Provision of Public Education* (Wash., D.C., November 1978).

3. For a discussion of the history of federal involvement in educational finance, see Advisory Commission on Intergovernmental Relations, *Intergovernmentalizing the Classroom: Federal Involvement in Elementary and Secondary Education* (Wash., D.C., 1981); Carl F. Kaestle and Marshall S. Smith, "The Federal Role in Elementary and Secondary Education," *Harvard Educational Review* 52 (November 1982): 384–408; Rosemary C. Salomone, "Equal Educational Opportunity and the New Federalism: A Look Backward and Forward," *Urban Education* 17 (1982): 213–32.

4. 347 U.S. 483 (1954).

5. Ibid., at 493.

6. From 1961 to 1963, the Kennedy Administration had pressed vigorously for federal education funding in the form of "general aid." Those efforts, as previous ones, had become mired in partisan wrangling over a host of legal and political concerns—the church-state issue, racial desegregation, constitutional challenges to congressional authority, and fear of loss of local control. See Hugh Davis Graham, *The Uncertain Triumph: The Kennedy and Johnson Years* (Chapel Hill: University of North Carolina Press, 1984) for a comprehensive analysis of the federal role during the Kennedy and Johnson Administrations.

7. For the architects of the Great Society programs, human skills and knowledge were a form of capital in which society ought to invest for the general welfare. They derived this concept from Theodore W. Schultz, "Investment in Human Capital," *American Economic Review* 52 (1961): 13–32.

8. 42 U.S.C. §2000d et seq. (Supp. 1984).

9. See Michael Timpane, ed., "Federal Aid to Education: Prologue and Prospects," in *The Federal Interest in Schooling*, ed. Michael Timpane (Cambridge, MA: Ballinger Pub. Co., 1975).

10. *Congressional Record*, vol. 111, p.5736 (1965) (statement of Rep. Perkins).

11. Ibid., p.5735.

12. *Aid to Elementary and Secondary Schools, Hearings Before the House Subcommittee on Education,* 89th Cong., 1st Sess. (1965) (statement of Francis Keppel, Commissioner of Education, Department of Health, Education, and Welfare).

13. *Message from the President of the United States Transmitting Education Program,* 89th Cong., 1st Sess. (January 12, 1965).

14. Keppel, *The Necessary Revolution,* p.109.

15. Perkins, *Congressional Record,* p.5734.

16. Stephan K. Bailey and Edith Mosher, *ESEA: The Office of Education Administers a Law* (Syracuse: Syracuse University Press, 1968), p.2.

17. Marilyn Gittell, "Localizing Democracy Out of the Schools," *Social Policy* 12 (Sept./Oct. 1981): 5.

18. C. Kent McGuire, *State and Federal Programs for Special Student Populations* (Denver, CO: Education Commission of the States, April 1982).

19. National Clearinghouse for Bilingual Education, *State-Funded Bilingual Education Programs* (Rosslyn, VA, 1983).

20. Christiane Citron, *The Rights of Handicapped Students* (Denver, CO: Education Commission of the States, 1982).

21. 20 U.S.C. §1681 et seq. (Supp. 1984).

22. 29 U.S.C. §794 (Supp. 1984).

23. Exec. Order No. 12250 delegates to the Justice Department under the Attorney General the responsibility for coordinating the implementation and enforcement by Executive agencies of various provisions of Title VI, Title IX, and §504. *Federal Register,* vol. 45, p.72,995 (1980).

24. Under the Department of Education Organization Act, P.L. 96-88, 93 Stat. 695, the Department of Health, Education and Welfare (HEW) was dismantled as of October 1, 1979. 20 U.S.C. §3411 (Supp. 1984). Most of the former HEW's education rulemaking and enforcement functions subsequently were transferred to the newly formed Department of Education as of May 9, 1980.

25. See Stephen L. Wasby, "Is 'Planned Litigation' Planned?" Paper presented at the Annual Meeting of the American Political Science Association, New York, September 1983.

26. 20 U.S.C. §1401 et seq. (Supp. 1984). The procedural protections built into the law and the concept of "appropriate" educational services grew out of two lower court decisions, *Mills v. Board of Education,* 348 F.Supp. 866 (D.D.C. 1972) and *Pennsylvania Association for Retarded Children (PARC) v. Pennsylvania,* 343 F.Supp. 279 (E.D.Pa. 1972) (consent decree).

27. 20 U.S.C. §1703(f) (Supp. 1984). The Act codified into statutory law a standard of "effective participation" adopted by the Supreme Court earlier that same year in *Lau v. Nichols,* 414 U.S. 563 (1974).

28. David L. Kirp, "Law, Politics and Equal Educational Opportunity: The Limits of Judicial Involvement," *Harvard Educational Review* 47 (May 1977): 137.

29. Abram Chayes. "The Role of the Judge in Public Law Litigation," *Harvard Law Review* 89 (1976): 1281–1316.

30. Owen Fiss, "The Supreme Court 1978 Term, Forward: The Forms of Justice," *Harvard Law Review* 93 (1979): 1.

31. Mark G. Yudof, "Implementation Theories and Desegregation Realities," *Alabama Law Review* 32 (Winter 1981): 463.

32. Abram Chayes, "The Supreme Court 1981 Term, Forward: Public Law Litigation and the Burger Court," *Harvard Law Review* 96 (1982): 60.

33. Gary L. McDowell, *Equity and the Constitution* (Chicago: University of Chicago Press, 1982), chap. 7.

34. Nathan Glazer, "Individual Rights Against Group Rights," in *Ethnic Dilemmas* (New York: Basic Books, 1983), pp.254–73.

35. Nathan Glazer, "Towards an Imperial Judiciary?," *The Public Interest* 41 (1975): 45.

36. Raoul Berger, *Government by Judiciary* (Cambridge, MA: Harvard University Press, 1977).

37. The year 1983 appeared to be the "year of the report." The major studies published during that year that have given substance to the current debate are: National Commission on Excellence in Education, *A Nation at Risk* (Wash., DC: U.S. Government Printing Office, 1983); John I. Goodlad, *A Place Called School: Prospects for the Future* (New York: McGraw-Hill, 1983); Twentieth Century Fund Task Force on Federal Elementary and Secondary Education Policy, *Making the Grade* (New York: Twentieth Century Fund, 1983); Ernest L. Boyer, *High School* (New York: Harper and Row, 1983); Education Commission of the States Task Force on Education for Economic Growth, *Action for Excellence* (Denver, CO: Education Commission of the States, 1983).

38. American Association of Colleges for Teacher Education, "Public Dilemma: Equity vs. Excellence," *Education Week*, November 28, 1984, p.20.

39. A. Harry Passow, "Tackling the Reform Reports of the 1980s," *Phi Delta Kappan* 65 (June 1984): 680.

40. Harold Howe II, "Education Moves to Center Stage: An Overview of Recent Studies, *Phi Delta Kappan* 65 (November 1983): 171.

41. Keppel, *The Necessary Revolution*, p.29.

42. John Gardner, "The Pursuit of Excellence: Education and the Future of America," *Prospects for America: The Rockefeller Panel Reports* (Garden City, NY: Doubleday, 1961): 356–57. See also John Gardner, *Excellence: Can We Be Equal and Excellent Too?* (New York: Harper & Row, 1961).

Chapter I

1. "Equality, Moral and Social," in *The Encyclopedia of Philosophy*, ed. Paul Edwards (New York: Collier Macmillan, 1972), p.39.

2. See Stanley Benn, "Egalitarianism and the Equal Consideration of Interests," in *IX Nomos: Equality*, eds. J. Roland Pennock and J.W. Chapman (New York: Atherton Press, 1967), p.61. According to Benn, things can be equal in three different ways—descriptive, evaluative, and distributive. On the descriptive plane, objects are ordered according to some common natural property or attribute that can be possessed in varying degrees, e.g., cabbages ordered by weight. On the evaluative scale, objects may be equal or unequal according to some standard of value of merit, e.g., the grading of student essays. Finally, as a matter of distribution, equality may be measured by such criteria as need, entitlement, or dessert.

3. Hugo Bedau, "Egalitarianism and the Ideal of Equality," in *IX Nomos: Equality*, eds. Pennock and Chapman, p.3.

4. John Rawls, *A Theory of Justice* (Cambridge, MA.: Harvard University Press, 1971).

5. For a comprehensive discussion of recurring patterns of egalitarian thought throughout modern history, see Stanley Lakoff, *Equality in Political Philosophy* (Cambridge, MA: Harvard University Press, 1964); J. R. Pole, *The Pursuit of Equality in American History* (Berkeley: University of California Press, 1978). For a discussion of redistribution of economic goods and the expansion of participatory opportunities as contrasting and conflicting themes in the liberal egalitarian tradition, see Amy Gutman, *Liberal Equality* (Cambridge: Cambridge University Press, 1980). Gutman argues that an adequate egalitarian theory must unite both ideals into a single vision without sacrificing either one.

6. Aristotle, *Politics,* trans. Benjamin Jowett (Oxford: Clarendon Press, 1921).

7. Aristotle, *The Nichomachean Ethics,* trans. W. D. Ross (New York: Oxford University Press, 1925).

8. John A. Schaar, "Some Ways of Talking about Equality," *Journal of Politics* 26 (1964): 868.

9. Fred R. Dallmayr, "Functionalism, Justice, Equality," *Ethics* 78 (1978): 10. See William A. Banner, "Compensatory Justice and the Meaning of Equity," in *Social Justice and Preferential Treatment,* eds. William T. Blackstone and Robert D. Helsep (Athens: University of Georgia Press, 1977).

10. Robert Spaemann, "Remarks on the Problem of Equality," *Ethics* 87 (1977): 364.

11. The concept of "arithmetical equality" is related to modern-day arguments for "minimal rights" to certain governmental benefits in order to meet basic human needs, e.g., health, housing, and education. See Frank Michelman, "Forward: On Protecting the Poor through the Fourteenth Amendment," *Harvard Law Review* 83 (1969): 7–59; Betsy Levin, "Education as a Constitutional Entitlement: A Proposed Judicial Standard for Determining How Much is Enough," *Washington Law Quarterly* (1979): 703–13.

12. William Frankena, "The Concept of Social Justice," in *Social Justice,* ed. R. B. Brandt (Englewood Cliffs, NJ: Prentice-Hall, 1962), p.11.

13. Thomas F. Green, "Equal Educational Opportunity: The Durable Injustice," in *Proceedings of the 27th Annual Meeting of the Philosophy of Education Society,* ed. Robert D. Helsep (Edwardsville, IL: Southern Illinois University Press, 1971), p.123.

14. Rawls, *A Theory of Justice,* p.15.

15. Michael Walzer, *Spheres of Justice* (New York: Basic Books, 1983).

16. Walzer's other goods or benefits that society bestows on its members include membership (citizenship), security and welfare, money and commodities, office, hard work, free time, kinship and love, divine grace, recognition, and political power.

17. For a critical review of *Spheres of Justice,* see Brian Barry, book review, *Columbia Law Review* 84 (1984): 806–15.

18. Robert Nozick, *Anarchy, State, and Utopia* (New York: Basic Books, 1974).

19. For a critique of Nozick's theory see Samuel Scheffler, "Natural Rights, Equality, and the Minimal State," *Canadian Journal of Philosophy* 6 (March 1976): 59–77.

20. This is based on a typology as outlined in Thomas Nagel, "The Meaning of Equality," *Washington Law Quarterly* (1979): 25–31.

21. For a discussion of legal equality and its link to the Fourteenth Amendment, see Ralph K. Winter, Jr., "Changing Concepts of Equality: From Equality before the Law to the Welfare State," *Washington University Law Quarterly* (1979): 741–55. According to Winter, alternative conceptions of equality that call for equality in social-political-economic status have weakened confidence in the democratic political process. For a more balanced discussion of the evolution of the anti-discrimination principle from a process-oriented to a group-oriented interpretation, see Owen Fiss, "The Fate of an Idea Whose Time Has Come: Antidiscrimination Law in the Second Decade after *Brown v. Board of Education*," *University of Chicago Law Review*, 41 (1974): 742–73.

22. The concept of *constructive exclusion* has been argued most effectively on behalf of educational opportunities for linguistic minorities and the handicapped. According to this rationale, the instruction traditionally offered such students is so inappropriate to their needs as to be meaningless, thereby constructively excluding them from any education at all.

23. See R. H. Tawney, *Equality*, 4th ed. (London: Allen and Unwin, 1964). Democratic socialists such as Tawney viewed this formal principle as an attempt to evade the moral decision regarding ultimate equality and inequality. According to Tawney, this attempt intensifies the cruelties of competition and leads in practice to domination and inequality feeding upon itself. He criticized equality of opportunity as based on a conception of society that he described as the "tadpole philosophy." The consolation that such a society offers for social evils is that exceptional individuals can succeed in evading them.

> It is possible that intelligent tadpoles reconcile themselves to the inconveniences of their position, by reflecting that, though most of them will live and die as tadpoles and nothing more, the more fortunate of the species will one day shed their tails, distend their mouths and stomachs, hop nimbly on to dry land, and croak addresses to their former friends on the virtues by which tadpoles of character and capacity can rise to be frogs. Ibid., pp.108–09.

24. See Charles Frankel, "Equality of Opportunity," *Ethics* 81 (1970–71): 111–30.

25. Some scholars including the sociologist Daniel Bell regard Rawls' theory to be extremely radical and in fact, part of the "socialist ethic." Daniel Bell, *The Coming of Post-Industrial Society* (New York: Basic Books, 1973). Marxists, on the other hand, would disagree and take strong exception to Rawls' neglect of the class struggle necessary to achieve equality. For them, the ruling class with wealth and power would have little desire for the social cooperation demanded by the difference principle. Richard Miller, "Rawls and Marxism," *Philosophy and Public Affairs* 3 (Winter 1974): 167–191.

26. Norman Daniels, "Introduction," in *Reading Rawls,* ed. Norman Daniels (New York: Basic Books, 1975).

27. This theoretical starting point contrasts sharply with classical utilitarianism, which is the one major philosophical framework other than contract theory that builds a social order from the choice of rational actors. For utilitarians, each

person acts from the particular position in which actually found and thereby pursues a self-interest.

28. Rawls, *A Theory of Justice*, p.302.

29. Ibid., p.303.

30. Ibid., pp.106–07. Rawls defines "efficiency" as Pareto optimality in the economic sense whereby a distribution is efficient if it is impossible to change it so as to make at least one person better off without making at least one person worse off. Ibid., p.68.

31. Ibid., p.66.

32. Ibid., p.505.

33. Ibid., p.73.

34. Ibid., p.74.

35. Ibid., p.75.

36. Ibid., p.101.

37. Maxine Greene, *Landscapes of Learning* (New York: Teachers College Press, 1978), p.130.

38. Rawls, *A Theory of Justice*, p.101.

39. Terry Eastland and William J. Bennett, *Counting by Race* (New York: Basic Books, 1979), p.6.

40. Formerly 20 U.S.C. §241 (1978). Chapter 1 of the Education Consolidation and Improvement Act of 1981, P.L. 97-35, 20 U.S.C. §2701 et. seq. (Supp. 1984) replaced Title I of the Elementary and Secondary Education Act of 1965. Both the original Title I and the current Chapter 1 provide federal aid on a formula per capita basis for remedial instruction to educationally and economically disadvantaged students.

41. House of Representatives, Report No. 143, 89th Cong., 1st Sess., (1965) (statement of Francis Keppel, U.S. Commissioner of Education).

42. Although Coleman has found certain inconsistencies in Rawls' theory when applied to social realities, he has hailed the work as having brought moral philosophy into direct confrontation with recent developments in sociological research and theory. Coleman, "Inequality, Sociology, and Moral Philosophy," pp.741–42.

43. James S. Coleman et al., *Equality of Educational Opportunity*, 2 vols. (Wash., D.C.: Office of Education, U.S. Department of Health, Education, and Welfare, 1966).

44. The most comprehensive discussion of the Coleman report took place in a three-year seminar at Harvard University initiated by Sen. Daniel P. Moynihan who was then a Harvard faculty member. The papers analyzing the report and Coleman's reply to his critics were published in Frederick Mosteller and Daniel P. Moynihan, eds., *On Equality of Educational Opportunity* (New York: Vintage Books, 1972). For historical background on the Coleman report and the debate it provoked particularly among the Harvard faculty, see Godfrey Hodson, "Do Schools Make a Difference?" in *The Inequality Controversy: Schooling and Distributive Justice*, eds. Donald M. Levine and Mary Jo Bane (New York: Basic Books, 1975), pp.22–43. For a more recent discussion of the report and its implications for racial integration, see Diane Ravitch, *The Troubled Crusade* (New York: Basic Books, 1983).

45. For a critique of the Coleman report, see Daniel Bell, "On Meritocracy and Equality," *The Public Interest* 29 (Fall 1982): 43–48.

46. James S. Coleman, "Equal Schools or Equal Students," *The Public Interest* 4 (Summer 1966): 70–75. In a later essay, Coleman suggests that a concept of equal educational opportunity which focused on the effects of schooling began to take shape as early as 1954 in the Supreme Court's decision in *Brown*. He states that the decision was in fact a confusion of two unrelated premises—a newly developed concept that looked at the results of schooling and the legal premise that the use of race violates fundamental freedoms. See James S. Coleman, "The Concept of Equal Educational Opportunities," *Harvard Educational Review* 38 (Winter 1968): 303–04.

47. James S. Coleman, "Equality of Opportunity and Equality of Results," *Harvard Educational Review* 43 (February 1973): 137.

48. Christopher Jencks et al., *Inequality: A Reassessment of the Effects of Family and Schooling in America* (New York: Basic Books, 1972).

49. James S. Coleman, "Inequality, Sociology, and Moral Philosophy," *American Journal of Sociology* 80 (November 1974): 739–64. He maintains that in a pluralistic society such as ours, no single contract can suffice to cover all interactions between the individual and the state. In fact, he advances a new theory built on a society of distinct corporate actors only one of which is the state. Ibid., p.758. See also Robert Nisbet, "The Pursuit of Equality," *The Public Interest,* 35 (Spring 1974): 103–20. Nisbet states that Rawls is "far better in his elaboration of equality, of justice as fairness, than in what he writes at great length about freedom." Accordingly, "the book would have been a better one if he had frankly abandoned the first principle of liberty, so called, and concerned himself entirely with developing the theme of equality." Ibid., p.117.

50. James S. Coleman, "Inequality, Sociology, and Moral Philosophy, p.753.

51. See Vernon Van Dyke, "Justice as Fairness: For Groups?," *American Political Science Review* 69 (1975): 607–14. Van Dyke advances a compelling argument that a theory of justice must take into account an intermediate level of group rights between the individual and the state. In fact, he advances a new theory built on a society of distinct corporate actors only one of which is the state. Ibid., p.758.

52. Rawls, *A Theory of Justice,* p.101.

53. Ibid., p.101.

54. See Peter Westen, "The Empty Idea of Equality," *Harvard Law Review* 95 (1982): 537–96; Kent Greenawalt, "How Empty is the Idea of Equality," *Columbia Law Review* 83 (1983): 1167–85; Peter Westen, "To Lure the Tarantula from Its Hole: A Response," *Columbia Law Review* 83 (1983): 1186–1208. Westen proposes that equality is simply derivative from other moral and legal rights that people have. He argues that the language of equality obscures crucial judgments about substantive rights and should therefore be banished from moral and legal discourse. Greenawalt, on the other hand, argues on behalf of substantive norms of equality that exist in our legal and moral order. He further expresses skepticism as to abandoning the language of equality because a substantial body of law has developed under norms that use equality language. See Kenneth Karst, "Why Equality Matters," *Georgia Law Review* 17 (1983): 245–89. Karst contends that the idea of equality "carries a meaning that is removed from the empty tautology that like cases should be treated alike . . . The ideal not only has substantive content, it is a statement of substantive values, with moral underpin-

nings solidly based in a particular society's religious and philosophical traditions." Ibid., pp.249–50.

Chapter II

1. Gunnar Myrdal, *An American Dilemma*, vol. I (New York: Pantheon Books, 1944), pp. xix–xx.

2. See e.g., Gary Orfield, ed., *Symposium on School Desegregation and White Flight* (Wash., D.C.: Center for National Policy Review, August 1975); James S. Coleman et al., *Trends in School Segregation 1968–73* (Wash., D.C.: Urban Institute, August 1975); Reynolds Farley and Clarence Wordock, *Can Government Policies Integrate Schools* (Ann Arbor: Population Studies Center, 1977); Christine H. Rossell, "Assessing the Unintended Impacts of Public Policy: School Desegregation and Resegregation" (Boston: Boston University, 1978); David Armour, "White Flight and the Future of School Desegregation," in *School Desegregation: Past, Present, and Future*, eds. Walter Stephan and Joe Feagin (New York: Plenum Press, 1980); Christine H. Rossell and Willis D. Hawley, "Understanding School Desegregation and Doing Something About It," in *Effective School Desegregation: Equity, Quality, and Feasibility*, ed. Willis D. Hawley (Beverly Hills, CA: Sage Publications, 1981).

3. See e.g., Nancy St. John, *School Desegregation: Outcomes for Children* (New York: Wiley Interscience, 1975); Meyer Weinberg, "The Relationship Between School Desegregation and Academic Achievement," *Law and Contemporary Problems* 39 (1975): 241–70; Robert L. Crain and Rita E. Mahard, *Desegregation Plans that Raise Black Achievement: A Review of the Research* (Santa Monica, CA: The Rand Corp., June 1982.) St. John analyzed 64 studies and found no strong evidence that desegregation closes the white-black achievement gap. However, she notes that desegregation has rarely lowered and sometimes raised the achievement scores of black children. Weinberg found that overall desegregation does, in fact, have a positive effect on minority achievement levels. In a more recent meta-analysis of desegregation studies, Crain and Mahard made similar findings. They propose that desegregation is most effective when begun in the early grades, when the desegregated schools are predominantly but not overwhelmingly white, and when the entire metropolitan area is included. See also William Taylor, "*Brown* in Perspective," in *Effective School Desegregation*, ed. Hawley, p.15; Willis D. Hawley, "Increasing the Effectiveness of School Desegregation: Lessons from the Research," in *Race and Schooling in the City*, eds. Adam Yarmolinsky et al. (Cambridge, MA: Harvard University Press, 1981).

4. The research appears to support the use of voluntary measures, such as magnet schools, in conjunction with mandatory strategies. See e.g., Eugene Royster, Catherine Baltzell, and Fran Simmons, *Study of the Emergency School Aid Act Magnet Schools Programs* (Cambridge, MA: Abt Associates, 1979); Christine H. Rossell, "Magnet Schools as a Desegregation Tool: The Importance of Contextual Factors in Explaining Their Success," *Urban Education* 14 (1979): 303–20; Mark A. Smylie, "Reducing Racial Isolation in Large School Districts: The Comparative Effectiveness of Mandatory and Voluntary Desegregation Strategies," *Urban Education* 17 (1982): 477–502; Rols K. Blank, Robert A. Dentler, Catherine Baltzell, and Kent Chabotar, *Survey of Magnet Schools: Analyzing A*

Model for Quality Integrated Education (Cambridge, MA: Lowry Associates, September 1983).

5. The Thirteenth Amendment to the U.S. Constitution states in part that "neither slavery nor involuntary servitude, except as punishment for crime whereof the party shall have been duly convicted, shall exist within the United States, or any place subject to their jurisdiction."

6. The Fourteenth Amendment to the U.S. Constitution states in part that "(n)o state shall . . . deprive any person of life, liberty, or property without due process of law; nor deny to any person within its jurisdiction the equal protection of the laws."

7. 109 U.S. 3 (1883).

8. 18 Stat. 335. Section One of the law provided:

> That all persons within the jurisdiction of the United States shall be entitled to the full and equal enjoyment of the accommodations, advantages, facilities and privileges of inns, public conveyances on land or water, theaters and other places of public amusement subject only to the conditions and limitations established by law, and applicable alike to citizens of every race and color, regardless of any previous condition of servitude.

9. Henry J. Abraham, *Freedom and the Court*, 3rd ed. (New York: Oxford University Press, 1977), p.358.

10. 163 U.S. 537 (1896).

11. Ibid., at 559.

12. U.S. Commission on Civil Rights, *With All Deliberate Speed: 1954–19??*. (Wash., D.C.: U.S. Government Printing Office, November 1981).

13. Abraham, p.362.

14. Richard Kluger, *Simple Justice* (New York: Vintage Books, 1977), p. 134.

15. Ibid., at 136–37. See also Jeanne Hahn, "The NAACP Legal Defense and Education Fund: Its Judicial Strategy and Tactics," in *American Government and Politics*, ed. Stephen L. Wasby (New York: Charles Scribner's Sons, 1973).

16. 305 U.S. 337 (1938).

17. 332 U.S. 631 (1948).

18. 339 U.S. 629 (1950).

19. 339 U.S. 637 (1950).

20. *Sweatt*, 339 U.S. at 634.

21. At the time of the Court's ruling in *Brown*, 11 southern states and the District of Columbia mandated segregated schools by law. Four states, including Kansas, permitted local communities the option of segregation. Kluger, *Simple Justice*, p.156.

22. 347 U.S. 484 (1954). The District of Columbia case, *Bolling v. Sharpe*, 347 U.S. 497 (1954), was decided under the Fifth Amendment. Here the Court read the concept of "equal protection of the laws" into the Fifth Amendment due process clause. It has since followed that interpretation in subsequent cases.

23. 347 U.S. 484, 493.

24. Ibid., at 494.

25. Ibid., at 494 n. 11. To support this conclusion that racial segregation in public schools has a psychologically detrimental effect on black children, the Court cited the following authorities: K.B. Clark, *Effect of Prejudice and Discrim-*

ination on Personality Development (Midcentury White House Conference on Children and Youth, 1950); Witmer & Kotinsky, *Personality in the Making* (1952), c. VI: Deutscher & Chein, "The Psychological Effects of Enforced Segregation: A Survey of Social Science Opinion," 26 *J. Psych.* 259 (1948); Chein, "What Are the Psychological Effects of Segregation Under Conditions of Equal Facilities?," 3 *Int. J. Opinion & Attitude Res.* 229 (1949); Brameld, "Education Costs," in *Discrimination and National Welfare* 44–48 (MacIver ed. 1949); Frazier, *The Negro in the United States* 674–81 (1949); and generally, Myrdal, *An American Dilemma* (1944).

26. Ibid., at 494. The Court's apparent reliance on social science data to support what critics have argued was essentially a value judgment and not an empirical fact has been the subject of heated debate. For an overview of the key arguments surrounding that debate, see generally, Betsy Levin and Willis D. Hawley, eds., *The Courts, Social Science, and the Judicial Process* (New York: Teachers College Press, 1977).

27. The inability of the Court to justify its decision on legal grounds generated strong criticism among legal scholars. In a now classic article, Columbia Law School professor Herbert Wechsler, a consultant to the NAACP lawyers in *Brown*, chided the Court for its bare, unreasoned conclusion that separate schools were "inherently unequal." According to Wechsler, the Justices had ignored their primary responsibility to neutral reasoning in order to achieve a desired outcome in the case. Wechsler, "Toward Neutral Principles of Constitutional Law," *Harvard Law Review* 73 (1959):1-35.

28. *New Orleans City Park Improvement Assn. v. Detiege*, 358 U.S. 54 (1958) (memorandum decision).

29. *Gayle v. Browder*, 352 U.S. 903 (1956) (memorandum decision).

30. *Boynton v. Virginia*, 364 U.S. 454 (1960).

31. *Holmes v. City of Atlanta*, 350 U.S. 879 (1955) (memorandum decision).

32. *Watson v. Memphis*, 373 U.S. 526 (1963); *Mayor & City Council of Baltimore City v. Dawson*, 350 U.S. 877 (1955) (memorandum decision).

33. *Turner v. Memphis*, 369 U.S. 762 (1962).

34. *Thomas v. Mississippi*, 380 U.S. 524 (1965); *Boynton v. Virginia*, 364 U.S. 903 (1956) (memorandum decision).

35. *Brown v. Louisiana*, 383 U.S. 131 (1966).

36. *Burton v. Wilmington Parking Auth.*, 365 U.S. 715 (1961).

37. *Johnson v. Virginia*, 373 U.S. 61 (1963).

38. See William L. Taylor, "Brown in Perspective," p.17. Taylor notes that early in the *Brown* opinion the Court quotes from an 1879 decision, *Strauder v. West Virginia*, 100 U.S. 303, in which the Court had set forth the purposes of the Fourteenth Amendment: to provide blacks with the right to exemption from unfriendly legislation. . . . from legal discriminations, implying inferiority in civil society . . ." Ibid., at 303.

39. 349 U.S. 294 (1955).

40. Fiss, "Forms of Justice," p. 3.

41. Mark G. Yudof, "Implementing the Desegregation Decrees," in *Effectve School Desegregation*, ed. Willis D. Hawley, pp. 249-50.

42. Gary Orfield, *The Reconstruction of Southern Education* (New York: Wiley-Interscience, 1969), p. 16.

43. Written correspondence from William L. Taylor, October 15, 1984.

44. 358 U.S. 1 (1958).

45. Ibid., at 18.

46. U.S. Commission on Civil Rights, *With Liberty and Justice for All* (Wash., D.C.: U.S. Government Printing Office, 1959), pp. 119, 123. See also Stephen L. Wasby, Anthony A. D'Amato and Rosemary Metrailler, *Desegregation from Brown to Alexander* (Carbondale, IL: Southern Illinois University Press, 1977).

47. 377 U.S. 218 (1964).

48. Ibid., at 234.

49. 391 U.S. 430 (1968).

50. J. Harvie Wilkinson, III, *From Brown to Bakke* (New York: Oxford University Press, 1979), p.109.

51. William L. Taylor, book review of *Disaster by Decree, Columbia Law Review* 77 (1977): 810.

52. 391 U.S. at 437.

53. Ibid., at 439.

54. Mark G. Yudof, "School Desegregation: Legal Realism, Reasoned Elaboration, and Social Research in the Supreme Court," *Law and Contemporary Problems* 42 (1978): 84.

55. For a forceful but flawed argument in opposition to integration and court ordered busing see, Lino A. Graglia, "From Prohibiting Segregation to Requiring Integration," in *School Desegregation: Past, Present, and Future*, eds. Stephan and Feagin, pp. 77–78; and *Disaster by Decree: The Supreme Court Decisions on Race and the Schools* (Ithaca, NY: Cornell University Press, 1976). Graglia argues that the standard of effectiveness laid out by the Court in *Green* was a "racist requirement" that set the Court on a course of increasingly "unprincipled and unscrupulous" decision making. Ibid., pp. 68–73. However, he fails to take note of the discriminatory actions on the part of school officials that such court intervention was designed to counteract. Nor does he recognize any of the political or social events that undoubtedly shaped the scope of federal intervention strategies during the 1960s and 1970s. See Taylor, book review of *Disaster by Decree*.

56. 396 U.S. 19 (1969).

57. Ibid., at 20.

58. E. Edmund Reutter, *The Supreme Court's Impact on Public Education* (Topeka, KS: Phi Delta Kappa and National Organization on Legal Problems of Education, 1982), p.71.

59. 402 U.S. 1 (1971).

60. Ibid., at 30.

61. Owen Fiss, "The Charlotte-Mecklenburg Case—Its Significance for Northern Desegregation," *University of Chicago Law Review* 38 (1971): 705.

62. Fiss, "Forms of Justice," pp. 46-55.

63. 413 U.S. 189 (1972).

64. Ibid., at 208.

65. Three years later, in *Washington v. Davis,* 426 U.S. 229 (1976), the Court extended the intent standard outside the reach of school desegregation cases and into the realm of employment discrimination. That standard has since been applied uniformly to Fourteenth Amendment equal protection claims. The Court

clarified the elements of proof incident to the intent standard the following year in *Village of Arlington Heights v. Metropolitan Housing Development Corporation*, 429 U.S. 252 (1977). There the Court presented five factors that might be considered in determining whether "invidious discriminatory purpose was a motivating factor." Included among these were : (1) the impact of the official action, that is, whether it bears more heavily upon one race; (2) a clear pattern of governmental discrimination unexplainable on grounds other than race; (3) the historical background of the decision, particularly the specific sequence of events leading up to the challenged decision; (4) departures from the normal procedural sequence; and (5) legislative or administrative history, particularly contemporaneous statements made by members of the decisionmaking body. Ibid., at 265–68.

66. See Peter Roos, "Bilingual Education: The Hispanic Response to Unequal Educational Opportunity," *Law and Contemporary Problems* 42 (1978): 111–40; Gary Orfield, "The Rights of Hispanic Children," in *Must We Bus?: Segregated Schools and National Policy* (Wash., D.C.: The Brookings Institution, 1978).

67. 413 U.S. 189, 208 (Powell, J., concurring in part and dissenting in part). See Note, "Reading the Mind of the School Board: Segregative Intent and the De Jure/De Facto Distinction," *Yale Law Journal* 86 (1976): 317–55.

68. 413 U.S. 189, 233.

69. Ibid., at 246.

70. Orfield, "Integration of Housing," in *Must We Bus?*, pp. 77-101. See also, Gary Orfield, "If Wishes were Houses Then Busing Could Stop: Demographic Trends and Desegregation Policy, *Urban Review* 10 (Summer 1978): 108–24.

71. 411 U.S. 913 (1973).

72. 418 U.S. 717 (1974).

73. Ibid., at 745.

74. Ibid., at 782 (Marshall, J., dissenting).

75. Ibid., at 814.

76. Taylor maintains that of the three legal theories left open after *Milliken*—interdistrict effect, boundary manipulation, and housing and racial containment, the last presents the most promising evidentiary path for litigants to pursue. William L. Taylor, "The Supreme Court and Urban Reality: A Tactical Analysis of *Milliken v. Bradley*," *Wayne Law Review* 21 (1975): 751–78. See also Gary Orfield, "Housing Patterns and Desegregation Policies," in *Effective School Desegregation*, ed. Willis D. Hawley, pp. 186–221. Orfield reaffirms the need to involve suburban school districts in desegregation plans as limiting such plans to cities may merely increase the rate of ghettoization. He suggests that desegregation advocates initiate combined school and housing litigation "to demonstrate the unavoidable historic and contemporary relationship between school and housing segregation." He further suggests that the federal government provide funds for voluntary desegregation plans. Ibid., p.216.

77. *Newbury Area Council v. Jefferson County Bd. of Educ.*, 510 F.2d 1360 (6th Cir.), *cert. denied*, 421 U.S. 931 (1974).

78. *Delaware State Bd. of Educ. v. Evans*, 635 F.2d 1124 (4th Cir.), *cert. denied sub nom. Evans v. United States*, 452 U.S. 943 (1980). For a discussion of the events surrounding the Wilmington, Delaware desegregation case, see Jeffrey A. Raffel, *The Politics of School Desegregation: The Metropolitan Remedy in Delaware* (Philadelphia: Temple University Press, 1980).

79. *Bd. of School Comm'rs of Indianapolis v. Metropolitan Dev. Comm'n of Marion County*, 637 F.2d 1101 (7th Cir.), *cert. denied sub nom. Metropolitan School Dist. of Perry Township, Marion County v. Buckley*, 449 U.S. 839 (1980).

80. *Hoots v. Pennsylvania*, 672 F.2d 1107 (3rd Cir.), *cert. denied*, 459 U.S. 824 (1982).

81. *Coloma Community School Dist. v. Berry*, 698 F.2d 813 (6th Cir. 1983), *cert. denied*, 104 S.Ct. 235 (1983). The Court also refused to consider a separate petition for review by 190 area parents. *Fellner v. Berry*, 698 F.2d, 813 (6th Cir.), *cert. denied*, 104 S.Ct. 236 (1983). One issue that the Court in *Milliken* clearly left unresolved is whether an interdistrict remedy may be pegged totally to violations by the state without proof of discriminatory acts with cross-district effects on the part of the outlying districts. That issue is presently in litigation in *Jenkins v. Missouri* (No. 77-0420-CV-W-4) (D.Mo. Jan. 25, 1985).

82. *Milliken v. Bradley*, 433 U.S. 267 (1977).

83. *Orr v. State Bd. of School Comm'rs*, 677 F.2d 1185 (6th Cir.), *cert. denied*, 459 U.S. 1086 (1982).

84. *Reed v. Rhodes*, 662 F.2d 1219 (6th Cir. 1981).

85. *Columbus Bd. of Educ. v. Penick*, 663 F.2d 24 (6th Cir. 1981).

86. 731 F.2d 1294 (8th Cir. 1984), *cert. denied*, 104 S. Ct. 2676 (1984).

87. The Eighth Circuit had refused to approve the district court order insofar as it required the state to fund student transfers between suburban school districts and to fund magnet schools or integrative programs in those districts. In a subsequent rehearing en banc, the Eighth Circuit held that the state was obligated to fund the plan's quality education programs in nonintegrated schools only to the extent that the programs were in effect at the time of the en banc decision. The state must pay one-half the cost of such programs in the integrated schools only to the extent that they were approved in the prior opinion or necessary for the city schools to retain their Class AAA bond status. *Liddell v. Bd. of Educ. of City of St. Louis*, No. 84-2175 (8th Cir. Mar. 26, 1985).

88. 418 U.S. 717, 741–42 (1974).

89. 433 U.S. 267, 287 (1977).

90. 423 U.S. 1335 (1976).

91. Wilkinson, *From Brown to Bakke*, pp. 245–46.

92. 433 U.S. 406 (1977).

93. Commentators disagree on the significance of *Dayton I*. Some see it as a godsend to northern school districts and maintain that the Court's emphasis on isolated violations runs counter to *Keyes*. Wilkinson, *From Brown to Bakke*, p. 246. Others argue that *Dayton I* does not depart from basic principles laid down by the Court in the northern cases. There simply were not adequate findings in the case to trigger the *Keyes* presumption. William L. Taylor, "The Supreme Court and Recent School Desegregation Cases: The Role of Social Science in a Period of Judicial Retrenchment," *Law and Contemporary Problems* 42 (1978): 37–56.

94. 433 U.S. 406, 410.

95. 433 U.S. 449 (1979).

96. 443 U.S. 526 (1979).

97. "The Supreme Court, 1978 Term," *Harvard Law Review* 93 (1979): 128–29.

98. 458 U.S. 527 (1982).

99. Ibid., at 540.

100. Ibid., at 542.

101. 458 U.S. 457 (1982).

102. Ibid., at 481 citing 418 U.S. 717, 741.

103. Ibid., at 484.

104. Stuart A. Sheingold, *The Politics of Rights* (New Haven: Yale University Press, 1974), pp. 117–18. For Sheingold, power is indispensable when it comes to getting large numbers of people to conform to norms they oppose. Ibid., p. 123. When legal rights run counter to prevailing power relationships, it cannot be assumed that such rights will be redeemed on demand. In fact, it is not even certain that they will serve as a base line for reasoned discourse. Ibid., p. 86.

105. "The Southern Manifesto: Declaration of Constitutional Principles," reprinted in Hubert H. Humphrey, ed., *School Desegregation: Documents and Commentaries* (New York: Thomas Y. Crowell, 1964), pp.32–35.

106. 42 U.S.C. §1975 et seq. (Supp. 1984).

107. Attorney General's Order No. 155–57 (Dec. 9, 1957).

108. 42 U.S.C. §2000 et seq. (Supp. 1984).

109. 42 U.S.C. §2000d-6 (Supp. 1984).

110. 42 U.S.C. §2000d (Supp. 1984).

111. For a discussion of desegregation during the decade following *Brown,* see Orfield, *the Reconstruction of Southern Education.* See also Walter A. Gellhorn, "A Decade of Desegregation—Retrospect and Prospect," *Utah Law Review* 9 (1964): 3–17; Benjamin Muse, *Years of Prelude* (New York: Viking Press, 1964).

112. Wilkinson, p.108.

113. In the mid-1970s, University of Chicago sociologist James S. Coleman, published a series of papers, articles, and reports in which he maintained that court-ordered busing and the instability created by the assignment of large numbers of disadvantaged children to middle-class schools in the big cities had accelerated white flight to the suburbs and thereby increased racial segregation in the schools. See e.g. James S. Coleman, Sara D. Kelly, and John A. Moore, "Recent Trends in School Integration," paper presented at the Annual Meeting of the American Educational Research Association, Washington, D.C., April 1975; James S. Coleman, Sara D. Kelly, and John A. Moore, "Trends in School Segregation, 1963–73," unpublished paper (Washington, D.C.: The Urban Institute, July 1975). This research appeared as a rethinking of Coleman's position a decade earlier which in effect had served as a catalyst to desegregation efforts. See James S. Coleman et. al., *Equality of Educational Opportunity* (Wash., D.C.: U.S. Government Printing Office, 1966). Coleman's thesis elicited a hue and cry from the civil rights and scholarly communities which maintained that his research was methodologically and conceptually flawed and provided little basis for his conclusion that urban desegregation leads to white flight. See generally Thomas F. Pettigrew and Robert L. Green, School Desegregation in Large Cities: A Critique of the Coleman 'White Flight' Thesis," *Harvard Educational Review* 46 (February 1976): 17–69.

114. In a 1972 Gallup poll on the public's attitudes toward court-ordered busing to achieve racial balance in the schools, 70 percent opposed, 21 percent favored, and 9 percent had no opinion on the concept. U.S. Commission on Civil Rights, *Public Knowledge and Busing Opposition* (Wash., D.C.: U.S. Govern-

ment Printing Office, 1973), p. A–1. A similar national poll taken in 1976 found that 71 percent of those interviewed opposed "racial integration of the schools . . . even if it requires busing." *New York Times*–CBS Survey, *New York Times*, Feb. 13, 1976.

115. *Swann v. Charlotte-Mecklenburg Bd. of Educ.*, 402 U.S. 1 (1971).

116. 20 U.S.C.S. §§1601-19 (1976) (repeal effective Sept. 30, 1979).

117. *Congressional Almanac Quarterly*, June 19, 1970, p.1585.

118. *Congressional Almanac Quarterly*, Dec. 11, 1970, p.2946.

119. 20 U.S.C. §1652 (a) (Supp. 1984).

120. *Keyes v. School Dist. No. 1, Denver Colo.*, 413 U.S. 1189 (1973).

121. 20 U.S.C. §1701 et seq. (Supp. 1984).

122. 20 U.S.C. §1704 (Supp. 1984).

123. 20 U.S.C. §1720 (Supp. 1984).

124. 20 U.S.C. §1713 (Supp. 1984).

125. 20 U.S.C. §1755 (Supp. 1984).

126. See note 115 *supra*.

127. Interview in *TV News*, September 20–26, 1975; reprinted in *Congressional Record* (daily edition), October 2, 1975, p. S17372.

128. 20 U.S.C. §1228(a) (Supp. 1984).

129. 20 U.S.C. §1714(a) (Supp. 1984).

130. 20 U.S.C. §1714(a) as amended by P.L. 94–206 §209 (1976).

131. 20 U.S.C. §1652 (Supp. 1984).

132. 627 F.2d 1221 (D.C.Cir. 1980).

133. H.R. 3462, the Department of Justice Authorization for FY 1983 as passed by the House of Representatives, contained the Collins Amendment. It was passed in the House on June 9, 1981 and received in the Senate on June 15, 1981 but never acted upon. During 1980-81 alone, 19 bills of this nature were introduced in Congress.

134. S.951. The Amendment consisted of two sections. The first was the Helms Amendment whose provisions were identical to the Collins Amendment. The second was the Johnson Amendment which was known officially as the "Neighborhood Schools Act." This latter provision would have limited court-ordered busing to the school nearest the student's home or to a school within five miles or fifteen minutes of home.

135. *Education Week*, Nov. 2, 1983, p.2.

136. See Citizens Committee on Civil Rights, *There is No Liberty . . . A Report on Congressional Efforts to Curb the Federal Courts and to Undermine the Brown Decision* (Wash., DC, October 1982).

137. 42 U.S.C. §2000d-1 (Supp. 1984).

138. 34 C.F.R. §100.8(a) (1984).

139. U.S. Office of Education, "General Statement of Policies," reprinted in *Guidelines for School Desegregation*, Hearings before a special subcommittee of the House Judiciary Committee (Wash., DC: U.S. Government Printing Office, 1966), pp. A20–24.

140. 34 C.F.R. §100.8(a) (1984). The regulations included a provision that was later incorporated into the Act, 42 U.S.C. §2000d-5 (Supp. 1984), whereby a school district subject to a desegregation order issued by a federal court would be deemed in compliance if it "provides an assurance that it will comply with such

order, including any future modification of such order . . ." 34 C.F.R. §100.4(c) (1) (1984). In the early stages of Title VI enforcement, some civil rights advocates criticized this court order standard of compliance on the grounds that court-ordered desegregation plans often fell far short of the HEW guidelines. See U.S. Commission on Civil Rights, *Federal Enforcement of School Desegregation* (Wash., D.C.: U.S. Government Printing Office, 1969), p. 10. See also Note, "The Courts, HEW, and Southern School Desegregation," *Yale Law Journal* 77 (1967): 321-65. Others have since argued that subsequent circuit court decisions showing deference to the HEW guidelines have rendered these early findings of little consequence. The Fifth Circuit opinion in *United States v. Jefferson County Bd. of Educ.*, 372 F.2d 836 (5th Cir. 1966), *aff'd en banc*, 380 F.2d 385, *cert. denied*, 389 U.S. 840 (1967), is most frequently cited to support this proposition. See Richard I. Slippen, "Administrative Enforcement of Civil Rights in Public Education: Title VI, HEW, and the Civil Rights Reviewing Authority," *Wayne Law Review* 21 (1975): 951-52.

141. 34 C.F.R. §100.3(b)(vii)(6)(1984).

142. *Revised Statement of Policies for School Desegregation Plans Under Title VI of the Civil Rights Act of 1964* (Wash., D.C., March 1966 as amended in December 1966).

143. Harold Howe II, *On the 1966 Desegregation Guidelines*, Address before the Mississippi State Advisory Committee, Civil Rights Commission, April 16, 1966, Jackson, Mississippi. U.S. Department of Health, Education, and Welfare, Office for Civil Rights.

144. 391 U.S. 430 (1968).

145. U.S. Department of Health, Education, and Welfare, Office for Civil Rights, *Policies on Elementary and Secondary School Compliance with Title VI of the Civil Rights Act of 1964* (Wash., D.C.: U.S. Government Printing Office, March 1968). Section 12(a) of the guidelines states:

In many school systems a start towards the elimination of a dual structure has been made by requiring parents or students to choose the school the student will attend (free choice). Usually, however, additional steps . . . are necessary to complete the desegregation of schools. If, under a free choice plan, vestiges of a dual school structure remain, the school system is responsible for taking whatever additional steps are necessary to complete the desegregation of its schools.

146. See Marion Wright Edelman, "Southern School Desegregation from 1954-1973: A Judicial-Political Overview," in *Blacks and the Law, Annals of the American Academy of Political and Social Science* (May 1973).

147. Orfield, *The Reconstruction of Southern Education*, pp.151-207.

148. Kluger, *Simple Justice*, p.764.

149. Augustus J. Jones, *Law, Bureaucracy and Politics: The Implementation of Title VI of the Civil Rights Act of 1964* (Wash., D.C.: University Press of America, 1982), p.155.

150. 351 F. Supp. (D.D.C. 1972), modified, 356 F. Supp. 92 (D.D.C.), *aff'd*, 480 F.2d 1159 (D.C. Cir. 1973) (en banc).

151. 417 F. Supp. 1215 (D.D.C. 1976).

152. In 1976, WEAL intervened in the *Adams* litigation maintaining that HEW was not enforcing Title IX. During that year, four Mexican-American students attending public schools intervened asserting violations of their Title VI right to be free from national origin discrimination. The following year, the National Federation of the Blind intervened asserting violations of §504 of the Rehabilitation Act of 1973 with regard to the rights of the handicapped. As a result, from 1977 on, the *Adams* litigation has embraced HEW enforcement of Title VI, Title IX, and §504.

153. *Adams v. Califano*, 430 F. Supp. 119 (D.D.C. 1977).

154. *Education Daily*, May 8, 1981, p.6.

155. *Peer Perspective*, July 1982, p.5.

156. *Higher Education Daily*, Aug. 18, 1982, p.1.

157. *WEAL v. Bell* (No. 74-1720) (D.D.C. Mar. 11, 1983) 47 Fed. Reg. 15,509 (1983); *Adams v. Bell* (No. 3095-70) (D.D.C. Mar. 11, 1983) 47 Fed. Reg. 15,509 (1983).

158. In October 1983, the Office for Civil Rights submitted two massive reports to the lawyers representing the plaintiffs in the lawsuits. The reports described in detail OCR's enforcement activities over the previous six years and outlined its budget and staffing decisions over the previous year.

159. In September 1983, OCR stated that it had acted on 702 cases. In five of these, letters had been sent ordering immediate corrective action. A total of 592 cases had been closed but the Department gave no breakdown of the reasons. Under the court order, OCR was required to settle by March 11, 1984 the 105 cases that had not been resolved. In March 1984, the Justice Department argued on appeal that the district court order of March 1983 had "unreasonably restricted" the operations of the Education Department's Office for Civil Rights and the Department of Labor's Office of Federal Contract Compliance Programs. *Chronicle of Higher Education*, Sept. 21, 1983, p.19.

160. Brief for Appellants, *Adams v. Bell* and *WEAL v. Bell*, 743 F.2d 42 (D.C. Cir. 1984).

161. *WEAL v. Bell* and *Adams v. Bell*, 743 F.2d 42 (D.C. Cir. 1984).

162. Washington Council of Lawyers, *Reagan Civil Rights: The First Twenty Months* (Wash., D.C., 1982), p.2.

163. Drew S. Days, "Turning Back the Clock: The Reagan Administration and Civil Rights," *Harvard Civil Rights—Civil Liberties Law Review* 19 (1984): 309.

164. William Bradford Reynolds, *Address to the Education Commission of the States, National Project on Desegregation Strategies Workshop*, Chicago, Illinois, September 27, 1981, p.8.

165. *Court Ordered Busing: Hearings on S.528, S.1005, S.1147, S.1647, S.1743 and S.1760 Before Subcommittee on Separation of Powers of the Senate Committee on the Judiciary*, 97th Cong., 1st Sess. 592–93 (1981) (statement of William Bradford Reynolds, Assistant Attorney General, Civil Rights Division).

166. William Bradford Reynolds, *Remarks Before the Metropolitan Center for Educational Research, Development and Training, New York University, Brown Plus Thirty Conference*, September 13, 1984, pp.12–14.

167. 413 U.S. 189 (1973).

168. Reynolds, *Court Ordered Busing*, p.592.

169. *United States v. Bd. of Educ. of City of Chicago*, 554 F. Supp. 912 (N.D. Ill. 1983).

170. *ESC (Education Commission of the States) Progress Review,* Feb. 1983, p.9.

171. *United States v. Bakersfield City School Dist. et al,* No. CVF-84-39 (E.D. Cal. filed Jan. 25, 1984) (consent decree). OCR began administrative proceedings against the school district in 1975. In 1978, an administrative law judge concluded that school officials had intentionally created a dual system. The Education Department referred the case to the Justice Department for judicial enforcement in 1982. At that time, the district had 18,194 students of which 36 percent were Hispanic, 16 percent black, 46 percent white, and two percent from other racial groups. *New York Times,* Jan. 26, 1984, p.A1.

172. Ibid., p.A1.

173. 498 F. Supp. 580 (M.D.La. 1980).

174. Motion by the United States to Stay Further Proceedings in the Court of Appeals, *Davis v. East Baton Rouge Parish School Bd.,* No. 81-3476 (5th Cir. August 16, 1982).

175. 687 F.2d 814 (1982), *cert. denied,* 103 S.Ct. 834 (1983).

176. 420 U.S. 1 (1971).

177. Brief Amicus Curiae of the Department of Justice, *Riddick v. School Bd. of the City of Norfolk,* No. 84-1815 (4th Cir. filed Dec. 6, 1984).

178. *Education Week,* Jan. 23, 1985, p.10.

179. Brief Amicus Curiae of the Lawyers Committee for Civil Rights Under Law at 39-40, *Riddick v. School Bd. of the City of Norfolk,* No. 84-1815 (4th Cir. filed Oct. 19, 1984).

180. Ibid., at 41–42.

181. *Congressional Record,* vol. 128, pp.S2890-91 (daily ed. March 29, 1982).

182. S.951, 97th Cong., 2d Sess. (1982). See U.S. Commission on Civil Rights, *Statement of School Desegregation,* p.16.

183. Letter from Attorney General William French Smith to Hon. Peter W. Rodino, Chairman, Committee on the Judiciary, May 6, 1982.

184. 567 F. Supp. 1037 (E.D.Mo. 1983), *aff'd,* 731 F.2d 1294 (8th Cir. 1984). In 1983, the city school system enrolled 60,500 students of whom 78.9 percent were black. In 1984, the first year the plan was in operation, 5,500 students were enrolled in suburban schools and more than 500 suburban students were enrolled in city magnet schools.

185. David S. Tatel and William L. Taylor, "St. Louis School Desegregation: Worth Watching," *Los Angeles Daily Journal,* Aug. 17, 1983, p. 4. See also David L. Kirp, "After 30 Years, Some Progress With School Desegregation," *Los Angeles Daily Journal,* May 15, 1983, p.4.

186. For a strong argument in support of magnet schools and their essential elements of commitment and choice, see Denis P. Doyle and Marsha Levine, "Magnet Schools: Choice and Quality in Public Education," *Phi Delta Kappan* 66 (Dec. 1984): 265–69.

187. Eugene Royster, Catherine Baltzell, and Fran Simmons, *Study of the Emergency School Aid Magnet Schools Program* (Cambridge, MA: Abt Associates, 1979).

188. Christine H. Rossell, Magnet Schools as a Desegregation Tool: The Importance of Contextual Factors in Explaining Their Success," *Urban Education* 14 (1979): 303–20. This was a reanalysis of the Royster data.

189. Mark A. Smylie, "Reducing Racial Isolation in Large School Districts:

The Comparative Effectiveness of Mandatory and Voluntary Desegregation Strategies," *Urban Education* 17 (1982): 477–502. Smylie compared 51 desegregation plans that relied primarily on either mandatory student assignment or voluntary strategies.

190. Rols K. Blank, Robert A. Dentler, Catherine Baltzell, and Kent Chabotar, *Survey of Magnet Schools: Analyzing a Model for Quality Integrated Education* (Cambridge, MA: Lowry Associates, 1984). The study examined 45 of the more than 1,000 magnet schools in the country. These were located in 15 of the more than 130 largest urban school districts.

191. Specifically, in congressional testimony, William Bradford Reynolds announced that the Civil Rights Division of the Justice Department would aim future enforcement policies not at eliminating segregation by all permissible means but by remedying "substantial disparities in the tangible components of education" between minority and white students. *School Desegregation: Hearings Before the House Subcommittee on Civil and Constitutional Rights of the Committee on the Judiciary*, 97th Cong., 1st Sess. (1981).

192. See Jomills Braddock, Robert Crain, and James McPartland, "A Long-Term View of School Desegregation," *Phi Delta Kappan* 66 (Dec. 1984): 259–64. Here the researchers report preliminary findings of a 15-year study of black students educated in predominantly white suburban schools. As compared with comparable students educated in predominantly black city schools, such students were more likely to attend primarily white colleges, to live and work in racially mixed communities, and to have white friends.

193. 20 U.S.C. §§3191-3207 (Supp. 1978) (repeal effective Oct. 1, 1982).

194. P.L. 98-377, Title VII of the Education for Economic Security Act, Magnet Schools Assistance Program, 98th Cong., 2d Sess. (1984). The purpose of the Act is to encourage voluntary desegregation plans and provide funds to school districts in support of magnet school programs. Congress funded the Act at $75 million for fiscal year 1985.

Chapter III

1. For a discussion of language policy and its educational implications, see Bernard Spolsky, *Educational Linguistics* (Rowley, MA: Newbury House Publishers, 1978); Joti Bhatnagar, *Educating Immigrants* (New York: St. Martin's Press, 1981). For a more specific treatment, see Joshua A. Fishman, *Language Loyalty in the United States* (The Hague: Mouton & Co., 1966).

2. Susan G. Schneider, *Revolution, Reaction or Reform* (New York: Las Americas, 1977), p.7. The figure was down to 19 in 1969 and 12 in 1975. Rosemary C. Salomone, *An Analysis of the Effects of Language Acquisition Context* (New York: Arno Press, 1978), p.8.

3. 262 U.S. 390 (1923).

4. 268 U.S. 510 (1925).

5. U.S. Office of Education, *The Condition of Bilingual Education in the Nation* (Wash., D.C.: U.S. Government Printing Office, 1976), p.21.

6. 1980 Census, U.S. Bureau of the Census, 1982. Spanish speakers are concentrated in three states, California, Texas, and New York.

7. *New York Times*, Aug. 12, 1983, Section B, p.1.

8. U.S. Department of Education, *The Condition of Bilingual Education in the Nation, 1984* (Wash., D.C.: U.S. Government Printing Office, 1984), p. 13, Table II-3.

9. Over the past 20 years, the Supreme Court has developed a "two-tier" doctrinal structure for reviewing classifications under the equal protection clause. Under current doctrine, state action is subject to strict scrutiny if it impinges on a *fundamental right* or discriminates against a *suspect class*. The state must then demonstrate that its action was necessary to advance a compelling state interest and that no less drastic means of achieving that interest were available to the decisionmaker. If the state's action adversely affects neither a fundamental right nor a suspect class, *minimal scrutiny* or *rational basis* is applied and the state merely must demonstrate that the classification is reasonably related to any legitimate governmental interest. Traditionally, the Court has afforded decisionmakers wide discretion as to the interest promoted under this lesser standard of review. More recently, the Court has developed a middle-tier of *intermediate scrutiny* for classifications based particularly on gender-discrimination but also on illegitimacy. Here the classification must be substantially necessary to promote an important governmental interest. See e.g., *Craig v. Boren*, 429 U.S. 190 (1976)(gender) and *Trimble v. Gordon*, 430 U.S. 762 (1967) (illegitimacy).

10. In addition to those rights guaranteed in the Bill of Rights, the Court has granted fundamental rights status to criminal defendants' rights, *Williams v. Illinois*, 399 U.S. 235 (1970); interstate travel, *Shapiro v. Thompson*, 394 U.S. 618 (1969); and voting rights, *Harper v. Board of Elections*, 383 U.S. 663 (1966).

11. 411 U.S. 1 (1973).

12. Ibid., at 28.

13. Ibid., at 37.

14. 414 U.S. 563 (1974).

15. See Betsy Levin, "The Courts, Congress and Educational Adequacy: The Equal Protection Predicament," *Maryland Law Review* 39 (1979): 187–263.

16. Penelope Preovolos, "Rodriguez Revisited: Federalism, Meaningful Access, and the Right to Education," *Santa Clara Law Review* 20 (1980): 75–121.

17. Robert W. Bennett, "The Burger Court and the Poor," in *The Burger Court: The Counterrevolution That Wasn't*, ed. Vincent Blasi (New Haven: Yale University Press, 1983), p. 55.

18. 457 U.S. 202 (1982).

19. Ibid., at 221.

20. Ibid., at 223.

21. 20 U.S.C. §3221 et seq. (Supp. 1984).

22. The Johnson Administration supported the concept of bilingual education but did not actively support separate legislation. In testimony before Congress, Commissioner of Education Harold Howe II argued that experimental bilingual education programs were already being mounted under various titles of the Elementary and Secondary Education Act of 1965 and that there was danger in the "spotlight" approach to special legislation for every group. See *Bilingual Education Programs, Hearings Before the Special Subcommittee on Education of the Committee on Education and Labor*, 90th Cong., 1st Sess. (1967)(statement of Commissioner of Education Harold Howe II), pp.46–49. Secretary of Health, Education and Welfare John Gardner echoed Howe's position, arguing that

existing titles and appropriations already provided not only more flexible authority but more money than the proposed bill, that intensive ESL instruction was a promising approach which would be excluded under the bill's requirement of native language instruction, and that the bill was straying into the dangerous area of ethnic entitlements. See Gardner to Capitol Hill, n.d. EXLE/FA$_2$, WHCF, LBJ Library, University of Texas at Austin, cited in Hugh Davis Graham, *The Uncertain Triumph: The Kennedy and Johnson Years* (Chapel Hill: University of North Carolina Press, 1984), p.158.

23. *Bilingual Education Act, Hearings* (statement of Rep. Augustus F. Hawkins), pp.90–91.

24. See National Education Association, *The Invisible Minority* (Washington, D.C., 1967).

25. American Institutes for Research, *Interim Report, Evaluation of the Impact of ESEA Title VII Spanish/English Bilingual Education Programs* (Palo Alto, CA, February 1977).

26. See Tracy C. Gray, *Response to the AIR Study, Evaluation of the Impact of ESEA Title VII Spanish/English Bilingual Education Programs*, memorandum (Wash., D.C.: Center for Applied Linguistics, April 18, 1977).

27. Noel Epstein, *Language, Ethnicity, and the Schools: Policy Alternatives for Bilingual-Bicultural Education* (Wash., D.C.: Institute for Educational Leadership, August 1977). See note 32 and accompanying text for a discussion of the *immersion* approach.

28. See Stanley S. Seidner and Maria Medina Seidner, "In the Wake of Conservative Reaction: An Analysis," in *Theory, Technology and Public Policy in Bilingual Education,* ed. Raymond V. Padilla (Rosslyn, VA: National Clearinghouse for Bilingual Education, 1983), pp.325–49.

29. The Bilingual Education Improvements Act of 1983 was introduced in the Senate on April 13, 1983 as S. 1041 by Sen. Orrin Hatch (R., UT) and in the House on April 21, 1983 as H.R. 2682 by Reps. John N. Erlenborn (R., IL) and William F. Goodling (R., PA).

30. Keith Baker and Adriana de Kanter, *Effectiveness of Bilingual Education: A Review of the Literature,* unpublished report (Washington, D.C.: U.S. Department of Education, September 1981). The researchers examined 39 evaluation studies of bilingual programs. Of those, ten indicated that transitional bilingual education (TBE) had positive effects on language performance; 26 found no difference between TBE students and others; two found that TBE enhanced students' acquisition of mathematics; and three reported a negative effect of TBE on mathematics achievement.

31. See Russell N. Campbell and Tracy C. Gray, *Critique of the U.S. Department of Education Report on Effectiveness of Bilingual Education: Review of the Literature,* memorandum (Wash., D.C.: Center for Applied Linguistics, June 8, 1981).

32. *Immersion* differs from the older method of *submersion* whereby diverse groups of non-English proficient students were placed together in an English-only classroom with an English monolingual teacher. Immersion programs group students according to native language and require a classroom teacher who is bilingual and able to teach English through the content areas. In the Canadian model, English-speaking students begin their schooling with native French-

speaking teachers who also speak English but use French exclusively for instruction. All subject matter is taught in French and content becomes the vehicle for language acquisition. Students are introduced to English language arts anywhere from the second to the fourth grade at which point about half of the instruction is in English. Thereafter the English component is taught by native English speaking teachers. The success of these programs has been well documented. See Wallace E. Lambert and G. Richard Tucker, *Bilingual Education of Children: The St. Lambert Experiment* (Rowley, MA.: Newbury House Publishers, 1972); Merrill Swain and Sharon Lapkin, *Bilingual Education in Ontario: A Decade of Research* (Toronto: The Minister of Education, Ontario, 1981).

33. For a discussion of the critical implications of the Canadian immersion model for bilingual education in this country, see G. Richard Tucker, "Implications for U.S. Bilingual Education: Evidence from Canadian Research," *Focus* (National Clearinghouse on Bilingual Education), No. 2, February 1980; Eduardo Hernandez-Chavez, "The Inadequacy of English as an Educational Approach for Language Minority Students in the United States," in *Studies on Immersion Education* (Sacramento, CA: California State Education Department, 1984), pp.144–83.

34. *Education Daily,* Mar. 28, 1983, p.3.

35. *Education Daily,* June 8, 1983, p.1.

36. *Education Week,* August 19, 1983, p.1.

37. Letter from Gloria Zamora, President, NABE to Secretary of Education Terrel Bell, August 17, 1985.

38. For a discussion of the events surrounding the development of the Kildee-Corrada bill, see James J. Lyons, *NABE News,* Vol. VIII, No. 2, Winter 1985, pp.1, 19–22.

39. *Hearings on Bilingual Education, H.R. 11 and H.R. 5231, Before the Subcommittee on Elementary, Secondary, and Vocational Education of the Committee on Education and Labor,* 98th Cong., 2d Sess. 60 (1984) (statement of Gumecindo Salas, President, Michigan State Board of Education).

40. Ibid., p.79 (statement of Nguyen Ngoc Bich, president-elect, National Association for Vietnamese-American Education (NAVAE).

41. Ibid., p. 133 (prepared statement of the Navajo Nation).

42. Ibid., p. 137 (prepared statement of the National Education Association).

43. Ibid., p. 123 (prepared statement of Dr. M. Joan Parent, President, National School Boards Association).

44. Ibid., p.68 (prepared statement of Gerda Bikales, Executive Director, U.S. English).

45. Ca. Assembly Bill No. 201, *An Act to Add §276 to the Government Code Relating to Language* (introduced Jan. 8, 1985).

46. Va. Code §§22.1-212.1 (1981).

47. *Hearings on Bilingual Education,* pp. 64–66 (statement of S.I. Hayakawa).

48. Ibid., p.69 (statement of Gerda Bikales).

49. In order to inform House members of the merits of bilingual education and the needs of linguistic minority children, the Hispanic Caucus utilized a House procedure known as "Special Orders" to schedule speeches by 16 Caucus and non-Caucus members on the Kildee-Corrada bill. *Congressional Record,* vol. 130, pp. H2212-2221 (1984).

50. Lyons, *NABE News*, p.22.

51. U.S. Department of Education, *The Condition of Bilingual Education in the Nation, 1984* (Wash., D.C.: U.S. Government Printing Office, 1984), p.1.

52. 42 U.S.C. §2000d et seq. (Supp. 1984).

53. "Identification of Discrimination and Denial of Services on the Basis of National Origin," *Federal Register*, vol. 35, p.11,595 (1970).

54. 414 U.S. 563 (1974).

55. 34 C.F.R. §100.3(b)(2)(1984).

56. 414 U.S. at 563.

57. U.S. Department of Health, Education and Welfare, Office for Civil Rights, *Task Force Findings Specifying Remedies for Eliminating Past Educational Practices Ruled Unlawful under Lau v. Nichols*, (Wash., D.C., 1975).

58. No. A-77-216 (D. Alaska Sept. 29, 1978) (consent decree).

59. *Federal Register*, vol. 45, p.52,059 (1980) (proposed August 5, 1980).

60. Betsy Levin, "An Analysis of the Federal Attempt to Regulate Bilingual Education: Protecting Civil Rights or Controlling Curriculum?" *Journal of Law and Education* 12 (1983): 39.

61. See *Public Administration Times*, Dec. 15, 1980, p. 1.

62. 20 U.S.C. §1703(f) (Supp. 1984).

63. For a discussion of the role played by the Fifth Circuit in desegregating the South in the years following *Brown v. Board of Education*, see Jack W. Peltason, *Fifty-eight Lonely Men: Southern Federal Judges and School Desegregation* (Urbana: University of Illinois Press, 1971).

64. 516 F.2d 411 (5th Cir. 1975).

65. 455 F.Supp. 57 (E.D.N.Y. 1978).

66. 480 F.Supp. 14 (E.D.N.Y. 1978).

67. Ibid., at 23.

68. 587 F.2d 1022 (9th Cir. 1978).

69. Ibid., at 1030.

70. 473 F.Supp. 1371 (E.D. Mich. 1978).

71. Ibid., at 1382.

72. Ibid., at 1382.

73. 506 F.Supp. 405 (E.D. Texas 1981), *rev'd in part*, 680 F.2d 356 (5th Cir. 1982).

74. Ibid., at 432.

75. Ibid., at 433.

76. Ibid., at 433.

77. Bilingual and Special Language Programs Act, *Texas Education Code* §§21.451-21.463 (Vernon 1981).

78. 648 F.2d 989 (5th Cir. 1981).

79. Ibid., at 1009.

80. Ibid., at 1010.

81. Ibid., at 1011.

82. *Keyes v. School District No. 1, Denver, Colorado*, 576 F.Supp. 1503 (D. Colo. 1983). This represents an ongoing desegregation suit begun in 1969 in which Hispanic groups later intervened. The district court stopped at the second *Castaneda* factor where it found the district's bilingual program to be inadequate so that an examination of the program's results would have been premature. However, the court noted two indicators of instructional failure that might be used

as guides for judging non-compliance with §1703: first, the high number of Hispanic dropouts peaking at grade 10; and second, the use of "levelled" English handouts (materials that are below grade level in readability) in the secondary schools. Ibid., at 1518.

83. Ibid., at 1515.

84. In *Guardians Ass'n v. Civil Service Comm. of New York*, 463 U.S. 582 (1983), a majority of the Supreme Court held that a violation of Title VI requires proof of discriminatory intent. A different majority held, however, that proof of discriminatory effect suffices to establish liability when the suit is brought to enforce regulations issued pursuant to the statute rather than the statute itself. For a discussion of the arguments supporting an effect standard, see Rosemary C. Salomone, "Title VI and the Intent/Impact Debate: A Critical Look at 'Coextensiveness,' " *Hastings Constitutional Law Quarterly* 10 (Fall 1982): 15–79.

85. Nathan Glazer, "Bilingualism: Will it Work?," in *Ethnic Dilemmas* (New York: Basic Books, 1983), p.151.

86. Abigail M. Thernstrom, "E Pluribus Plura—Congress and Bilingual Education," *The Public Interest* 60 (Summer 1980): 21.

87. Eileen M. Gardner, ed., *A New Agenda for Education* (Wash., D.C.: The Heritage Foundation, 1985), p.41.

88. Twentieth Century Fund Task Force on Federal Elementary and Secondary Education Policy, *Making the Grade* (New York: the Twentieth Century Fund, 1983), p.12.

89. Some of the early research comparing the effects of bilingual and English monolingual instruction on the development of English language skills controlled for many of the variables operating, which the more recent broadscale studies have not, and lend support for bilingual methodology. See Nancy Modiano, "National or Mother Tongue Language in Beginning Reading: A Comparative Study," *Research in the Teaching of English* 2 (1968): 32–43; Andrew D. Cohen, *A Sociolinguistic Approach to Bilingual Education* (Rowley, MA.: Newbury House Publishers, 1975); Rosemary C. Salomone, *An Analysis of the Effects of Language Acquisition Context* (New York: Arno Press, 1978).

90. See George Weber, *Inner City Children Can Be Taught to Read: Four Successful Schools* (Wash., D.C.: Council for Basic Education, 1971); Wilbur B. Brookover et al., *School Systems and Student Achievement* (New York: Praeger, 1979); Ronald Edmonds, "Effective Schools for the Urban Poor," *Educational Leadership*, 37 (1979): 15–24; Michael Rutter et al., *Fifteen Thousand Hours* (London: Open Books, 1979).

91. Far West Development Educational Laboratory, *Significant Bilingual Instructional Features (SBIF)* (San Francisco, 1981). See also, Courtney Cazden, *Effective Instructional Practices in Bilingual Education*, draft report (Wash., D.C.: National Institute of Education, January 1984).

92. See Christina Bratt Paulston, "Ethnic Relations and Bilingual Education: Accounting for Contradictory Data," in *English as a Second Language in Bilingual Education*, eds. James Alatis and Kristie Twaddell (Wash., D.C.: Teachers of English to Speakers of Other Languages, 1976).

93. For a full discussion of this theory, see Jim Cummins, *Interdependence and Bicultural Ambivalence: Regarding the Pedagogical Rationale for Bilingual Education* (Rosslyn, VA.: National Clearinghouse for Bilingual Education, 1982).

94. According to preliminary findings of a May 1980 study of high school sophomores and seniors, bilingual programs reduce the difference in the dropout rate between Hispanics and other students by one-half. Among Hispanic students not participating in bilingual programs, the dropout rate can be high as 20 percent or more. Lutz Ebring, *High School and Beyond Summary Report: An Overview of Outcomes in Secondary Education,* mimeographed report (Wash., D.C.: National Opinion Research Center, 1980), p. 12. According to a more recent report, 45 percent of Mexican-American and Puerto Rican students who enter high school never finish and 40 percent of those who leave do so before the tenth grade. National Commission on Secondary Education for Hispanics, *Make Something Happen: Hispanics and High School Reform,* 2 vols. (Wash., D.C.: Hispanic Policy Development Project, 1984).

Chapter IV

1. See Maxine Greene, *Landscapes of Learning* (New York: Teachers College Press, 1978), pp.225–26.

2. For a history of sex discrimination and the evolution of the women's movement in the United States, see Albie Sachs and Joan Hoff Wilson, *Sexism and the Law* (New York: The Free Press, 1979), pp.67–231.

3. William Boyd, ed., *The Emile of Jean Jacques Rousseau* (New York: Teachers College Press, 1960), pp.134–35.

4. Alexis de Tocqueville, *Democracy in America,* vol. II, ed. Phillips Bradley (New York: Vintage Books, 1945), pp.222–225.

5. Ibid., p.223.

6. 20 U.S.C. §1681 et seq. (Supp. 1984).

7. 34 C.F.R. §106 (1984).

8. As to sex discrimination against faculty members, Title VII of the Civil Rights Act of 1964, 42 U.S.C. §2000e et seq., has proven a far more effective tool. (Title VII prohibits employment discrimination on the basis of race, national origin, sex, and religion.) For the first ten years after its enactment, Title IX's employment coverage was open to question and litigants had a far better chance of seeing their case through under Title VII. The issue of whether Title IX covers employees and not just students was finally resolved in the affirmative in 1982 in *North Haven Bd. of Educ. v. Bell,* 456 U.S. 512 (1982).

9. Margaret A. Berger, *Litigation on Behalf of Women* (New York: The Ford Foundation, 1980), pp.8–9.

10. 83 U.S. 130 (1873).

11. Ibid., at 141 (Bradley, J., concurring).

12. *State v. Hall,* 187 So.2d 861, 863 (1966).

13. *Hollander v. Conn. Interscholastic Athletic Conf.,* No. 124427 (Conn. Sup. Ct., New Haven County, 1971), *appeal dismissed,* 295 A.2d 671 (Conn. 1972).

14. Berger, *Litigation on Behalf of Women,* p.7.

15. Each of these groups seems to have focused on a particular area of litigation. For example, the ACLU brought a significant body of public benefits litigation throughout the mid 1970s with Ruth Bader Ginsburg briefing cases that

challenged disparities in Social Security benefits. On the other hand, the Center for Law and Social Policy Women's Rights Project (now the National Women's Law Center) has consistently viewed education as one of its high priority areas.

16. 426 U.S. 229 (1976).

17. See generally Leslie Friedman Goldstein, *The Constitutional Rights of Women: Cases in Law and Social Change* (New York: Longman, 1979); Karen O'Connor, *Women's Organizations' Use of the Courts* (Lexington, MA: Lexington Books, 1980); Ruth Bader Ginsburg, "The Burger Court's Grapplings with Sex Discrimination," in *The Burger Court: the Counterrevolution That Wasn't,* ed. Vincent Blasi (New Haven: Yale University Press, 1980), pp. 133–56.

18. 404 U.S. 71 (1971).

19. Laurence H. Tribe, *American Constitutional Law* (Mineola, NY: The Foundation Press, 1978), p.1063; Gerald Gunther, "The Supreme Court, 1971 Term—Forward: In Search of Evolving Doctrine on a Changing Court: A Model of a Newer Equal Protection," *Harvard Law Review* 86 (1972): 34.

20. 411 U.S. 677 (1973). *Frontiero* was brought under the Fifth Amendment which protects individuals from impermissible action by the federal government and not the Fourteenth Amendment which reaches action by states and their political subdivisions. The Supreme Court in recent years, has recognized an implied equal protection provision within the due process clause of the Fifth Amendment similar to that expressly contained in the Fourteenth Amendment equal protection clause. See *Bolling v. Sharpe,* 347 U.S. 497 (1954).

21. Ibid., at 692.

22. *Weisberger v. Weisenfeld,* 420 U.S. 636 (1975) (survivors benefits allowed to widows but not widowers responsible for dependent children); *Stanton v. Stanton,* 421 U.S. 7 (1975) (parents obligated to support sons until age 21 but daughters only until age 18).

23. 429 U.S. 190 (1976).

24. Ibid., at 197.

25. See e.g., *Rostker v. Goldberg,* 453 U.S. 57 (1981) (upholding the constitutionality of the Military Selective Service Act which authorizes the President to require the draft registration of males but not females). In a 6-3 decision, the Court maintained that the sex classification was substantially related to an important governmental interest in preparing the country for combat—a task for which Congress and the President deem women not similarly situated with men.

26. 458 U.S. 718 (1982).

27. Ibid., at 728.

28. For a comprehensive discussion of litigation on behalf of women with particular emphasis on education, see Nancy Duff Campbell, Marcia D. Greenberger, Margaret A. Kohn, and Shirley J. Wilcher, *Sex Discrimination in Education,* 2 vols. (Wash., D.C.: National Women's Law Center, 1983).

29. 309 F.Supp. 184 (E.D. Va. 1970).

30. 501 F.2d 1264 (9th Cir. 1974).

31. 337 F.Supp. 934 (D.Mass. 1972).

32. 341 F.Supp. 258 (D.Neb. 1972).

33. 457 F.2d 1292 (8th Cir. 1973).

34. 377 F.Supp. 1233 (D.Kan. 1974). But see *Hollander v. Conn. Interscholastic Athletic Conf.,* No. 124427 (Conn. Sup. Ct., New Haven County, 1971), *appeal*

dismissed, 295 A.2d 671 (Conn. 1972)—cross country; *Morris v. Mich. State Bd. of Education,* 472 F.2d 1207 (6th Cir. 1973)—tennis; and *Ritacco v. Norwin School District,* 361 F.Supp. 930 (W.D. Penn. 1973)—all interscholastic noncontact sports. These cases have typically been brought against statewide high school athletics associations that establish rules governing interscholastic athletic competition among high schools in the particular state. Courts have generally found that there is a sufficient nexus between the association and the state to find "state action" for purposes of the Fourteenth Amendment. In such cases, defendants typically have justified the total exclusion of women as well as separate teams based on physiological differences between males and females that prevent them from competing on an equal level. Evidence has been introduced at trial concerning sex-related differences in height, weight, muscle mass, size of heart, and even running ability as related to the construction of the pelvic area. Other arguments have hinged on a benign intent to preserve athletic opportunities for women by maintaining a separate competition. The courts have been more inclined to accept this latter argument in the case of male students challenging separate teams in sports traditionally dominated by females. See e.g., *Gomes v. Rhode Island Interscholastic League,* 469 F.Supp. 659 (D.R.I., 1979) (as long as a separate team available for males); and *Petrie v. Ill. H.S. Athletic Ass'n,* 394 N.E.2d 885 (1979) (even where no separate competition offered for males).

35. 645 F.2d 578 (7th Cir.), *cert. denied,* 454 U.S. 1084 (1981).

36. 444 F.Supp. 117 (E.D. Wis. 1978).

37. 430 F.Supp. 164 (D.Colo. 1977).

38. 430 U.S. 703 (1977), *aff'g by an equally divided court* 532 F.2d 880 (3rd Cir. 1976). A 1981 survey taken by the Office for Civil Rights revealed that among the 6,000 school districts nationwide included in the study, there were 86 all-male and 106 all-female schools. The majority of the boys' schools were vocational-technical while many of the girls' schools were for pregnant students. *Education Week,* Feb. 2, 1983, p.12.

39. The appeals court discussed at considerable length the Equal Educational Opportunities Act of 1974, 20 U.S.C. §1701 (Supp. 1984) and its impact on sex-segregated schools. The statute states that "the maintenance of dual school systems in which students are assigned to schools solely on the basis of . . . sex denies those students the equal protection of the laws guaranteed by the Fourteenth Amendment." The statute further includes the prohibition that, "no state shall deny equal education opportunity to an individual on account of his or her . . . sex." The majority of the appeals court maintained that the Philadelphia system was not a dual system, a phrase generally applied to racial separation. According to the Third Circuit, the school district was neither assigning students solely on the basis of sex nor was it denying females "equal education opportunity." The key issue is how to define equality of opportunity.

40. 9 Phil.Cty.Rep. 556 (1983).

41. Ibid., at 570.

42. Ibid., at 575.

43. In recent years in response to pressure from women's groups, 12 state legislatures have passed specific laws promoting sex equity in education. An additional 11 states have included statements in other equity laws that specifically bar sex discrimination in education. *Education Week,* Sept. 14, 1983, p. 2. For a

general discussion of the increased use of state constitutional provisions in view of federal court backsliding, see William Brennan, "State Constitutions and the Protection of Individual Rights," *Harvard Law Review* 90 (1977): 489-504.

44. Justice O'Connor's opinion in *Mississippi Univ. for Women v. Hogan* may leave that option open. See *supra* note 26 and accompanying text. At this point in time there has been insufficient constitutional litigation on the merits to compare remedies across cases. Aside from constitutional rights, the Title IX regulations specifically permit, although they do not require, recipients of federal aid to "take affirmative action to overcome the effects of conditions which resulted in limited participation therein by persons of a particular sex." 34 C.F.R. §106 (1984).

45. See Anne N. Costain and Douglas Costain, "The Women's Lobby: The Impact of a Movement on Congress," in *Interest Group Politics,* eds. Allan J. Cigler and Burdett A. Loomis (Wash., D.C.: Congressional Quarterly, Inc., 1981).

46. Sam Wasserstrom, "Racism, Sexism and Preferential Treatment," *UCLA Law Review* 24 (1977): 604.

47. Anne N. Costain, "Eliminating Sex Discrimination in Education: Lobbying for Implementation of Title IX," in *Race, Sex and Policy Problems,* eds. Marian Lief Palley and Michael B. Preston (Lexington, MA: Lexington Books, 1979), p.10, n.7.

48. Some of the arguments advanced concerned drafting women into the armed forces, forcing women to share bathroom facilities in public institutions, and denying women alimony and support payments. See Sachs and Wilson, *Sexism and the Law,* pp.219–21.

49. 20 U.S.C. §1681 states:

(a) No person in the United States shall, on the basis of sex, be excluded from participation in, be denied the benefits of, or be subjected to discrimination under any education program or activity receiving Federal financial assistance.

The discussion of the enactment of the Title IX law and regulations is drawn primarily from Andrew Fischel and Janice Pottker, *National Politics and Sex Discrimination in Education* (Lexington, MA: Lexington Books, 1977).

50. 42 U.S.C. §2000e et seq. (Supp. 1984).

51. In 1972, P.L. 92–318 inserted "sex" following "religion" (codified as amended at 20 U.S.C. §2000c-6(a)(2) (Supp. 1984). The Justice Department has no independent authority with regard to sex discrimination apart from admissions. The Department of Education may refer such cases to Justice if ED has been unsuccessful in negotiating voluntary compliance and seeks to resolve the matter through litigation.

52. 29 U.S.C. §206(a)(Supp. 1984).

53. Costain, "Eliminating Sex Discrimination," p.5.

54. 20 U.S.C. §§1682-83 (Supp. 1984). All agencies that provide federal funds for education are obligated to enforce Title IX. Several other agencies, including the Departments of Agriculture and Energy, have issued Title IX regulations. However, the Department of Education's Office for Civil Rights, and prior to that the HEW Office for Civil Rights, are the only agencies that have taken an active role in this area.

55. 20 U.S.C. §1681(a)(3)(Supp. 1984).

56. 20 U.S.C. §1681(a)(4)(Supp. 1984).

57. 20 U.S.C. §1681(a)(1)(Supp. 1984). These exemptions are by implication. The statute specifically states that Title IX "shall apply only to institutions of

vocational education, professional education, and graduate education, and to public institutions of undergraduate higher education."

58. 20 U.S.C. §1681(a)(5)(Supp. 1984).

59. 20 U.S.C. §1681(a)(6)(Supp. 1984).

60. 20 U.S.C. §1681(a)(7)(Supp. 1984).

61. 20 U.S.C. §1681(a)(8)(Supp. 1984).

62. 20 U.S.C. §1681(a)(9)(Supp. 1984).

63. According to a newly enacted "laying before" procedure for promulgating administrative regulations for education statutes, the agency (HEW) was required to submit the regulations for congressional review. If not rejected by Congress within 45 days, the regulations would become law. Administrative Procedure Act, 5 U.S.C. §533 (Supp. 1984).

64. Groups represented in the Education Task Force included the Federation of Organizations for Professional Women; Council on National Priorities; American Alliance for Health, Physical Education and Recreation; League of Women Voters; Cooperative College Registry; Intercollegiate Association for Women Students; Project on the Status and Education of Women of the Association of American Colleges; National Association of State Universities and Land Grant Colleges; Women's Lobby; National Student Lobby; Education Commission of the State Equal Rights for Women in Education; National Student Association; Project on Equal Education Rights; Women's Legal Defense Fund; National Council of Jewish Women; Resource Center on Sex Roles in Education; National Association for Women Deans, Administrators and Counselors; American Association of University Women; Teacher Rights; National Education Association; National Association for Girls and Women in Sports; ACLU Women's Rights Project; Association for Intercollegiate Athletics for Women; American Association of University Professors; Women's Equity Action League; Women's Rights Project; American Association of School Administrators; American Council on Education; Business and Professional Women's Federation; and National Organization for Women. Costain, "Eliminating Sex Discrimination," p.11, n.11.

65. The day after HEW issued the final regulations to Title IX, Senator Jesse Helms (R., NC) introduced a concurrent resolution to disapprove the Title IX regulations in their entirety. Shortly thereafter Representative James Martin (R., NC) introduced a similar resolution in the house. Both resolutions were buried in committee. During that same period, the House Special Subcommittee on Education passed a bill introduced by Representative James O'Hara (D., MI), who headed the Subcommittee, to amend the Title IX law by removing revenue-producing sports from coverage and thereby preventing the law from integrating physical education classes. The bill died in subcommittee. Ibid., pp.8–9.

66. 34 C.F.R. Part 106 (Supp. 1984).

67. 34 C.F.R. §106.21(b)(2)(Supp. 1984).

68. 34 C.F.R. §106.23 (Supp. 1984).

69. 34 C.F.R. §106.23 (Supp. 1984).

69. 34 C.F.R. §106.36 (Supp. 1984).

70. 34 C.F.R. §106.41 (Supp. 1984).

71. 34 C.F.R. §106.34(c) (1984).

72. 34 C.F.R. §106.41(b) (1984).

73. 34 C.F.R. §106.41(c) (1984).

74. 34 C.F.R. §106.4 (1984).

75. 34 C.F.R. §106.3(c) (1984).

76. 34 C.F.R. §106.71 (1984) adopts and incorporates by reference the procedural provisions applicable to Title VI as found in 34 C.F.R. §§100.6-100.11 and 34 C.F.R. Part 101 (1984).

77. 34 C.F.R. §100.6(b) (1984).

78. 34 C.F.R. §100.6(c) (1984).

79. 34 C.F.R. §100.7(a) (1984).

80. 34 C.F.R. §100.7(b) (1984).

81. Project on Equal Education Rights, NOW Legal Defense and Education Fund, *Stalled at the Start: Government Action on Sex Bias in the Schools* (Wash., D.C., 1978), p.19.

82. Plaintiffs' Women's Equity Action League et. al.'s Motion for Order to Show Cause at 3-5, *WEAL v. Bell,* Civ. No. 74-1720 (D.D.C. Mar. 11, 1983).

83. Prepared response to Question 20, supplied in HEW response to self-administered questionnaire sent by U.S. Commission on Civil Rights in December 1979 to assist in preparation of the report entitled, *Enforcing Title IX* (Wash., D.C.: U.S. Government Printing Office, October 1980).

84. Ibid., prepared response to Question 18, supplied in HEW response. These figures primarily reflect the fact that HEW had suspended processing in three major policy areas while awaiting policy development: intercollegiate athletics (policy interpretation published in 1979, *Federal Register,* vol. 44, no. 239, Dec. 11, 1979, p. 71413), rules of appearance (regulation contained in 34 C.F.R. §106.31(6)(5) that prohibited discrimination in the application of codes of personal appearance revoked, *Federal Register,* vol. 47, no. 145, July 28, 1982, p. 32526), and employment (resolved by Supreme Court decision in *North Haven Bd. of Educ. v. Bell,* 456 U.S. 512 (1982), *Enforcing Title IX,* p. 19.

85. Correspondence with Margaret A. Kohn, attorney, National Women's Law Center, August 24, 1984.

86. 441 U.S. 677 (1979). In the follow-up action, the Seventh Circuit Court of appeals ruled that complainants must prove intentional discrimination in order to establish a prima facie case under Title IX. *Cannon v. University of Chicago,* 648 F.2d 1104 (7th Cir.), *cert. denied,* 454 U.S. 1128 (1981).

87. 456 U.S. 512 (1982).

88. Ibid., at 540.

89. 104 S.Ct. 1211 (1984). The case traces back to 1977 when the college refused to sign the assurance of compliance form as required under Title IX. The college argued that it received no direct federal aid and therefore was not subject to Title IX mandates. When threatened with termination of federal student aid funds, the college for itself and on behalf of four students sued HEW. The Third Circuit, in August 1982, ruled that private educational institutions such as Grove City College are covered as a whole when they or any of their students receive federal scholarship loans or grants. 687 F.2d 689 (3rd Cir. 1982).

90. In the years immediately preceding *Grove City,* the definition of "program or activity" under Title IX had been the object of conflicting decisions among the lower federal courts. Federal district courts in Virginia (*University of Richmond v. Bell,* 543 F.Supp. 321 (E.D.Va. 1982)) and Michigan (*Othen v. Ann Arbor School Board,* 507 F.Supp. 1376 (E.D. Mich. 1981) *aff'd on other grounds,* 699 F.2d 309 (6th Cir. 1983)), as well as the First Circuit Court of Appeals (*Rice v.*

President and Fellows of Harvard, 663 F.2d 336 (1st Cir. 1982), *cert. denied,* 456 U.S. 928 (1982)), and the Sixth Circuit (*Hillsdale College v. HEW,* 696 F.2d 418 (6th Cir. 1982), *vacated and remanded,* 104 S.Ct. 1673 (1984)), had ruled that Title IX bans discrimination only in those education programs that receive federal aid and not the entire institution. The Eleventh Circuit (*Iron Arrow Honor Society v. Heckler,* 702 F.2d 549 (11th Cir.), *appeal dismissed,* 464 U.S. 67 (1983)), the Fifth Circuit (*Bennett v. West Texas State University,* No. 81-1398 (5th Cir. Jan 31, 1983), *cert. denied,* 464 U.S. 963 (1983)), and the Third Circuit (*Haffner v. Temple University,* 688 F.2d 14 (3rd Cir. 1982) and *Grove City College v. Bell,* 687 F.2d 689 (3rd Cir. 1982), *rev'd in part,* 104 S.Ct. 1211 (1984)) had ruled otherwise.

91. H.R. Res. 190, 98th Cong., 1st Sess. (1983).

92. 104 S.Ct. 1211, 1222.

93. Ibid., at 1236 (Brennan, J., dissenting).

94. Faculty members of higher education institutions that are federal contractors may also have remedies available under Executive Order 11246, although the courts have not recognized a private right of action under that law. But none of these alternatives provides the same mechanisms or types of relief available under Title IX. With respect to Title VII and the Equal Pay Act, there is no guarantee that the administrative agency with which one initially files a complaint will actually undertake an investigation. Experience has proven that it is highly unlikely that the agency will carry the case to court or into any administrative proceedings. In contrast, under Title IX the complainant is guaranteed an investigation upon filing a bona fide complaint. If the Department of Education cannot resolve the discrimination, then it can refer the matter to the Justice Department for judicial enforcement or take steps to terminate funding. This fund termination remedy is not available under either Title VII or the Equal Pay Act.

95. *Education Week,* Mar. 2, 1984, p.1.

96. Memorandum from Assistant Secretary for Civil Rights Harry M. Singleton to Regional Civil Rights Directors, "Analysis of the Decision in *Grove City v. Bell* and Initial Guidance on Its Application to OCR Enforcement Activities," July 31, 1984.

97. *New York Times,* June 3, 1984, p.36.

98. Project on Equal Education Rights, NOW Legal Defense and Education Fund, *Injustice Under the Law: The Impact of the Grove City College Decision on Civil Rights* (Wash., D.C., February 1985). In June 1984, the American Association of University Women, the National Education Association, the Women's Equity Action League, and two students initiated litigation against the Department of Education, charging that officials had implemented an unwritten policy in an inconsistent manner based on an incorrect interpretation of the *Grove City* decision, *AAUW et al. v. U.S. Department of Education,* No. 84-1881 (D.D.C. filed June 19, 1984). The following month, the Department published Title IX policy guidelines.

99. S.2568, 98th Cong., 1st Session (1984).

100. H.R.5490, 98th Cong., 2d Sess. (1984).

101. *Congressional Record,* vol. 130, pp. S12142-12176 (1984).

102. S. 431 and H. 700, 99th Cong., 1st Sess. (1985). S. 431 has 45 co-sponsors in the Senate while H.700 has 100 House co-sponsors.

103. S.272, 99th Cong., 1st Sess. (1985).

104. Hearings Before the House Education and Labor Committee and the Civil and Constitutional Rights Subcommittee, 99th Cong., 1st Sess. (1985)(statement of William Bradford Reynolds, Assistant Attorney General for Civil Rights).

105. U.S. Commission on Civil Rights, Statement on Civil Rights Act of 1985, March 5, 1985.

106. 20 U.S.C. §1866 (Supp. 1984). For a discussion of WEEA's history, programs, and budget, see Citizens Council on Women's Education, *Catching Up: A Review of the Women's Educational Equity Act Program* (Wash., D.C., March 1984). WEEA represents the one program for which the federal government has earmarked a specific amount of funds for programs that address sex equity. Other programs have placed some emphasis on the elimination of sex bias and sex stereotyping among broader program priorities, e.g., The Career Education Incentive Act, 20 U.S.C. §2601-2612 (1978) (repealed 1981) and the Guidance and Counseling provisions of the Education Amendments of 1976, 20 U.S.C. §3121-3123 (1978) (repealed 1981). Both of these were merged into the state block grant under Chapter 2 of the Education Consolidation and Improvement Act of 1981. In 1984, Congress enacted the Carl D. Perkins Vocational Education Act, 20 U.S.C. §2301 et seq., as amended by P.L. 98-524, 98th Cong., 2d Sess. (1984). The Act provides funds to the states for vocational education with the states reallocating the funds to local school districts primarily on a discretionary basis. The only funds earmarked for sex equity are contained in a requirement that states spend at least $60,000 of their annual allotment on the employment of a sex equity coordinator.

107. National Federation of State High School Associations, *Sports Participation Survey,* (Kansas City, MO, 1981). For a thorough discussion with supporting data on women and athletics, see U.S. Commission on Civil Rights, *More Hurdles to Clear: Women and Girls in Competitive Athletics,* (Wash., D.C.: U.S. Government Printing Office, July 1980).

108. *Education Daily,* Feb. 25, 1982 p. 1.

109. National Advisory Council on Women's Education Programs, *Title IX: The Half Full, Half Empty Glass* (Wash., D.C. 1979), p.30.

110. Project on Equal Education Rights, NOW Legal Defense and Education Fund, *Survey of Prominent Issues in the 1984 Elections* (Wash., D.C. 1983), p.7.

111. National Advisory Council on Women's Education Programs, *The Half Full, Half Empty Glass,* p.44.

112. Project on Equal Education Rights, NOW Legal Defense and Education Fund, *Silver Snail Awards: PEER's Analysis of Females in Public Education* (Wash., D.C., February 1982), Chart 1.

113. Project on Equal Education Rights, *Survey on Prominent Issues,* p.3.

Chapter V

1. 20 U.S.C. §1401 et seq. (Supp. 1984).

2. For an overview of legal issues, see generally David L. Kirp, "Schools as Sorters: The Constitutional and Policy Implications of Student Classification," *University of Pennsylvania Law Review* 121 (April 1973): 705–97; Jack B. Weinstein, "Education of Exceptional Children," *Creighton Law Review* 12 (1979):

987–1039; Betsy Levin, "Equal Educational Opportunity for Special Pupil Populations and the Federal Role," *West Virginia Law Review* 85 (1982–83): 159–85.

3. The due process clause of the Fifth Amendment states that "[n]o person shall . . . be deprived of life, liberty, or property, without due process of law." The Fourteenth Amendment applies that prohibition to the states. Section One provides in part that "[n]o state shall . . . deprive any person of life, liberty, or property without due process of law.

4. 343 F.Supp. 279 (E.D. Pa. 1972) (consent decree).

5. 348 F.Supp. 866 (D.D.C. 1972).

6. 343 F.Supp. 279 at 285. According to the consent agreement approved by the court, "it is the commonwealth's obligation to place each mentally retarded child in a free, public program of education and training appropriate to the child's capacity."

7. Ibid., at 878

8. See Margaret P. Burgdorf and Robert Burgdorf, "A History of Unequal Treatment: The Qualification of Handicapped Persons as a 'Suspect Class' under the Equal Protection Clause," *Santa Clara Law Review* 15 (1975): 855–910. The Supreme Court has never ruled on the issue of whether the handicapped, in general, are entitled to greater judicial protection. However, in *City of Cleburne v. Cleburne Living Center,* 105 S. Ct. 3249 (1985), the Court held that mental retardation is not a quasi-suspect classification, such as gender, calling for more exacting judicial review than is normally accorded economic and social legislation. The Court noted the vast array of federal statutes protecting the rights of the handicapped as evidence of legislative attention to their difficulties, thereby negating a need for more intrusive judicial oversight.

9. 348 F.Supp. 866 at 876.

10. 458 U.S. 176 (1982).

11. 345 F.Supp. 1306 (N.D. Ca. 1972), (order granting preliminary injunction), *aff'd,* 502 F.2d 963 (9th Cir. 1974). In deciding the case on the merits, the district court found that such tests are racially and culturally biased. The court prohibited school districts from using them in the placement of children in classes for the educable mentally retarded. When used as the primary means of placement, these tests violate both P.L. 94-142 and §504, 495 F.Supp. 926 (N.D. Cal. 1979), *aff'd,* 52 U.S.L.W. 2456 (U.S. Jan. 23, 1984) (No. 80-4027).

12. Erwin C. Hargrove et al., *Regulations and Schools: The Implementation of Equal Education for Handicapped Children* (Nashville: Vanderbilt University, Institute of Policy Studies, March 1981).

13. 29 U.S.C. §701 et seq. (Supp. 1984).

14. 20 U.S.C. §1401 et seq. (Supp. 1984).

15. See H.R.12154, 92nd Cong., 1st Sess. *Congressional Record,* vol. 117, p. 45945 (1971).

16. See S.3044, *Congressional Record,* vol. 118, pp. 525–26 (1972).

17. *Cherry v. Mathews,* 419 F.Supp. 922 (D.D.C. 1976). While §503 of the Rehabilitation Act expressly requires federal agencies to promulgate regulations to implement that section's prohibition of employment discrimination against the handicapped, the 1973 version of the Act was silent as to any regulatory authority or duty under §504. However, Congress amended the Act in 1978, incorporating enforcement mechanisms available under Title VI of the Civil Rights Act of 1964.

18. 34 C.F.R. Part 104 (1984).

19. NARC was organized in 1950 as a coalition of several state organizations of parents and families of handicapped individuals. Membership grew from 62,000 in 1960 to 218,000 in 1975. CEC was founded in 1922 by faculty and students at Teachers College, Columbia University. Its membership, which consists mainly of special education professionals, grew from 6,000 in 1950 to 7,000 in the mid-1970s. In addition to NARC and CEC, other specialized groups presented testimony, including the Association for Children with Learning Disabilities, the American Federation for the Blind, and the American Speech and Hearing Association. Erwin L. Levine and Elizabeth M. Wexler *P.L. 94-142: An Act of Congress* (New York: Macmillan, 1981), pp.15–16, 28.

20. Ibid., pp.20–21.

21. Correspondence with Edwin W. Martin, former director Bureau of the Education for the Handicapped, January 10, 1985.

22. Levine and Wexler, pp. 25-26.

23. P.L. No. 89-750, 80 Stat. 1204-08 (1966).

24. For a discussion of the establishment of BEH and its early role in promoting equality for the handicapped, see Edwin W. Martin, "Breakthrough for the Handicapped: Legislative History," *Exceptional Children* 33 (March 1968): 493–503.

25. Correspondence with Edwin W. Martin.

26. Elementary and Secondary Education Act of 1970, P.L. No. 91-230, 84 Stat. 241 (1970).

27. H.R.5823 and S.1319, 93rd Cong., 1st Sess. (1973).

28. The political power of these two groups would be tested again in the 1980s by executive attempts to consolidate Title I and P.L. 94-142 programs into a block grant to be administered by the states.

29. Education of the Handicapped Act of 1974, P.L. No. 93-380, §611, 20 U.S.C. §1401 (Supp. 1984).

30. Gerald R. Ford, *Weekly Compilation of Presidential Documents*, vol. 11, (1975) p.1335.

31. 20 U.S.C. §1401(19) (Supp. 1984).

32. 20 U.S.C. §1415(b-c) (Supp. 1984).

33. 20 U.S.C. §1401(17) (Supp. 1984).

34. 20 U.S.C. §1412(5)(A) (Supp.1984).

35. For a discussion of legal problems in implementing P.L. 94-142, see Richard Weatherly and Michael Lipsky, "Street Level Bureaucrats and Institutional Innovation: Implementing Special Education Reform," *Harvard Educational Review* 47 (May 1977): 171-97; Richard Weatherly, *Reforming Special Education: Policy Implementation from State Level to Street Level* (Cambridge MA: MIT Press, 1979); Anne W. Wright, *Local Implementation of P.L. 94-142: Second Year Report of a Longitudinal Study* (Menlo Park, CA: Stanford Research Institute, 1980). For a discussion of the issues surrounding the mainstreaming debate, see Barbara K. Keough and Marc L. Levitt, "Special Education in the Mainstream: A Confrontation of Limitations," *Focus on Exceptional Children* 8 (March 1976): 1-10; Seymour Sarason and Doris John, "Mainstreaming: Dilemmas, Opposition, Opportunities," in *Futures in Education for Exceptional Students*, ed. Maynard Reynolds (Reston, VA: Council for Exceptional Children, 1978).

36. 20 U.S.C. §1411 (a)(1) (Supp. 1984).

37. Educational Priorities Panel, *Special Education Funding: A Story of Broken Promises* (New York, February 1981).

38. During 1979–80, the identified special population as a percent of total public school enrollment was 8.6 percent nationally. That figure was higher in large urban areas, with Boston at 18.4 percent, Buffalo at 15.2 percent, Baltimore at 14.9 percent, Philadelphia at 12.4 percent, Chicago at 11.7 percent, Los Angeles at 8.3 percent, and New York at 7.5 percent. Joseph P. Viteritti, *Across the River: Politics and Education in the City* (New York: Holmes & Meier, 1983), p. 183.

39. Jeffrey J. Zeitel, "Implementing the Right to a Free Appropriate Education," in *Special Education in America: Its Legal and Governmental Foundations*, eds. Joseph Ballard, Bruce A. Ramirez, and Fredrick J. Weintraub (Wash., D.C.: Council for Exceptional Children, 1983), p.24. Despite these gains in the numbers of children served, the total number of school-aged handicapped children in the United States has been estimated at 5.8 million. U.S. Office of Education, Bureau of the Education for the Handicapped, *Probable Upper Limits on the Number of Handicapped Children in the United States*, draft (Wash., D.C., 1978).

40. U.S. Department of Education, *Seventh Annual Report to Congress on the Implementation of Public Law 94-142: The Education for All Handicapped Children Act* (Wash., D.C.: U.S. Government Printing Office, 1985).

41. Educational Priorities Panel, *Special Education Funding*, p.6.

42. 20 U.S.C. §1401(1)(Supp. 1984).

43. 34 C.F.R. Part 104 app. A at 346-47 (1984).

44. 20 U.S.C. §1401(16),(18)(Supp. 1984).

45. 34 C.F.R. §104.33(b)(1)(1984).

46. Levine and Wexler, *An Act of Congress*, p.111.

47. In 1982 in the case of *New Mexico Association for Retarded Citizens (N.M.A.R.C.) v. State of New Mexico*, 495 F.Supp. 391 (D.N.M. 1982), *rev'd in part*, 678 F.2d 847 (10th Cir. 1982), the Tenth Circuit reversed and sent back to the lower court a 1980 ruling that the state had discriminated against handicapped children in violation of §504. According to the appeals court, the district court had failed to address the Supreme Court's 1979 opinion in *Southeastern Community College v. Davis*, 442 U.S. 397 (1979). In that case, the Court had ruled that the purpose of §504 is to prohibit discrimination against handicapped persons, not to mandate affirmative action for such individuals. That decision, the appeals court said, "eroded somewhat the breadth of Section 504 compliance regulations" and "plainly suggests that the distinction between affirmative action unnecessary under Section 504 and discrimination made unlawful by [it] are sometimes unclear." However, a federally funded education system may not engage in practices that "preclude the handicapped from obtaining system benefits realized by the non-handicapped." Ibid., at 852–53. To support its "benefits" standard, the appeals court relied not only on *Davis* but also on *Lau v. Nichols*, 414 U.S. 563 (1974) and *Serna v. Portales*, 499 F.2d 1147 (10th Cir. 1974), two cases that had been brought under Title VI of the Civil Rights Act of 1964 on behalf of linguistic minority students. According to the Tenth Circuit in *NMARC*, those cases indicated that discrimination may occur where students derive fewer benefits than their English-speaking classmates, even where the education programs are administered "evenhandedly." Ibid., at 853. For the lower court to conclude that discrimination has occurred, the appeals court stated, plaintiffs must prove the

following: that the state's existing education programs preclude the handicapped from activities and benefits enjoyed by the nonhandicapped; that program modifications would result in the handicapped obtaining these benefits; and, that program modification would not jeopardize the overall capacity of the state's education system. In February 1984, realizing that the refusal of special education funds under P.L. 94-142 would not release the state from §504 requirements, the New Mexico legislature approved a bill that would require the state education department to apply for funds under P.L. 94-142.

48. On the other hand, the §504 statute expressly allows attorney's fees. 29 U.S.C §794(b) (Supp. 1984) provides that, "In any action or proceeding to enforce or charge a violation of a provision of this subchapter, the court, in its discretion, may allow the prevailing party, other than the United States a reasonable attorney's fee as part of the costs."

49. 442 U.S. 397 (1979). For a comprehensive discussion of §504, see Judith Welsh Wegner, "The Antidiscrimination Model Reconsidered: Ensuring Equal Opportunity without Respect to Handicap under Section 504 of the Rehabilitation Act of 1973," *Cornell Law Review* 69 (1984): 401–516.

50. Ibid., at 406.

51. Ibid., at 411.

52. Ibid., at 412.

53. 105 S.Ct. 712 (1985) (challenge brought by medicaid recipients against state's reduction from 20 to 14 in the number of inpatient hospital days for which state medicaid would pay hospitals on behalf of medicaid recipients each year).

54. Ibid., at 720.

55. Ibid., at 721, n.21.

56. Ibid., at 721, n.20.

57. 458 U.S. 176 (1982).

58. Ibid., at 189.

59. Ibid., at 192.

60. Ibid., at 198.

61. Ibid., at 200.

62. Ibid., at 207.

63. 411 U.S. 1 (1973).

64. 458 U.S. 176 at 208.

65. The *Rowley* decision has generated considerable commentary. See Note, "The Education for All Handicapped Children Act of 1975: What's Left After *Rowley*," *Williamette Law Review* 19 (1983): 715–36; Note, "Crippling the Education for All Handicapped Children Act: *Board of Education v. Rowley,* 102 S.Ct. 3034," *Stetson Law Review* 12 (1983): 791–813; Note, "Education—*Board of Education v. Rowley:* The Supreme Court Takes a Conservative Approach to the Education of Handicapped Children," *North Carolina Law Review* 16 (1983): 881–903; Note, "The Education for All Handicapped Children Act: What is a 'Free Appropriate Public Education'?" *Wayne Law Review* 29 (1983): 1285–1300; Mark G. Yudof, "Education for the Handicapped: *Rowley* in Perspective," *American Journal of Education* 92 (February 1984): 163–77.

66. 20 U.S.C. §1401(17) (Supp. 1984).

67. 34 C.F.R. §300.13(b)(10)(1984).

68. 104 S.Ct. 3371 (1984).

69. Ibid., at 3376–77.

70. Ibid., at 3378.

71. Ibid., at 3379.

72. Ibid., at 3376–77, n.6. Subsequent to its decision in *Tatro,* the Court declined to review a federal appeals court ruling requiring a school district to pay for psychotherapy treatments for an emotionally disturbed child as a 738 F.2d 425 (3rd Cir.), "related service" under P.L. 94-142. *Piscataway Township Bd. of Educ. v. T.G.,* 738 F.2d 425 (3rd *Cir.*), *cert. denied,* 105 S.Ct. 592 (1984).

73. 104 S.Ct. 3457 (1984).

74. 42 U.S.C. §1988 (Supp. 1984) permits the court in its discretion to award attorney's fees to prevailing plaintiffs seeking to vindicate federal statutory or constitutional rights in civil rights cases, including those brought under §1983, Title IX (sex discrimination) and Title VI (race discrimination). Section 505 of the Rehabilitation Act of 1973 incorporates the legislative history of §1988 for claims brought under §504.

75. 42 U.S.C. §1983 (Supp. 1984) provides a remedy for a deprivation, under color of state law, "of any rights, privileges, or immunities secured by the Constitution and laws." For the plaintiffs in *Robinson,* the underlying constitutional claims were based upon denial of Fourteenth Amendment due process and of a free appropriate education under the equal protection clause.

76. §505(b) of the Rehabilitation Act of 1973, 29 U.S.C. §794(a)(b)(Supp. 1984) allows the court in its discretion to award reasonable attorney's fees to a prevailing party in a §504 handicapped discrimination case.

77. H.R. 1523 and S. 415, 99th Cong., 1st Sess. (1985).

78. Paul T. Hill and Doren L. Madey, *Educational Policymaking through the Civil Justice System* (Santa Monica, CA: The Rand Corp., Institute for Civil Justice, 1982). That report cited the important effects the civil justice system has had on special education services. It has made school officials more responsive to parental claims and has made parents more knowledgeable and aggressive concerning their children's rights. Ibid., p. 21.

79. The Handicapped Children's Protection Act of 1985, Hearings Before the House Subcommittee on Select Education, 99th Cong., 1st Sess. (1985) (statement on behalf of the Consortium for Citizens with Developmental Disabilities Task Force on Education).

80. Ibid., (statement of Jean Bilger Arnold, Board of Directors, NSBA Council of School Attorneys).

81. Letter from William J. Bennett, Secretary of Education to Representative Augustus F. Hawkins, Chairman, Committee on Education and Labor, April 2, 1985. The Department's response to the pending legislation focused on four points. First, it opposed any wholesale incorporation of the §504 regulations into statutory law. Second, it recommended clarification that parents not be allowed to bypass the administrative procedures established under P.L. 94-142 and the §504 regulations by filing a complaint under 42 U.S.C. §1983 and the Constitution. Third, it opposed the retroactive application of the legislation to cases pending as of the date of the Court's decision in *Robinson.* And fourth, it opposed the award of attorney's fees for admininstrative proceedings on the grounds that such allowance would disrupt the speedy and consensual resolution of disputes, impose financial burdens on state and local governments, and foster additional litigation

solely on the question of attorney's fees. The Department further suggested that attorney's fees be allowed not only to prevailing parents, but to state and local governments where individuals' claims are found to be frivolous. The National School Boards Association expressed a related concern and suggested that school districts be held to a "good faith" standard of liability. According to NSBA, to permit attorney's fees whenever a plaintiff prevails overlooks the problems school districts face in implementing a law whose meaning is subject to diverse interpretations in an area where experts disagree on the most appropriate educational services. Letter from Thomas A. Shannon, Executive Director, and Mack J. Spears, President, NSBA to Representative Pat Williams, Subcommittee on Select Education, Committee on Education and Labor, April 12, 1985.

82. 20 U.S.C. §1401 (16) (Supp. 1984).

83. *Battle v. Pennsylvania,* 629 F.2d (3rd Cir. 1980), *cert. denied sub nom. Scanlon v. Battle,* 452 U.S. 968 (1981); *Crawford v. Pittman,* 708 F.2d 1028 (5th Cir. 1983) (Mississippi); *Yaris v. Special School District of St. Louis County,* 728 F.2d 1055 (8th Cir. 1984) (Missouri); *Georgia Assoc. of Retarded Children (GARC) v. McDaniel,* 716 F.2d 1565 (11th Cir. 1983). On review, the Supreme Court vacated and remanded the case for further consideration in light of *Smith v. Robinson,* 104 S.Ct. 3581 (1984) and the Eleventh Circuit modified its previous opinion on attorney's fees and the §504 claim, 740 F.2d 902 (11th Cir. 1984). In February 1985, the Supreme Court denied a second petition for review filed by both the state and the local school system of Savannah. Petitioners had based their argument on the high price tag of additional schooling. 105 S.Ct. 1228 (1985).

84. 708 F.2d 1028, 1035.

85. 716 F.2d 1565, 1576.

86. 728 F.2d 1055, 1057.

87. 720 F.2d 463, 466 (6th Cir. 1983).

88. For a discussion of the extended school year in view of *Rowley,* see Laurie Mesibov, "An Extended School Year for Handicapped Students?," *West's Education Law Reporter* 14 (1984): 867–86.

89. Education Commission of the States, Department of Research and Information, unpublished tabulations (Denver, CO, September 1982).

90. For an overview of competency testing issues, see Merle McClung, "Competency Testing Programs: Legal and Educational Issues," *Fordham Law Review* 47 (1979): 651–712; Martha M. McCarthy, "Minimum Competency Testing for Students: Educational and Legal Issues," *Educational Horizons* 62–63 (Spring 1984): 103–110. For a discussion of the legal issues surrounding competency testing, see George Madaus, *The Courts, Validity and Competency Testing* (Boston: Kluwer-Nijhoff, 1983).

91. The leading case on competency testing is *Debra P. v. Turlington,* 474 F.Supp. 244 (N.D. Fla. 1979), *aff'd in part and rev'd and remanded in part,* 644 F.2d 397 (5th Cir. 1981), 564 F.Supp. 177 (N.D. Fla. 1983), *aff'd,* 730 F.2d 1405 (11th Cir. 1984). Here the Fifth Circuit upheld the trial court's determination that due process demands that students be given adequate notice prior to the invocation of the diploma sanction. The appeals court further ruled that the state could not deny diplomas until it proved that the test had "curricular validity," that is, that it actually reflected the curriculum as taught in the schools. On remand, the

trial court found that the functional literacy test did in fact cover the material taught in Florida classrooms. The appeals court upheld that conclusion.

92. 458 N.Y.S.2d 680 (1982), aff'd, 60 N.Y.2d 758 (1983), cert. denied, 104 S.Ct. 1598 (1984). According to regulations of the State Commissioner of Education, local school districts can award a certificate of completion to students who do not pass the state competency tests in reading and mathematics but who successfully complete an appropriate individualized education program. School districts must report the names of students receiving such certificates to the State Department of Education shortly after the close of the school year. The tests were first administered in New York State in 1979. Rather than comply with the regulation, the school district of Northport-East Northport filed suit against the State Department of Education.

93. 458 N.Y.S.2d 680, 689.

94. 697 F.2d 179 (7th Cir. 1983).

95. The court, however, noted that the individual students challenging the requirement lacked exposure to as much as 90 percent of the material tested. The court ruled on due process grounds that the 18-month notice of the testing requirements prior to graduation was inadequate for the school to have specifically incorporated the test objectives into the student's IEPs. The court recognized that ordinarily the proper remedy for such a violation would be free, remedial, special education classes to ensure exposure to the material tested. However, the eleven students in question had been out of school for over two years and could not attend remedial classes without undue hardship. Consequently, the court ordered the school district to award diplomas to these students but upheld the competency testing requirement for future application.

96. 635 F.2d 342 (5th Cir. 1981), cert. denied, 454 U.S. 1030 (1981). Two lower court decisions that predated the appeals court opinion in Turlington had held similarly. See Stuart v. Nappi, 443 F.Supp. 1235 (D. Conn. 1978) (prohibited expulsion but upheld suspension); Doe v. Koger, 480 F.Supp. (N.D. Ind. 1979), rev'd on other grounds, 710 F.2d 1209 (7th Cir. 1983).

97. 682 F.2d 595 (6th Cir, 1982).

98. 419 U.S. 565 (1975). In Goss, the Supreme Court stated that students suspended for ten days or less must be afforded due process under the Fourteenth Amendment to the U.S. Constitution. Due process in such cases demands oral or written notice of the charges and an informal hearing or opportunity to rebut those charges.

99. 531 F.Supp. 148 (D.Ill. 1982).

100. Ibid., at 151.

101. Ibid., at 150.

102. For a discussion of related legal and policy issues, see Note, "The Application of 94-142 to the Suspension and Expulsion of Handicapped Children," Arizona Law Review 24 (1982): 685–701; Note, "Disciplinary Exclusion of Handicapped Students: An Examination of the Limitations Imposed by the Education for All Handicapped Children Act of 1975," Fordham Law Review 51 (1982): 168–95; Note, "School Discipline and the Handicapped Child," Washington Law Review 39 (1982): 1453–67.

103. Federal Register, vol. 47, p.33,836 (1982) (proposed August 4, 1982).

104. *Education Week*, Nov. 11, 1983, p.12.
105. *Education Week*, Mar. 17, 1983, p.1.
106. *Education Week*, Nov. 18, 1983, p.11.
107. 103 S.Ct. 3221 (1983).
108. 104 S.Ct. 1211 (1984).

Chapter VI

1. According to Chester Finn, the membership of the liberal consensus has included the Ford and Carnegie Foundations and some smaller ones, the elite graduate schools, the major national education organizations, the various groups represented in the Leadership Council for Civil Rights, the large labor unions, political appointees in the federal executive agencies, key members of Congress, a variety of "think tanks" such as the Brookings Institution and the Aspen Institute, the editorial writers for major metropolitan newspapers, and some distinguished individual citizens and scholars. See Chester E. Finn, Jr., "The Future of Education's Liberal Consensus," *Change* 12 (September 1980): 25.

2. For a coherent statement of policy recommendations emanating from that ideology, see Stuart M. Butler, W. Bruce Weinrod, and Michael Sanera, eds., *Mandate for Leadership: Policy Management in a Conservative Administration* (Wash., D.C.: The Heritage Foundation, 1981). This 1,092-page report published by the conservative "think tank" was used by the Reagan Administration as a blueprint for its first term. For a more recent statement of policy recommendations, see Eileen M. Gardner, ed., *A New Agenda for Education* (Wash., D.C.: The Heritage Foundation, 1985). The theme of this report is that "centralized control of education has failed." Among its recommendations are those supporting a national voluntary school integration plan in lieu of forced busing, the conversion of Chapter 1 remedial programs into a voucher system or the consolidation of that program into a state block grant, the enactment of more general tuition tax credit and voucher legislation, and state adoption of tuition tax deduction laws. The report is also critical of Title I compensatory programs, P.L. 94-142 handicapped programs, bilingual education, and women's equity projects. See also Thanksgiving Statement Group, *Developing Character: Transmitting Knowledge* (Posen, IL.: ARL, 1984) for a less radical neo-conservative statement made by an ad hoc group of 27 scholars, educators, and policymakers. This paper focuses specifically on youth character but includes a recommendation for providing parents and children with greater choice among forms of schools and school systems.

3. Republican National Convention, Republican Party Platform, July 14, 1980, Detroit, Michigan.

4. Inaugural Address, January 21, 1985, Washington, D.C.

5. National Education Association, Research Estimates of School Statistics Data File.

6. Denis P. Doyle and Terry W. Hartle, "Ideology, Pragmatic Politics, and the Education Budget," in *Maintaining the Safety Net: Income Redistribution Programs in the Reagan Administration*, ed. John C. Weicher (Wash., D.C.: American Enterprise Institute, 1984), p.144, Table 6–2.

7. The Council of the Great City Schools, *Analysis of the Effect of the FY82 and FY83 Reagan Budget Proposals on Urban Schools* (Wash., D.C., 1982), p. 7. In August 1981, Congress enacted the Education Consolidation and Improvement Act as Subtitle D of Title V of the Omnibus Budget Reconciliation Act of 1981, P.L. 97-35. Chapter 1 of the Act amends Title I of ESEA as to program design, parental involvement, fiscal requirements, and accountability provisions. 20 U.S.C. §3801 (Supp. 1984).

8. U.S. Department of Education, budget documents, selected years.

9. Congressional Research Service, *Impact of Budget Cuts on Major Education Programs During the Reagan Administration.* CRS Report No. 84-EPW (Wash., D.C., August 1984).

10. National School Boards Association, Council of Urban Boards of Education, *The Impact of Reductions in Federal Education Expenditures* (Alexandria, VA, 1984). This figure is based on responses of 39 (55%) of CUBE member districts.

11. The Council of the Great City Schools, *Analysis of the Effect of the FY82 and FY83 Reagan Budget Proposals on Urban Schools* (Wash., D.C., 1982), p. 2.

12. According to the National Assessment of Educational Progress, between 1971 and 1980, 9-, 13-, and 17-year-old black students, particularly those in the lowest quartiles of achievement, increased in both reading and mathematics performance. In contrast to these gains, white students demonstrated a significant increase in reading achievement only at grade 9 while demonstrating a decrease in mathematics achievement at all three grade levels. National Assessment of Educational Progress, *Reading, Science and Mathematics Trends: A Closer Look* (Denver, CO: Education Commission of the States, December 1982), p. 3, Table 1. See also, Roy H. Forbes, "Academic Achievement of Historically Lower-Achieving Students during the Seventies," *Phi Delta Kappan* 66 (April 1985): 542-44. The "Sustaining Effects Study" conducted under U.S. Department of Education sponsorship provides additional evidence of compensatory education's benefits. This project collected data from approximately 120,000 students in over 300 elementary schools nationwide for three years beginning with the 1976-77 school year. Findings revealed that, when compared with students in need of such services but not receiving them, Title I participating students showed greater improvement in reading in grades 1, 2, and 3 and in all grades in math. Launor F. Carter, *A Study of Compensatory and Elementary Education: The Sustaining Effects Study.* Final Report (Santa Monica, CA: System Development Corp., 1983). See also Launor F. Carter, "The Sustaining Effects Study of Compensatory Education," *Educational Researcher* 13 (Aug./Sept. 1984): 4–9. For a more general discussion of the 20 year history of Title I, see Virginia R. L. Plunkett, "From Title I to Chapter 1: the Evolution of Compensatory Education," *Phi Delta Kappan* 66 (April 1985): 533–37.

13. Kathleen Adams, *A Changing Federalism: The Condition of the States* (Denver, CO: Education Commission of the States, April 1982).

14. *Serrano v. Priest*, 557 P.2d 929 (Cal. 1976). For a thorough discussion of the legal and political aspects of school finance reform in California, see Richard Elmore and Milbrey W. McLaughlin, *Reform and Retrenchment: The Politics of California School Finance Reform* (Cambridge, MA: Ballinger Pub. Co., 1982).

15. Since the early 1970s, at least 27 of the 50 states have passed school

finance reform laws. Fourteen of these were involved in litigation prior to final enactment of reform measures. Reform states include Arizona, California, Colorado, Florida, Illinois, Indiana, Iowa, Kansas, Maine, Maryland, Michigan, Minnesota, Missouri, Montana, New Jersey, New Mexico, North Dakota, Ohio, Oklahoma, South Carolina, Tennessee, Texas, Utah, Virginia, Washington, and Wisconsin. Allan Odden, "School Finance Reform: Redistributive Education Policy at the State Level," in *New Directions in the Federal-State Partnership in Education,* eds. Joel D. Sherman, Mark A. Kutner and Kimberley J. Small (Wash., D.C.: Institute for Educational Leadership, 1982).

16. National Education Association, Reseach Estimates of School Statistics Data File.

17. Ibid.

18. See James Catterall and Timothy Thresher, *Proposition 13: The Campaign, the Vote, and the Immediate Aftereffects for California Schools* (Palo Alto, CA: Stanford University, Institute for Research on Education Finance and Governance, March 1979).

19. See Rosemary C. Salomone, "Primary and Secondary Education and the Poor," in *The State and the Poor in the 1980s,* eds. Mary Jo Bane and Manuel Carballo (Boston: Auburn House Publishers, 1984), pp.90–94.

20. As noted by Michael Kirst, evidence of changing politics was the unwillingness of legislators and taxpayers to increase school aid to match inflation. The result of these changes has been described as "steady-state funding for education." Michael W. Kirst, "A New School Finance for a New Era of Fiscal Constraint," in *School Finance and School Improvement: Linkages for the 1980s,* eds. Allan W. Odden and Dean L. Webb (Cambridge, MA: Ballinger Pub. Co., 1983).

21. National Association of State Budget Officers and National Governors' Association, *Fiscal Survey of the States* (Wash., D.C., February 1985).

22. *Education Daily,* Mar. 7, 1986, p.1.

23. Paul E. Peterson and Barry G. Rabe, "The Role of Interest Groups in the Formation of Educational Policy: Past Practice and Future Trends," *Teachers College Record* 84 (Spring 1983): 723.

24. Most education programs are forward funded so the budget for fiscal year 1982, which would begin on October 1, 1981, contained funds to be expended during the 1982–83 school year.

25. 20 U.S.C. §3811 (Supp. 1984). Most of these categorical grant programs for elementary and secondary education were formerly authorized under Titles II-IX of ESEA. Others included the Alcohol and Drug Abuse Education Act, Part A and §532 of Title V of the Higher Education Act of 1965, the Follow-Through Act (on a phased-in basis), the National Science Foundation Act as it relates to precollege science teacher training, and the Career Education Incentive Act.

26. See Linda Darling-Hammond and Ellen L. Marks, *The New Federalism in Education* (Santa Monica, CA: the Rand Corp., February 1983). Based on a 1982 study of 9 states preparing to assume new responsibilities under ECIA, the researchers concluded that states would not abandon previously inefficient and cumbersome methods of service delivery without clear guidance from the federal government as to compliance standards. They recommended that program requirements be clearly specified and that federal, state, and local functions be more clearly sorted out.

27. Harold Wolman, "The Effects of Block Grants: Lessons from Experience," in *New Directions in the Federal-State Partnership,* eds. Joel D. Sherman, Mark A. Kutner, and Kimberly J. Small (Wash., D.C.: Institute for Educational Leadership, 1982), p.141.

28. For a discussion of the shift in public and private school allocations in Massachusetts under Chapter 2, see Salomone, "Primary and Secondary Education and the Poor," p.104. Of the formerly categorical programs merged into Chapter 2, only ESEA Title IV-B provided substantial funds on an entitlement basis to the private schools prior to consolidation. The Title IV-B program provided for library resources and counseling services.

29. David R. Mandel, "ECIA Chapter 2: Education's First Taste of the New Federalism," *Education and Urban Society* 16 (November 1983): 40.

30. American Association of School Administrators, *Private School Participation in Chapter 2* (Arlington, VA, April 1984).

31. National Committee for Citizens in Education, *Anything Goes: An Analysis of the Education Department's Monitoring of Chapter 2 in 21 States* (Columbia, MD, April 1985).

32. Initially, public school officials nationwide feared that funds drawn to a district on the basis of its high-cost public school population would be allocated to private schools that have no-high cost population. Regulations issued by the Department of Education provide for the equitable participation of public and private school students. However, in determining whether expenditures are equal, a school district "may not take into account the extent to which children in private schools generated a portion of the LEA's allocation under Section 298.8(b)" (relating to high cost children). Nevertheless, the AASA study found that many of the 34 districts surveyed did not share any of their high-cost allocations with private schools. A subsequent study conducted by the U.S. Department of Education found that among the 49 districts surveyed, 16 reported a failure to share such funds with the private schools. U.S. Department of Education, *Setting the Record Straight: What ED Knows about Private School Participation under ECIA Chapter 2* (Wash., D.C.: Planning and Evaluation Service, Office of Planning, Budget and Evaluation, 1984). These figures indicate that, contrary to the concerns of public school advocates, private school students may actually be receiving less than their due and not more under Chapter 2.

33. National Committee for Citizens in Education, *No Strings Attached: An Interim Report on the New Education Block Grants* (Columbia, MD, 1983), pp. 14–16.

34. House Committee on Government Operations, Conference Report No. 98-574 on P.L. 98-211, Education Consolidation and Improvement Act of 1981 Technical Amendments (November 18, 1983), p.15.

35. Letter from the Council of the Great City Schools and the Lawyer's Committee for Civil Rights Under Law to Secretary of Education Terrel Bell, January 4, 1984.

36. *Education Daily,* Mar. 20, 1984, p.1.

37. *Federal Register,* vol. 49, p. 28,213 (1984) (proposed July 10, 1984).

38. Michael D. Casserly, *City School Desegregation and Block Grant Legislation* (Wash., D.C.: The Council of the Great City Schools, September 1982).

39. *Education Times,* Feb. 1, 1982, p.6.

40. Casserly, *City School Desegregation,* p.5.

41. *Education Daily,* Apr. 27, 1983, p.3.

42. American Association of School Administrators, *The Impact of Chapter 2 on the Education Consolidation and Improvement Act on Local Education Agencies* (Arlington, VA, 1983).

43. *Education Week,* Feb. 16, 1983, p.10.

44. P.L. 98-377, Title VII of the Education for Economic Recovery Act, 98th Cong., 2d Sess. (1984).

45. 20 U.S.C. §1866 (Supp. 1984). The original WEEA legislation was drafted by a coalition of women's groups working under the aegis of the Women's Equity Action League (WEAL). The bill was introduced in Congress by Representative Patsy Mink (D, HI). and Senator Walter Mondale (D., MN). Despite Office of Education opposition, WEEA was enacted into law as part of the Special Projects Act of 1974.

46. 42 U.S.C. §§2000C-2-4 (Supp. 1984).

47. P.L. 98-511, Title V of the Education Amendments of 1984, 98th Cong., 2d Sess. (1984).

48. See National Advisory Council on Women's Educational Programs, *Evaluation of the Women's Educational Equity Act Program* (Wash., D.C., 1980).

49. U.S. Commission on Civil Rights, *Statement on the Fiscal Year 1983 Education Budget* (Wash., D.C.: U.S. Government Printing Office, October 1982), p.8; *School Finance News,* Nov. 3, 1983, p.3.

50. See Henry M. Levin, "Uniformity and Diversity: Democratic Ideals of Schooling," *IFG Policy Perspectives* (Palo Alto, CA: Stanford University, Institute for Research on Education Finance and Governance, Winter 1982).

51. For a discussion of the current church-state question, see Rosemary C. Salomone, *Church, State, and Education: A Preliminary Analysis of Legislative and Judicial Policymaking.* Final report to the National Institute of Education, Law and Government Program, January 1985.

52. James S. Catterall, "Politics and Aid to Private Schools," *Educational Evaluation and Policy Analysis* 6 (1984): 435. According to data extrapolated from National Center for Education Statistics (NCES) figures, a total of 5.95 million children will be attending private schools by 1990. While enrollment in Catholic schools declined by six percent from 1980 to 1983, the number of children attending either non-Catholic religious schools or non-religiously affiliated private schools increased by 40 percent. Bruce S. Cooper, Donald McLaughlin, and Bruno V. Manno, "The Latest Word on Private School Growth," *Teachers College Record* 85 (Fall 1983): 94.

53. Catterall, p.436.

54. U.S. Department of Education, Advisory Panel on Financing Elementary and Secondary Education, *Toward More Local Control: Financial Reform for Public Education* (Wash., D.C., February 1982).

55. *Tuition Tax Credits: Hearings on S. 528 Before the Senate Committee on Finance,* 98th Cong., 1st Sess. (1983).

56. Senator Moynihan had cosponsored similar legislation in previous years with Rep. Robert Packwood (R., OR). In fact, the Moynihan-Packwood proposals introduced in 1977 and 1978 helped frame the current debate over tuition tax credits. The 1977 proposal had 50 co-sponsors in the Senate, 26 Republicans and 24 Democrats covering the broad political spectrum from Senator George

McGovern (D., SD) to Senator Barry Goldwater (R., AZ). See Daniel Patrick Moynihan, "Government and the Ruin of Private Education," *Harper's* (April 1978): 28–38. Moynihan initially opposed the Reagan proposal on the grounds that it failed to provide a refundable credit for those with no tax libability and it did not include adequate assurances that private institutions would comply with civil rights mandates. Those two provisions were later added in floor amendments.

57. Joel D. Sherman et al., *Congressionally Mandated Study on School Finance: A Final Report to Congress, vol. 2, Private Elementary and Secondary Education* (Wash., D.C.: U.S. Department of Education, School Finance Project, July 1983), p.64.

58. *New York Times,* June 30, 1983, p.A1.

59. John Augenblick and C. Kent McGuire, *Tuition Tax Credits: Their Impact on the States* (Denver, CO: Education Commission of the States, October 1982), p.24.

60. James Catterall and Henry M. Levin, *Public and Private Schools: Evidence of Tuition Tax Credits* (Palo Alto, CA: Stanford University, Institute for Research on Educational Finance and Governance, February 1982), pp.11–15. The authors suggest that the most obvious way to circumvent the "no tax liability" problem is to provide a "refundable" credit, that is, one that would refund any eligible amount above the limited tax liability of the poor. See Thomas James and Henry M. Levin, *Public Dollars for Private Schools: The Case of Tuition Tax Credits* (Philadelphia: Temple University Press, 1983).

61. See Paul J. Weber, "Building on Sand: Supreme Court Construction and Educational Tax Credits," *Creighton Law Review,* 12 (1978): 531–65; Howard O. Hunter, "The Continuing Debate over Tuition Tax Credits," *Hastings Constitutional Law Quarterly,* 7 (1980): 523–78.

62. See Rosemary C. Salomone, "Equality, Liberty, and Community: Religion, Educational Policy, and the Burger Court." Paper presented at the Annual Meeting of the American Educational Research Association, Chicago, April 1985.

63. 463 U.S. 388 (1983). The Court's decision also shifted lobbying efforts from the federal to the state level. An informal 1984 survey of 50 states indicated that one-third of the state legislatures had taken up the battle for tuition tax credits and deductions. *Education Week,* Mar. 7, 1984, p.1.

64. 463 U.S. 582, 405 (Marshall, J., dissenting). This three-part test, originally enunciated by the Supreme Court in *Lemon v. Kurtzman,* 403 U.S. 602 (1971), was seemingly eroded by the Court in *Mueller.* However, the Court demonstrated the continued vitality of the test in the government funding context in two 6-3 opinions of the 1984-85 term: *Grand Rapids School Dist. v. Ball,* 105 S.Ct. 3216 (1985) (striking down a Michigan shared-time program in non-public schools) and *Aguilar v. Felton,* 105 S.Ct. 3232 (1985) (striking down New York City's use of Chapter 1 remedial funds to pay salaries of public school teachers who teach secular subjects in religiously affiliated schools).

65. For a discussion of empowerment in the context of the welfare state, see Peter L. Berger and Richard John Neuhaus, *To Empower People: The Role of Mediating Structures in Public Policy* (Wash., D.C.: American Enterprise Institute, 1977). The authors attempt to divest themselves of political ideological baggage and develop a theory that would expand government services without producing government oppressiveness. They advance a paradigm of *mediating*

structures, that is, structures that stand between the individual and the state—neighborhood, family, church, and voluntary association. They argue that if government utilized these to carry out some of its functions, then those at the lower rungs of the economic ladder could exercise greater control over their lives.

66. See Milton Friedman, *Capitalism and Freedom* (Chicago: University of Chicago Press, 1962).

67. See John E. Coons and Stephen D. Sugarman, *Education by Choice: The Case of Family Control* (Berkeley: Universuty of California Press, 1978). Coons and Sugarman have worked tirelessly but unsuccessfully to gather the necessary signatures to put their California Initiative for Family Choice before the voters of that state. For a general discussion of vouchers, see Henry M. Levin, *Educational Vouchers and Social Policy* (Stanford, CA: Stanford University, Institute for Educational Finance and Governance, 1979); Laura Hersh Salganik, *The Rise and Fall of Education Vouchers* (Baltimore, MD: Johns Hopkins University, Center for Social Organization of Schools, March 1980).

68. See Christopher C. Jencks, *Education Vouchers: A Report on Financing Elementary Education by Grants to Parents* (Cambridge, MA: Center for the Study of Public Policy, 1970).

69. Gary R. Bridge and Julie Blackman, *A Study of Alternatives in American Education, vol. IV: Family Choice in Schooling* (Santa Monica, CA: The Rand Corp., 1978).

70. Michael A. Olivas, "Information Access Inequities: A Fatal Flaw in Education Voucher Plans," *Journal of Law and Education* 10 (1981): 441–65.

71. For a discussion of the use of education vouchers to provide special education services in New York State, see Michael Rebell, "Educational Voucher Reform: Empirical Insights from the Experience of New York's Schools for the Handicapped," *Urban Lawyer,* 14 (1982): 441–67.

72. *Church and State,* June 1983, pp.6–8.

73. *Education Week,* June 5, 1985, p.1.

74. *Education Week,* May 8, 1985, p.1.

75. One approach that has been suggested is a statewide public school voucher system financed completely with state revenues. See Denis P. Doyle and Chester E. Finn, Jr., "American Schools and the Future of Local Control," *The Public Interest,* 77 (Fall 1984): 77–95. Under such a plan, public education funds would attach to individual students and not to institutions. The authors maintain that a voucher system of this nature has the potential to meet several important objectives—achieve school finance reform so that the quality of a child's education is not a function of family or community wealth, facilitate the establishment and enforcement of statewide quality standards, provide true educational choice for all children, and reinvigorate the principle of "local control" at the level of the individual school where research shows it to have the greatest significance. For a more theoretical discussion of the philosophy underlying this alternative, see Denis P. Doyle, *Beyond Instrumentalism: The Value of Education Choice and Education Choice as Value.* Education Policy Studies Occasional Papers, ESP 83, No. 2 (Wash., D.C.: American Enterprise Institute, March 1983). Here the author advances a compelling argument for choice and diversity based on moral and not just instrumental justifications. He argues that good education is rooted in values and must therefore be as diverse as its clients rather than provided by the bureaucratic assembly line of the present system.

Chapter VII

1. Vincent Blasi, "The Rootless Activism of the Burger Court," in *The Burger Court: The Counterrevolution That Wasn't*, ed. Vincent Blasi (New Haven: Yale University Press, 1983), p. 198.

2. *Martin Shapiro, "Fathers and Sons: The Court, the Commentators, and the Search for Values," in The Burger Court*, ed. Blasi, p.218.

3. Paul E. Peterson and Barry G. Rabe, "The Role of Interest Groups in the Formation of Educational Policy: Past Practice and Future Trends," *Teachers College Record* 84 (Spring 1983): 717.

4. For a discussion of the public's misperceptions of the Burger Court, see Paul J. Mishkin, "Equality," *Law and Contemporary Problems* 43 (1980): 51–65; Jesse H. Chopter, "The Burger Court: Misperceptions Regarding Judicial Restraint and Insensitivity to Individual Rights," *Syracuse Law Review* 30 (1979): 767–87; Stephen L. Wasby, *Continuity and Change: From the Warren Court to the Burger Court* (Pacific Palisades, CA: Goodyear Publishing Co., 1976).

5. See Abram Chayes, "The Role of the Judge in Public Law Litigation," *Harvard Law Review* 89 (1976): 1284–1316.

6. Nathan Glazer, "Towards an Imperial Judiciary?," *The Public Interest* 41 (1975): 104–23.

7. Russell W. Rumberger, "Dropping Out of High School: The Influence of Race, Sex, and Family Background" *American Educational Research Journal* 20 (Summer 1983): 199–220. For a general discussion of the economic and social consequences of ignoring the needs of the disadvantaged, see Henry M. Levin, *The Educationally Disadvantaged: A National Crisis*. Stanford, CA: Stanford University, Institute for Education Finance and Governance, July 1985.

8. National Center for Education Statistics, *The Condition of Education, 1984* (Wash., D.C.: U.S. Government Printing Office, 1984):52.

9. *Ibid.*, p. 54–56.

10. *Ibid.*, p. 16.

Bibliography

Books

Abraham, Henry J. *Freedom and the Court,* 3rd ed. New York: Oxford University Press, 1977.

Alatis, James and Kristie Twaddell, eds. *English as a Second Language in Bilingual Education.* Wash., D.C.: Teachers of English to Speakers of Other Languages, 1976.

Aristotle. *Politics,* trans. Benjamin Jowett. Oxford: Clarendon Press, 1921.

———. *The Nichomachean Ethics,* trans. W.D. Ross. New York: Oxford University Press, 1925.

Bailey, Stephan K. and Edith Mosher. *ESEA: The Office of Education Administers a Law.* Syracuse: Syracuse University Press, 1968.

Ballard, Joseph, Bruce A. Ramirez, and Frederick J. Weintraub. *Special Education in America: Its Legal and Governmental Foundations.* Wash., D.C.: Council for Exceptional Children, 1983.

Bane, Mary Jo and Manuel Carballo, eds. *The State and the Poor in the 1980s.* Boston: Auburn House Publishers, 1984.

Bell, Daniel. *The Coming of Post-Industrial Society.* New York: Basic Books, 1973.

Berger, Margaret A. *Litigation on Behalf of Women.* New York: The Ford Foundation, 1980.

Berger, Peter L. and Richard John Neuhaus. *To Empower People: The Role of Mediating Structures in Public Policy.* Wash., D.C.: American Enterprise Institute, 1977.

Berger, Raoul. *Government by Judiciary.* Cambridge, MA: Harvard University Press, 1977.

Bhatnagar, Joti. *Educating Immigrants.* New York: St. Martin's Press, 1981.

Blackstone, William T. and Robert D. Helsep, eds. *Social Justice and Preferential Treatment.* Athens: University of Georgia Press, 1977.

Blasi, Vincent, ed. *The Burger Court: The Counterrevolution that Wasn't.* New Haven: Yale University Press, 1983.

Brandt, R.B., ed. *Social Justice.* Englewood Cliffs, NJ: Prentice-Hall, 1962.

Boyd, William, ed. *The Emile of Jean Jacques Rousseau.* New York: Teachers College Press, 1960.

Boyer, Ernest L. *High School.* New York: Harper & Row, 1983.

Brookover, Wilbur B. et al. *School Systems and Student Achievement.* New York: Praeger, 1979.

Campbell, Nancy Duff, Marcia D. Greenberger, Margaret A. Kohn, and Shirley J. Wilcher. *Sex Discrimination in Education,* 2 vols. Wash., D.C.: National Women's Law Center, 1983.

Cigler, Allan J. and Burdett A. Loomis, eds. *Interest Group Politics*. Wash., D.C.: Congressional Quarterly, Inc., 1981.

Cohen, Andrew D. *A Sociolinguistic Approach to Bilingual Education*. Rowley, MA: Newbury House Publishers, 1975.

Coons, John E. and Stephen D. Sugarman. *Education by Choice: The Case of Family Control*. Berkeley: University of California Press, 1978.

Eastland, Terry and William J. Bennett. *Counting by Race*. New York: Basic Books, 1979.

Edwards, Paul, ed. *The Encyclopedia of Philosophy*. New York: Collier Macmillan, 1972.

Elmore, Richard and Milbrey W. McLaughlin. *Reform and Retrenchment: The Politics of California School Finance Reform*. Cambridge, MA: Ballinger Pub. Co., 1982.

Epstein, Noel. *Language, Ethnicity, and the Schools: Policy Alternatives for Bilingual-Bicultural Education*, Wash., D.C.: Institute for Educational Leadership, August 1977.

Fischel, Andrew and Janice Pottker. *National Politics and Sex Discrimination in Education*. Lexington, MA: Lexington Books, 1977.

Fishman, Joshua A. *Language Loyalty in the United States*. The Hague: Mouton & Co., 1966.

Freeman, Jo. *The Politics of Women's Liberation*. New York: David McKay, 1975.

Friedman, Milton. *Capitalism and Freedom*. Chicago: University of Chicago Press, 1962.

Gardner, John. *Excellence: Can We Be Equal and Excellent Too?* New York: Harper & Row, 1961.

Glazer, Nathan. *Ethnic Dilemmas*. New York: Basic Books, 1983.

Goldstein, Leslie Friedman. *The Constitutional Rights of Women: Cases in Law and Social Change*. New York: Longman, 1979.

Goodlad, John I. *A Place Called School: Prospects for the Future*. New York: McGraw-Hill, 1983.

Graglia, Lino A. *Disaster by Decree: The Supreme Court Decisions on Race and the Schools*. Ithaca, NY: Cornell University Press, 1976.

Graham, Hugh Davis. *The Uncertain Triumph: The Kennedy and Johnson Years*. Chapel Hill: University of North Carolina Press, 1984.

Greene, Maxine. *Landscapes of Learning*. New York: Teachers College Press, 1978.

Gutman, Amy. *Liberal Equality*. Cambridge: Cambridge University Press, 1980.

Hawley, Willis D., ed. *Effective School Desegregation: Equity, Quality, and Feasibility*. Beverly Hills, CA: Sage Publications, 1981.

Helsep, Robert D. *Proceedings of the 27th Annual Meeting of the Philosophy of Education Society*. Edwardsville, IL: Southern Illinois University Press, 1971.

Humphrey, Hubert H., ed. *School Desegregation: Documents and Commentaries*. New York: Thomas Y. Crowell, 1964.

Jaeger, Werner. *Paideia: The Ideals of Greek Culture*, 2nd ed. New York: Oxford University Press, 1945.

James, Thomas and Henry M. Levin. *Public Dollars for Private Schools: The Case of Tuition Tax Credits*. Philadelphia: Temple University Press, 1983.

Jencks, Christopher et al. *Inequality: A Reassessment of the Effects of Family and Schooling in America.* New York: Basic Books, 1972.

Jones, Augustus J. *Law, Bureaucracy and Politics: The Implementation of Title VI of the Civil Rights Act of 1964. Wash., D.C.: University Press of America,* 1982.

Keppel, Francis. *The Necessary Revolution.* New York: Harper & Row, 1966.

Kluger, Richard. *Simple Justice.* New York: Vintage Books, 1977.

Lakoff, Stanley. *Equality in Political Philosophy.* Cambridge, MA: Harvard University Press, 1964.

Lambert, Wallace E. and G. Richard Tucker. *Bilingual Education of Children: The St. Lambert Experiment.* Rowley, MA: Newbury House Publishers, 1972.

Levin, Betsy and Willis D. Hawley eds. *The Courts, Social Science, and the Judicial Process.* New York: Teachers College Press, 1977.

Levine, Donald M. and Mary Jo Bane, eds. *The Inequality Controversy: Schooling and Distributive Justice,* New York: Basic Books, 1975.

McDowell, Gary L. *Equity and the Constitution.* Chicago: University of Chicago Press, 1982.

McGuire, C. Kent. *State and Federal Programs for Special Student Populations.* Denver CO: Education Commission of the States, April 1982.

Madaus, George. *The Courts, Validity and Competency Testing.* Boston: Kluwer-Nijhoff Pub. Co., 1983.

Muse, Benjamin. *Years of Prelude.* New York: Viking Press, 1964.

Myrdal, Gunnar. *An American Dilemma,* vol. I. New York: Pantheon Books, 1944.

Nozick, Robert. *Anarchy, State, and Utopia.* New York: Basic Books, 1974.

O'Connor, Karen, *Women's Organizations' Use of the Courts.* Lexington, MA: Lexington Books, 1980.

Odden, Allan W. and Dean L. Webb, eds. *School Finance and School Improvement: Linkages for the 1980s.* Cambridge, MA: Ballinger Pub. Co., 1983.

Orfield, Gary. *The Reconstruction of Southern Education.* New York: Wiley-Interscience, 1969.

———. *Must We Bus?: Segregated Schools and National Policy.* Wash., D.C.: The Brookings Institution, 1978.

———. ed. *Symposium on School Desegregation and White Flight.* Wash., D.C.: Center for National Policy Review, August 1975.

Padilla, Raymond V., ed. *Theory, Technology and Public Policy in Bilingual Education.* Rosslyn, VA: National Clearinghouse for Bilingual Education, 1983.

Palley, Marian Lief and Michael B. Preston, eds. *Race, Sex and Policy Problems.* Lexington, MA: Lexington Books, 1979.

Peltason, Jack W. *Fifty-eight Lonely Men: Southern Federal Judges and School Desegregation.* Urbana: University of Illinois Press, 1971.

Pennock, J. Roland and J.W. Chapman, eds. *IX Nomos: Equality.* New York: Atherton Press, 1967.

Pole, J.R. *The Pursuit of Equality in American History.* Berkeley: University of California Press, 1978.

Raffel, Jeffrey A. *The Politics of School Desegregation: The Metropolitan Remedy in Delaware.* Philadelphia: Temple University Press, 1980.

Ravitch, Diane. *The Troubled Crusade*. New York: Basic Books, 1983.

Rawls, John. *A Theory of Justice*. Cambridge, MA: Harvard University Press, 1971.

Reutter, E. Edmund. *The Supreme Court's Impact on Public Education*. Topeka, KA: Phi Delta Kappa and National Organization on Legal Problems of Education, 1982.

Reynolds, Marnard, ed. *Futures in Education for Exceptional Students*. Reston, VA: Council for Exceptional Children, 1978.

Rutter, Michael et al. *Fifteen Thousand Hours*. London: Open Books, 1979.

Sachs, Albie and Joan Hoff Wilson. *Sexism and the Law*. New York: The Free Press, 1979.

Salomone, Rosemary C. *An Analysis of the Effects of Language Acquisition Context*. New York: Arno Press, 1978.

Schneider, Susan G. *Revolution, Reaction or Reform*. New York: Las Americas, 1977.

Sheingold, Stuart A. *The Politics of Rights*. New Haven: Yale University Press, 1974.

Sherman, Joel D., Mark A. Kutner, and Kimberly J. Small, eds. *New Directions in the Federal-State Partnership in Education*. Wash., D.C.: Institute for Educational Leadership, 1982.

Spolsky, Bernard. *Educational Linguistics*. Rowley, MA: Newbury House Publishers, 1978.

St. John, Nancy. *School Desegregation: Outcomes for Children*. New York: Wiley-Interscience, 1975.

Stephan, Walter and Joe Feagin, eds. *School Desegregation: Past, Present, and Future*. New York: Plenum Press, 1980.

Swain, Merrill and Sharon Lapkin. *Bilingual Education in Ontario: A Decade of Research*. Toronto: The Minister of Education, Ontario, 1981.

Tawney, R.H. *Equality*, 4th ed. London: Allen and Unwin, 1964.

Timpane, Michael, ed. *The Federal Interest in Schooling*. Cambridge, MA: Ballinger Pub. Co., 1979.

Tocqueville, Alexis de. *Democracy in America*, vol. II, ed. Phillips Bradley. New York: Vintage Books, 1945.

Tribe, Laurence H. *American Constitutional Law*. Mineola, NY: The Foundation Press, 1978.

Viteritti, Joseph P. *Across the River: Politics and Education in the City*. New York: Holmes & Meier, 1983.

Walzer, Michael. *Spheres of Justice*. New York: Basic Books, 1983.

Wasby, Stephen L. *Continuity and Change: From the Warren Court to the Burger Court*. Pacific Palisades, CA: Goodyear Pub. Co., 1976.

———, ed. *American Government and Politics*. New York: Charles Scribner's Sons, 1973.

Wasby, Stephen L., Anthony A. D'Amato, and Rosemary Metrailler. *Desegregation from Brown to Alexander*. Carbondale: Southern Illinois University Press, 1977.

Weatherly, Richard. *Reforming Special Education: Policy Implementation from State Level to Street Level*. Cambridge, MA: MIT Press, 1979.

Wexler, Elizabeth M. *P. L. 94–142: An Act of Congress*. New York: MacMillan Pub. Co., 1981.

Wilkinson, J. Harvie III. *From Brown to Bakke.* New York: Oxford University Press, 1979.

Yarmolinsky, Adam et al., eds. *Race and Schooling in the City.* Cambridge, MA: Harvard University Press, 1981.

Reports

Adams, Kathleen. *A Changing Federalism: The Condition of the States.* Denver, CO: Education Commission of the States, April 1982.

Advisory Commission on Intergovernmental Relations. *Intergovernmentalizing the Classroom: The Federal Involvement in Elementary and Secondary Education.* Wash., D.C: U.S. Government Printing Office, 1981.

American Association of School Administrators. *The Impact of Chapter 2 of the Education Consolidation and Improvement Act on Local Education Agencies.* Arlington, VA, 1983.

————. *Private School Participation in Chapter 2.* Arlington, VA, April 1984.

American Institutes for Research. *Interim Report of the Impact of ESEA Title VII Spanish/English Bilingual Education Programs.* Palo Alto, CA, February 1977.

Augenblick, John and C. Kent McGuire. *Tuition Tax Credits: Their Impact on the States.* Denver, CO: Education Commission of the States, October 1982.

Baker, Keith and Adriana de Kanter. *Effectiveness of Bilingual Education: A Review of the Literature,* unpublished report. Wash., D.C.: U.S. Department of Education, September 1981.

Blank, Rols K., Robert A. Dentler, Catherine Baltzell, and Kent Chabotar. *Survey of Magnet Schools: Analyzing a Model for Quality Integrated Education.* Cambridge, MA: Lowry Associates, September 1983.

Bridge, Gary K. and Julie Blackman. *A Study of Alternatives in American Education, vol. IV: Family Choice in Schooling.* Santa Monica, CA: The Rand Corp., 1978.

Butler, Stuart M., W. Bruce Weinrod, and Michael Sanera, eds. *Mandate for Leadership: Policy Management in a Conservative Administration.* Wash., D.C.: Heritage Foundation, 1981.

California State Department of Education. *Studies of Immersion Education.* Sacramento, CA., 1984.

Carter, Launor F. *A Study of Compensatory and Elementary Education: The Sustaining Effects Study,* final report. Santa Monica, CA: System Development Corp., 1983.

Casserly, Michael D. *City School Desegregation and Block Grant Legislation.* Wash., D.C.: The Council of the Great City Schools, September 1982.

Catterall, James and Timothy Thresher. *Proposition 13: The Campaign, the Vote, and the Immediate Aftereffects for California Schools.* Palo Alto, CA: Stanford University, Institute for Research on Education Finance and Governance, March 1979.

Catterall, James and Henry M. Levin. *Public and Private Schools: Evidence of Tuition Tax Credits.* Palo Alto, CA: Stanford University, Institute for Research on Education Finance and Governance, February 1982.

Cazden, Courtney. *Effective Instructional Practices in Bilingual Education,* draft report. Wash., D.C.: National Institute of Education, January 1984.

Citizens Committee on Civil Rights. *There is No Liberty . . . A Report on Congressional Efforts to Curb the Federal Courts and to Undermine the Brown Decision.* Wash., D.C., October 1982.

Citizens Council on Women's Education. *Catching Up: A Review of the Women's Educational Equity Act Program.* Wash., D.C., March 1984.

Citron, Christiane. *The Rights of Handicapped Students.* Denver, CO: Education Commission of the States, 1982.

Coleman, James S. et al. *Equality of Educational Opportunity.* Wash., D.C.: U.S. Government Printing Office, 1966.

Coleman, James et al. *Trends in School Segregation 1968-73.* Wash., D.C.: Urban Institute, August 1975.

Congressional Research Service. *Impact of Budget Cuts on Major Education Programs during the Reagan Administration.* CRS Report No. 84-EPW. Wash., D.C., August 1984.

Council of the Great City Schools. *Analysis of the Effect of the FY82 and FY83 Reagan Budget Proposals on Urban Schools.* Wash., D.C., 1982.

Crain, Robert L. and Rita E. Mahard. *Desegregation Plans that Raise Black Achievement: A Review of the Research.* Santa Monica, CA: The Rand Corp., June 1982.

Cummins, Jim. *Interdependence and Bicultural Ambivalence: Regarding the Pedagogical Rationale for Bilingual Education.* Rosslyn, VA: National Clearinghouse for Bilingual Education, 1982.

Darling-Hammond, Linda and Ellen L. Marks. *The New Federalism in Education.* Santa Monica, CA: The Rand Corp., February 1983.

Doyle, Denis P. *Beyond Instrumentalism: The Value of Education Choice and Education Choice as Value.* Educational Policy Studies Occasional Papers, ESP 83, No. 2. Wash., D.C.: American Enterprise Institute, March 1983.

East, Catherine. *Chronology of the Women's Movement in the U.S. 1961-75.* Wash., D.C.: National Commission on the Observation of International Women's Year, 1975.

Ebring, Lutz. *High School and Beyond Summary Report: An Overview of Outcomes in Secondary Education,* mimeographed report. Wash., D.C.: National Opinion Research Center, 1980.

Education Commission of the States Task Force on Education for Economic Growth. *Action for Excellence.* Denver, CO: Education Commission of the States, 1983.

Educational Priorities Panel. *Special Education Funding: A Story of Broken Promises.* New York, February 1981.

Far West Development Educational Laboratory. *Significant Bilingual Instructional Features (SBIF).* San Francisco, 1981.

Farley, Reynolds and Clarence Wordock. *Can Government Policies Integrate Schools?* Ann Arbor, MI: Population Studies Center, 1977.

Gardner, Eileen M., ed. *A New Agenda for Education.* Wash., D.C.: The Heritage Foundation, 1985.

Gray, Tracy C. *Response to the AIR Study, Evaluation of the Impact of ESEA Title VII Spanish/English Bilingual Education Programs,* memorandum. Wash., D.C.: Center for Applied Linguistics, April 18, 1977.

Hargrove, Edwin C. et al. *Regulations and Schools: The Implementation of Equal Education for Handicapped Children.* Nashville: Vanderbilt University, Institute of Policy Studies, March 1981.

Hill, Paul T. and Doren L. Madey. *Educational Policymaking through the Civil Justice System.* Santa Monica, CA: The Rand Corp., Institute for Civil Justice, 1982.

Jencks, Christopher C. *Education Vouchers: A Report on Financing Elementary Education by Grants to Parents.* Cambridge, MA: Center for the Study of Public Policy, 1970.

Levin, Henry M. *Educational Vouchers and Social Policy.* Stanford, CA: Stanford University, Institute for Education Finance and Governance, 1979.

――――. *The Educationally Disadvantaged: A National Crisis.* Stanford, CA: Stanford University, Institute for Education Finance and Governance, July 1985.

National Advisory Council on Women's Educational Programs. *Title IX: The Half Full, Half Empty Glass.* Wash., D.C., 1979

――――. *Evaluation of the Women's Equity Act Program.* Wash., D.C., 1980.

National Assessment of Educational Progress. *Reading, Science and Mathematics Trends: A Closer Look.* Denver, CO: Education Commission of the States, December 1982.

National Association of State Budget Officers and National Governors' Association, *Fiscal Survey of the States.* Wash., D.C., February 1985.

National Center for Education Statistics. *The Condition of Education, 1984.* Wash., D.C.: U.S. Government Printing Office, 1984.

National Clearinghouse for Bilingual Education, *State-Funded Bilingual Education Programs.* Rosslyn, VA, 1983.

National Commission on Excellence in Education, *A Nation at Risk.* Wash., D.C.: U.S. Government Printing Office, 1983.

National Commission on Secondary Education for Hispanics. *Make Something Happen: Hispanics and High School Reform,* 2 vols. Wash., D.C.: Hispanic Policy Development Project, 1984.

National Committee for Citizens in Education. *No Strings Attached: An Interim Report on the New Education Block Grants.* Columbia, MD, 1983.

――――. *Anything Goes: An Analysis of the Education Department's Monitoring of Chapter 2 in 21 States.* Columbia, MD, April 1985.

National Institute of Education. *State Legal Standards for the Provision of Public Education.* Wash., D.C.: U.S. Government Printing Office, November 1978.

National School Boards Association, Council of Urban Boards of Education. *The Impact of Reductions in Federal Education Expenditures.* Alexandria, VA, 1984.

Project on Equal Education Rights, NOW Legal Defense and Education Fund. *Stalled at the Start: Government Action on Sex Bias in the Schools.* Wash., D.C., 1978.

――――. *Silver Snail Awards: PEER's Analysis of Females in Public Education.* Wash., D.C., February 1982.

――――. *Injustice Under the Law: The Impact of the Grove City College Decision on Civil Rights.* Wash., D.C., February 1985.

Royster, Eugene, Catherine Baltzell, and Fran Simmons. *Study of the Emergency School Aid Act Magnet Schools Programs.* Cambridge, MA: Abt Associates, 1979.

Salganik, Laura Hersh. *The Rise and Fall of Education Vouchers.* Baltimore, MD: Johns Hopkins University, Center for Social Organization of Schools, March 1980.

Salomone, Rosemary C. *Church, State, and Education: A Preliminary Analysis of Legislative and Judicial Policymaking.* Final report to the National Institute of Education, Law and Government Program, January 1985.

Sherman, Joel D. et al. *Congressionally Mandated Study on School Finance: A Final Report to Congress, vol. 2, Private Elementary and Secondary Education.* Wash., D.C.: U.S. Department of Education, School Finance Project, July 1983.

Thanksgiving Statement Group. *Developing Character: Transmitting Knowledge.* Posen IL: ARL, 1984.

Twentieth Century Fund Task Force on Federal Elementary and Secondary Education Policy. *Making the Grade.* New York: Twentieth Century Fund, 1983.

United States Commission on Civil Rights. *With Liberty and Justice for All.* Wash., D.C.: U.S. Government Printing Office, 1959.

————. *Federal Enforcement of School Desegregation.* Wash., D.C.: U.S. Government Printing Office, 1969.

————. *Public Knowledge and Busing Opposition.* Wash., D.C.: U.S. Government Printing Office, 1973.

————. *More Hurdles to Clear: Women and Girls in Competitive Athletics.* Wash., D.C.: U.S. Government Printing Office, July 1980.

————. *With All Deliberate Speed: 1954–19??.* Wash., D.C.: U.S. Government Printing Office, November 1981.

————. *Statement on the Fiscal Year 1983 Education Budget.* Wash., D.C.: U.S. Government Printing Office, 1982.

United States Department of Education, Advisory Panel on Financing Elementary and Secondary Education. *Toward More Local Control: Financial Reform for Public Education.* Wash., D.C., February 1982.

United States Department of Education. *Setting the Record Straight: What ED knows about Private School Participation under ECIA Chapter 2.* Wash., D.C.: Planning and Evaluation Service, Office of Planning, Budget and Evaluation, 1984.

————. *The Condition of Bilingual Education, 1984.* Wash., D.C.: U.S. Government Printing Office, 1984.

————. *Seventh Annual Report to Congress on the Implementation of Public Law 94-142: The Education for All Handicapped Children Act.* Wash., D.C.: U.S. Government Printing Office, 1985.

————. *The Condition of Bilingual Education in the Nation.* Wash., D.C.: U.S. Government Printing Office, 1976.

————. *Probable Upper Limits on the Number of Handicapped Children in the United States,* draft. Wash., D.C., 1978.

Washington Council of Lawyers, *Reagan Civil Rights: The First Twenty Months.* Wash., D.C., 1982.

Weber, George. *Inner City Children Can Be Taught to Read: Four Successful Schools.* Wash., D.C.: Council for Basic Education, 1971.

Wright, Anne W. *Local Implementation of P.L. 94-142: Second Year Report of a Longitudinal Study.* Menlo Park, CA.: Stanford Research Institute, 1980.

Journal Articles

Bell, Daniel. "On Meritocracy and Equality." *The Public Interest* 29 (Fall 1982): 42–48.

Braddock, Jomills, Robert Crain, and James McPartland. "A Long-Term Look at School Desegregation." *Phi Delta Kappan* 66 (Dec. 1984): 259–64.

Brennan, William. "State Constitutions and the Protection of Individual Rights." *Harvard Law Review* 90 (1977): 489–504.

Burgdorf, Margaret P. and Robert Burgdorf. "A History of Unequal Treatment: The Qualification of Handicapped Persons as a 'Suspect Class' under the Equal Protection Clause." *Santa Clara Law Review* 15 (1975): 855–910.

Carter, Launor F. "The Sustaining Effects Study of Compensatory Education." *Educational Research* 13 (Aug./Sept. 1984): 4–9.

Catterall, James S. "Politics and Aid to Private Schools," *Educational Evaluation and Policy Analysis* 6 (1984): 435–40.

Chayes, Abram. "The Role of the Judge in Public Law Litigation." *Harvard Law Review* 89 (1976): 1281–1316.

———. "The Supreme Court 1981 Term, Foreward: Public Law Litigation and the Burger Court." *Harvard Law Review* 96 (1982): 4–60.

Choper, Jesse H. "The Burger Court: Misperceptions Regarding Judicial Restraint and Insensitivity to Individual Rights." *Syracuse Law Review* 30 (1979): 767–87.

Coleman, James S. "Equal Schools or Equal Students." *The Public Interest* 4 (Summer 1966): 70–75.

———. "The Concept of Equal Educational Opportunities." *Harvard Educational Review* 38 (Winter 1968): 297–310.

———. "Equality of Opportunity and Equality of Results." *Harvard Educational Review* 43 (February 1973): 129–37.

———. "Inequality, Sociology, and Moral Philosophy." *American Journal of Sociology* 80 (November 1974): 739–64.

Cooper, Bruce S., Donald McLaughlin, and Bruno V. Manno. "The Latest Word on Private School Growth." *Teachers College Record* 85 (Fall 1983): 89–98.

Crain, Robert L. and Rita E. Mahard. "Desegregation and Black Achievement: A Review of the Research." *Law and Contemporary Problems* 42 (1978): 17–56.

Dallmayr, Fred R. "Functionalism, Justice, Equality." *Ethics* 78 (October 1978): 1–16.

Days, Drew S. "Turning Back the Clock: The Reagan Administration and Civil Rights." *Harvard Civil Rights—Civil Liberties Law Review* 19 (1984): 309–47.

Doyle, Denis P. and Chester E. Finn, Jr. "American Schools and the Future of Local Control." *The Public Interest* 77 (Fall 1984): 77–95.

Edelman, Marion Wright. "Southern School Desegregation from 1954–1973: A Judicial-Political Overview," in *Blacks and the Law, Annals of the American Academy of Political and Social Science* 407 (May 1973): 32–42.

Edmonds, Ronald. "Effective Schools for the Urban Poor." *Educational Leadership* 37 (1979): 15–24.

Finn, Chester E., Jr. "The Future of Education's Liberal Consensus." *Change* 12 (September 1980): 25—30.

Fiss, Owen. "The Charlotte-Mecklenburg Case—Its Significance for Northern Desegregation." *University of Chicago Law Review* 38 (1971): 697–709.

——. "The Fate of an Idea Whose Time Has Come: Antidiscrimination Law in the Second Decade After *Brown v. Board of Education*." *University of Chicago Law Review* 41 (1974): 742–73.

——. "The Supreme Court 1978 Term, Foreward: The Forms of Justice." *Harvard Law Review* 93 (1979): 1–58.

Forbes, Roy H. "Academic Achievement of Historically Lower-Achieving Students during the Seventies." *Phi Delta Kappan* 66 (April 1985): 542–44.

Frankel, Charles. "Equality of Opportunity." *Ethics* 81 (1970–71): 111–30.

Gellhorn, Walter A. "A Decade of Desegregation—Retrospect and Prospect." *Utah Law Review* 9 (1964): 3–17.

Gittell, Marilyn. "Localizing Democracy Out of the Schools." *Social Policy* 12 (Sept./Oct. 1981): 4–11.

Glazer, Nathan. "Towards an Imperial Judiciary?" *The Public Interest* 41 (1975): 104–23.

Greenawalt, Kent. "How Empty is the Idea of Equality." *Columbia Law Review* 83 (1983): 1167–85.

Gunther, Gerald. "The Supreme Court, 1971 Term, Foreward: In Search of Evolving Doctrine on a Changing Court: A Model of a Newer Equal Protection." *Harvard Law Review* 86 (1972): 1–48.

Howe, Harold II. "Education Moves to Center Stage: An Overview of Recent Studies." *Phi Delta Kappan* 65 (November 1983): 167–72.

Hunter, Howard O. "The Continuing Debate over Tuition Tax Credits." *Hastings Constitutional Law Quarterly* 7 (1980): 523–78.

Kaestle, Karl F. and Marshall S. Smith. "The Federal Role in Elementary and Secondary Education." *Harvard Educational Review* 52 (November 1982): 348–408.

Karst, Kenneth. "Why Equality Matters." *Georgia Law Review* 17 (1983): 245–89.

Keough, Barbara K. and Marc L. Levitt. "Special Education in the Mainstream: A Confrontation of Limitations." *Focus on Exceptional Children* 8 (March 1976): 1–10.

Kirp, David L. "Schools as Sorters: The Constitutional and Policy Implications of Student Classification." *University of Pennsylvania Law Review* 121 (1973): 705–97.

——. "Law, Politics and Equal Educational Opportunity: The Limits of Judicial Involvement." *Harvard Educational Review* 47 (May 1977): 117–37.

Levin, Betsy. "Education as a Constitutional Entitlement: A Proposed Judicial Standard for Determining How Much Is Enough." *Washington Law Quarterly* (1979): 703–13.

——. "Equal Educational Opportunity for Special Pupil Populations and the Federal Role." *West-Virginia Law Review* 85 (Winter 1982-83): 159–85.

——. "An Analysis of the Federal Attempt to Regulate Education: Protecting Civil Rights or Controlling Curriculum?" *Journal of Law and Education* 12 (1983): 29–60.

Levin, Henry M. "Uniformity and Diversity: Democratic Ideals of Schooling." *IFG Policy Perspectives*. Palo Alto, CA.: Stanford University, Institute for Education Finance and Governance, Winter 1982.

McCarthy, Martha. "Minimum Competency Testing for Students: Educational and Legal Issues." *Educational Horizons* 62–63 (Spring 1984): 103–110.

McClung, Merle. "Competency Testing Programs: Legal and Educational Issues." *Fordham Law Review* 47 (1979): 651–712.

Mesibov, Laurie. "An Extended School Year for Handicapped Students?" *West's Education Law Reporter* 14 (1984): 867–86.

Michelman, Frank. "The Supreme Court 1968 Term, Foreward: On Protecting the Poor through the Fourteenth Amendment." *Harvard Law Review* 83 (1969): 7–59.

Miller, Richard. "Rawls and Marxism." *Philosophy and Public Affairs* 3 (Winter 1974): 167–91.

Modiano, Nancy. "National or Mother Tongue Language in Beginning Reading: A Comparative Study." *Research in the Teaching of English* 2 (1968): 32–43.

Moynihan, Daniel Patrick. "Government and the Ruin of Private Education." *Harper's* (April 1978): 28–38.

Nagel, Thomas. "The Meaning of Equality." *Washington Law Quarterly* (1979): 25–31.

Nisbet, Robert. "The Pursuit of Equality." *The Public Interest* 35 (Spring 1974): 103–20.

Olivas, Michael A. "Information Access Inequities: A Fatal Flaw in Education Voucher Plans." *Journal of Law and Education* 10 (1981): 441–65.

Orfield, Gary. "If Wishes Were Houses Then Busing Could Stop: Demographic Trends and Desegregation Policy." *Urban Review* 10 (Summer 1978): 108–24.

Passow, A. Harry. "Tackling the Reform Reports of the 1980s." *Phi Delta Kappan* 65 (June 1984): 674–83.

Peterson, Paul E. and Barry G. Rabe. "The Role of Interest Groups in the Formation of Educational Policy: Past Practice and Future Trends." *Teachers College Record* 84 (Spring 1983): 708–29.

Pettigrew, Thomas F. and Robert L. Green. "School Desegregation in Large Cities: A Critique of the Coleman 'White Flight' Thesis." *Harvard Educational Review* 46 (February 1976): 17–69.

Plunkett, Virginia R.L. "From Title I to Chapter 1: The Evolution of Compensatory Education." *Phi Delta Kappan* 66 (April 1985): 533–37.

Rebell, Michael. "Educational Voucher Reform: Empirical Insights from the Experience of New York's Schools for the Handicapped." *Urban Lawyer* 14 (1982): 441–67.

Roos, Peter. "Bilingual Education and the Hispanic Response to Unequal Educational Opportunities." *Law and Contemporary Problems* 42 (1978): 111–40.

Rossell, Christine H. "Magnet Schools as a Desegregation Tool: The Importance of Contextual Factors in Explaining Their Success." *Urban Education* 14 (1979): 303–20.

Rumberger, Russell W. "Dropping Out of School: The Influence of Race, Sex, and Family Background." *American Educational Research Journal* 20 (Summer 1983): 199–220.

Salomone, Rosemary C. "Equal Educational Opportunity and the New Federalism: A Look Backward and Forward." *Urban Education* 17 (1982): 213–32.

———. "Title VI and the Intent/Impact Debate: A New Look at 'Coextensiveness.'" *Hastings Constitutional Law Quarterly* 10 (Fall 1982): 15–79.

Schaar, John A. "Some Ways of Talking about Equality." *Journal of Politics* 26 (1964): 867–95.

Scheffler, Samuel. "Natural Rights, Equality, and the Minimal State." *Canadian Journal of Philosophy* 6 (March 1976): 59–77.

Schultz, Theodore W. "Investment in Human Capital." *American Economic Review* 52 (1961): 1–17.

Slippen, Richard I. "Adminstrative Enforcement of Civil Rights in Public Education: Title VI, HEW, and the Civil Rights Reviewing Authority." *Wayne Law Review* 21 (1975): 931–54.

Smylie, Mark A. "Reducing Racial Isolation in Large School Districts: The Comparative Effectiveness of Mandatory and Voluntary Desegregation Strategies." *Urban Education* 17 (1982): 477–502.

Spaemann, Robert. "Remarks on the Problem of Equality." *Ethics* 87 (July 1977): 363–69.

Taylor, William L. "The Supreme Court and Urban Reality: A Tactical Analysis of *Milliken v. Bradley." Wayne Law Review,* 21 (1975): 751–78.

———. "The Supreme Court and Recent Desegregation Cases: The Role of Social Science in a Period of Judicial Retrenchment." *Law and Contemporary Problems* 42 (1978): 37–56.

Thernstrom, Abigail M. "E Pluribus Plura—Congress and Bilingual Education." *The Public Interest* 60 (Summer 1980): 5–22.

Tucker, G. Richard. "Implications for U.S. Bilingual Education: Evidence from Canadian Research." *Focus* (National Clearinghouse on Bilingual Education) 2 (February 1980).

Van Dyke, Vernon. "Justice as Fairness: For Groups?" *American Political Science Review* 69 (1975): 607–14.

Wasserstrom, Sam. "Racism, Sexism and Preferential Treatment." *UCLA Law Review* 24 (1977): 581–622.

Weatherly, Richard and Michael Lipsky. "Street Level Bureaucrats and Institutional Innovation: Implementing Special Education Reform." *Harvard Educational Review* 47 (May 1977): 171–97.

Weber, Paul J. "Building on Sand: Supreme Court Construction and Educational Tax Credits." *Creighton Law Review* 12 (1978): 531–65.

Wechsler, Herbert. "Toward Neutral Principles of Constitutional Law." *Harvard Law Review* 73 (1959): 1–35.

Weinberg, Meyer. "The Relationship Between School Desegregation and Academic Achievement." *Law and Contemporary Problems* 39 (1975): 241-70.

Weinstein, Jack B. "Education of Exceptional Children." *Creighton Law Review* 12 (1979): 987–1039.

Westen, Peter. "The Empty Idea of Equality." *Harvard Law Review* 95 (1982): 537–96.

———. "To Lure the Tarantula from Its Hole: A Response." *Columbia Law Review* 83 (1983): 1186–1208.

Winter, Ralph K., Jr. "Changing Concepts of Equality: From Equality before the Law to the Welfare State." *Washington Law Quarterly* (1979): 741–55.

Yudof, Mark G. "School Desegregation: Legal Realism, Reasoned Elaboration, and Social Science Research in the Supreme Court." *Law and Contemporary Problems* 42 (1978): 57–110.

————. "Implementation Theories and Desegregation Realities." *Alabama Law Review* 32 (1981): 441–64.

————. "Education for the Handicapped: *Rowley* in Perspective." *American Journal of Education* 92 (February 1984): 163–77.

Notes

"The Courts, HEW, and Southern School Desegregation." *Yale Law Journal* 77 (1967): 321–65.

"Reading the Mind of the School Board: Segregative Intent and the De Jure/De Facto Distinction." *Yale Law Journal* 86 (1976): 317–55.

"Disciplinary Exclusion of Handicapped Students: An Examination of the Limitations Imposed by the Education for All Handicapped Children Art of 1975." *Fordham Law Review* 51 (1982): 168–95.

"School Discipline and the Handicapped Child." *Washington Law Review* 39 (1982): 1453–67.

"The Application of 94–142 to the Suspension and Expulsion of Handicapped Children." *Arizona Law Review* 24 (1982): 685–71.

"Crippling the Education for All Handicapped Children Act: *Board of Education v. Rowley*, 102 S.Ct. 3034." *Stetson Law Review* 12 (1983): 791–813.

"The Education for All Handicapped Children Act: What Is a 'Free Appropriate Public Education'?" *Wayne Law Review* 29 (1983): 1285–1300.

"Education—*Board of Education v. Rowley:* The Supreme Court Takes a Conservative Approach to the Education of Handicapped Children." *North Carolina Law Review* 16 (1983): 881–903.

"The Education for All Handicapped Children Act of 1975: What's Left After Rowley." *Williamette Law Review* 19 (1983): 715–36.

Papers and Speeches

Reynolds, William Bradford. Address to the Education Commission of the States, National Project on Desegregation Strategies Workshop. Chicago, Illinois, September 27, 1981.

————. Remarks Before the Metropolitan Center for Educational Research, Development and Training, New York University, *Brown* Plus Thirty Conference, September 13, 1984.

Rossell, Christine H. "Assessing the Unintended Impacts of Public Policy: School Desegregation and Resegregation." Boston University, Boston, Massachusetts, 1978.

Salomone, Rosemary C. "Equality, Liberty, and Community: Religion, Educational Policy, and the Burger Court." Paper presented at the Annual Meeting of the American Educational Research Association, Chicago, April 1985.

Wasby, Stephen L. "Is 'Planned Litigation' Planned?" Paper presented at the Annual Meeting of the American Political Science Association, New York, September 1983.

Newspaper Articles

American Association of Colleges for Teacher Education. "Public Dilemma: Equity vs. Excellence," *Education Week,* November 28, 1984.

Kirp, David L. "After 30 Years, Some Progress with School Desegregation," *Los Angeles Daily Journal,* May 15, 1983.

Tatel, David S. and William T. Taylor. "St. Louis School Desegregation: Worth Watching." *Los Angeles Daily Journal,* August 17, 1983.

Book Reviews

Barry, Brian. Review of *Spheres of Justice. Columbia Law Review* 84 (1984): 806–15.

Taylor, William L. Review of *Disaster by Decree* by Lino Graglia. *Columbia Law Review* 77 (1977): 810–17.

Index